Being Fair, Faring Better

DIRECTIONS IN DEVELOPMENT
Human Development

Being Fair, Faring Better

Promoting Equality of Opportunity for Marginalized Roma

Roberta Gatti, Sandor Karacsony, Kosuke Anan, Celine Ferré, and Carmen de Paz Nieves

WORLD BANK GROUP

ISBN (paper): 978-1-4648-0598-1
ISBN (electronic): 978-1-4648-0619-3
DOI: 10.1596/978-1-4648-0598-1

Cover photo: © Dorota Kowalska / World Bank. Further permission required for reuse.
Cover design: Debra Naylor, Naylor Design, Inc.

Library of Congress Cataloging-in-Publication Data
Names: Gatti, Roberta, author. | Karacsony, Sandor (Economist) | Anan, Kosuke, author. | Ferré,
   Celine author. | De Paz Nieves, Carmen author.
Title: Being fair, faring better : promoting equality of opportunity for marginalized Roma / Roberta Gatti,
   Sandor Karacsony, Kosuke Anan, Celine Ferré, and Carmen de Paz Nieves.
Description: Washington, DC : World Bank, 2016. | Series: Directions in development: human development
Identifiers: LCCN 2016022489| ISBN 9781464805981 | ISBN 9781464806193
Subjects: LCSH: Romanies—Europe, Eastern—Social conditions. | Romanies—Europe,
   Eastern—Economic conditions. | Romanies—Europe, Central—Social conditions. | Romanies—Europe,
   Central—Economic conditions.
Classification: LCC DX210 .G37 2016 | DDC 305.8914/97047—dc23
LC record available at https://lccn.loc.gov/2016022489

Contents

Boxes

Figures

Maps

Tables

Preface

The Roma are one of Europe's largest ethnic minorities. Many Roma households are among the poorest and most vulnerable Europeans, facing poverty, exclusion, and discrimination. With a geographical focus on those European Union member countries in Central and Eastern Europe (CEE) that have large Roma populations (Bulgaria, the Czech Republic, Hungary, Romania, and the Slovak Republic), this book aims to contribute to the debate on Roma inclusion in three complementary ways. First, it consolidates existing knowledge on key barriers to inclusion of marginalized Roma across these countries based on recent quantitative and qualitative evidence. Second, it does so around the unifying conceptual framework of equality of opportunity, which offers a lens to prioritize policy interventions. Finally, with a strong "how to" emphasis, it aims to promote awareness of good practices and policies, including for programming and implementing European Structural and Investment Funds.

Roma populations are very diverse in terms of identity, culture, and socioeconomic background. In line with the World Bank Group's goals of eradicating extreme poverty and promoting shared prosperity, this book focuses primarily on pathways for inclusion of disadvantaged Roma. The 2011 UNDP, World Bank, and EC Regional Roma Survey (RRS)—which constitutes the main evidence base for this study—was collected and sampled with the explicit purpose of providing information on the challenges faced by Roma and non-Roma living in areas of high Roma population density, and thus at relatively higher risk of marginalization. Hence, when drawn from the RRS, the book's comparisons between Roma and non-Roma should be understood as comparisons between Roma who live in areas at higher-than-average density of Roma populations and their non-Roma neighbors. This evidence is referred to throughout the book as evidence about "marginalized or disadvantaged Roma." When comparisons are drawn using national data, this is explicitly indicated.

This book enriches the comparative quantitative analysis with qualitative evidence drawn from case studies and with international examples of successful social inclusion interventions. Individual stories illustrate the life trajectories of young Roma who successfully overcame significant barriers. These life stories were collected based on a purposeful sample of Roma who were beneficiaries of the Roma Education Fund scholarships and have completed tertiary education.

The stories represent male and female experiences from a diverse set of countries and include urban and rural households.

The unifying framework of this work is centered on the notion of promoting *equality of opportunity* and on the set of policies that could help to level the playing field between Roma and non-Roma. As a result, the book has a strong emphasis on the next generation and on the development of inclusive education policies as a key instrument to change Roma children's opportunity set. At the same time, the focus on children is not exclusive, as children are the "entry point" for integrated policies aimed at improving household circumstances by fostering access to productive employment and upgrading living conditions.

While acknowledging that the multiplicity of barriers faced by marginalized Roma goes beyond schooling, jobs, and living conditions, this book does not provide a comprehensive review of policies in all sectors. Instead, and consistent with the prioritization laid out by the equality of opportunity approach, it focuses on directions for policy linked to the key three areas of education, jobs, and living conditions, while drawing links to complementary interventions (for example, health and nutrition).

Many relevant issues fall outside the scope of this work and could be the subject of future research. These include the role of perceptions, attitudes, biases, and social norms that affect discrimination against the Roma, and in-depth contextual studies, including cultural and social aspects at the country and community levels. This book also looks at the question of equality of opportunity primarily from an economic standpoint, without delving into the distinct yet important questions of social cohesion, empowerment, and citizenship. Finally, issues of Roma identity are very important in the debate around Roma and were highlighted as such in a number of comments received during the consultations on the draft version of this book. While the book touches upon some aspects of Roma identity in the different chapters, with its primary focus on quantitative evidence, the book does not discuss them in depth. These are key issues for future research.

The UNDP, World Bank, and EC Regional Roma Survey, 2011

The main source of data for this book was a survey carried out by the United Nations Development Programme (UNDP), the World Bank, and the European Commission during May–July 2011 in 12 countries of Central and Eastern Europe, including Albania, Bosnia and Herzegovina, Bulgaria, Croatia, the Czech Republic, Hungary, the former Yugoslav Republic of Macedonia, Moldova, Montenegro, Romania, Serbia, and the Slovak Republic. The survey was conducted on a sample of Roma and non-Roma households living in areas with a high density of Roma populations (20,018 Roma households and 9,782 non-Roma households living nearby).

The questionnaire was designed by a joint team from the UNDP and the World Bank, and was administered by the IPSOS polling agency in each country. It was translated into the local language and consisted of five main modules: (a) a management section, filled in by the interviewer, which covered his/her evaluation of the settlement and housing characteristics; (b) household members' profiles, answered by the head of household, which covered education level, health conditions, employment status, and sources of income; (c) an early childhood education and care section, answered by the children's primary caretaker, which covered child vaccination and assessment, nursery or preschool center attendance, parenting techniques, and preschool characteristics; (d) household status, answered by the head of household, which covered income, employment, and entrepreneurial activity, living standards, and economic security; and (e) individual status and attitudes administered to a random household member 16 years of age or older, which covered health, values and norms, migration, discrimination, and active citizen/trust.

The sampling frame for Roma settlements was based on information from the most recent population census available in the country, using the lowest administrative units with the equal or higher than national average proportion of Roma population on its total population. In some countries, other more up-to-date and widely acceptable information on the spatial distribution of Roma population was used for sampling (such as the 2004 *Atlas of Roma Communities in Slovakia*). By following a similar procedure as the 2004 survey, the 2011 RRS allows for some level of comparability across time. At the first stage of sampling, a list of settlements from census data was used. In a second stage, external or outsider's identification (local people, NGOs, and experts) was used to pinpoint areas where Roma households are located in a given municipality. In a third stage, the explicit willingness of the household's head to participate in a survey on Roma population (internal or self-identification) was requested. The sample was purposefully not representative of all Roma in these countries, but rather focused on those communities where the Roma population's share equals or is higher than the national share of Roma population. This covers 88 percent of the Roma population in Bulgaria, 90 percent in the Czech Republic, 78 percent in Hungary, 89 percent in Romania, and 83 percent in the Slovak Republic.

Source: World Bank. 2012. *Protecting the Poor and Promoting Employability: An Assessment of the Social Assistance System in the Slovak Republic.* World Bank, Washington, DC.

Acknowledgments

This book was written by a core team led by Roberta Gatti and comprising Kosuke Anan, Celine Ferré, Silvia Guallar Artal, Sandor Karacsony, Valerie Morrica, Carmen de Paz Nieves, and Abla Safir. It benefited from important contributions from Rosen Asenov, Vlad Grigoras, Marijana Jasarevic, Martina Kubanova, Claudia Rokx, and Andrej Salner.

While this is the product of a collaborative effort, primary authorship of chapters is as follows:

Overview	Roberta Gatti
Chapter 1	Roberta Gatti, Carmen de Paz Nieves, and Abla Safir, with input from Vlad Grigoras
Chapter 2	Sandor Karacsony
Chapter 3	Celine Ferré
Chapter 4	Kosuke Anan, with input from Carmen de Paz Nieves and Paula Restrepo
Chapter 5	Sandor Karacsony and Roberta Gatti, with input from Kosuke Anan and Valerie Morrica

Valerie Morrica and Claudia Rokx were responsible for weaving in, respectively, the gender and health angle throughout the book; Silvia Guallar Artal handled data management. The authorship of the spotlight annexes is as follows: Vlad Grigoras (Human Opportunity Index); Carmen de Paz Nieves and Veronica Silva (Chile Solidario); Sandor Karacsony with Vlad Grigoras (Targeting). Carmen de Paz Nieves and Lauri Scherer edited the document at different stages. Dorota Kowalska supported the team on communications and Isadora Nouel assisted the team.

We thank the young Roma university graduates who kindly shared their experiences during interviews with Rosen Asenov. We are deeply grateful to Tünde Buzetzky, Erzsébet Gulyás, Margareta Matache, Lászlo Ulicska, and the Roma Decade Secretariat for their insightful views and to participants at the Roma Decade Secretariat meeting in Sarajevo, September 29 and 30, 2014, for their comments on the conceptual framework of the book. We also would like to acknowledge the many good comments received from Ruth Barnett, Bill Bila, Katya Dunajeva, Delia Grigore, Francisco Monteiro, Maria-Carmen Pantea and Daniela Tarnovschi during the online consultation of the book. We also thank the participants joining and contributing to our live chat held on January 12, 2015.

Finally, we benefited from the ongoing advisory of Christian Bodewig, Plamen Danchev and of our peer reviewers Dominique Be, Enrica Chiozza, Joost de Laat, and Dena Ringold. We are grateful to Nina Arnhold, Polly Jones, and Juan Manuel Moreno for their detailed comments on early chapter drafts; and to Joao Wagner de Acevedo, Maitrey Das, Ellen Hamilton, Gábor Kertesi, Yoonhee Kim, Victoria Levin, Katarina Mathernova, Ana Maria Munoz Boudet, Mariana Moarcas, Ambar Narayan, Beata Olahova, Ismail Radwan, Veronica Silva, Kenneth Simler, Rob Swinkels, and Judit Szira for their insightful views and for useful discussions. All of these greatly improved the book.

This book was written under the strategic guidance of Mamta Murthi, Regional Director for Central and South Eastern Europe and the Baltics; Andrew Mason, Practice Manager for the Social Protection and Labor Global Practice; and in close collaboration with Elisabeth Huybens, Practice Manager for the Social, Urban, Rural, & Resilience Global Practice.

Executive Summary

Many Roma are among the poorest and most vulnerable Europeans, facing poverty, exclusion, and discrimination. In European Union member countries in Central and Eastern Europe (CEE) with substantial Roma populations, inequalities between Roma and non-Roma start early and are striking. Some of these inequalities reflect hard-wired family circumstances. For example, a Roma child is much more likely to grow up in a household at the very bottom of the income distribution, or have parents with little or no education. Other inequalities reflect limited opportunities such as access to basic goods and services (e.g., quality education and adequate living conditions), which are necessary not only for realizing one's potential in life, but also for living with dignity.

However, the context in which many Roma children are born and raised largely shapes lifelong opportunities and places them at a disadvantage early on. This process translates into significantly unequal outcomes over the life cycle, perpetuating inequality across generations. In many cases, the very design of institutions—including of education systems—as well as social norms and widespread discrimination, contribute to reinforce gaps. This happens despite the fact that Roma—contrary to what is often believed—report having similar aspirations to those of their non-Roma neighbors.

Inequality of opportunity is unfair and inefficient. Although there is much debate on whether and to which extent public policy should aim to level outcomes (for example, being poor), there is consensus that all individuals—irrespective of the socioeconomic circumstances into which they are born—should be allowed the same chances to be successful in life. Equality of opportunity is not only the right thing to do for societies that want to call themselves fair, but also a smart economic choice. A growing body of evidence shows that equity is associated with improved growth prospects. This is especially the case in the context of countries such as those in CEE, where aging, emigration, and low fertility are leading to a decline in working-age populations and where the young and growing Roma populations represent an increasing share of new labor market entrants.

This book focuses on identifying pathways to promote fair chances for disadvantaged Roma in CEE countries. Investing early, by promoting good nutrition, cognitive child development, and access to quality education is a policy with recognized high returns, especially for disadvantaged children.

While leveling the playing field for marginalized Roma puts emphasis on the next generation, the focus on children is not exclusive. Roma might continue to face unfair chances during key transitions in their lives, such as when looking for a job. Equally as important, for returns to education to materialize, a broader set of policies must address some of the disadvantaged circumstances in which a large share of Roma children grow up, including access to employment for their families and decent living conditions. As such, the equality of opportunity approach articulates a theory of change that centers on supporting healthy growth and access to inclusive education for children and provides a lens that helps to prioritize interventions across different sectors.

Addressing early childhood development gaps by sustaining parenting skills and improving the availability or affordability of quality services in the first 1,000 days of life could go a long way in enhancing opportunities for Roma children well into adulthood. Moreover, redesigning education systems toward a more inclusive structure—delaying tracking, promoting desegregation, enhancing incentives for teachers to work in marginalized areas, and providing remedial education support and mentoring—would continue to equalize opportunities in systems that to this day continue to stack chances against children from disadvantaged socioeconomic background, such as many Roma.

Early disadvantage and limited access to quality education, combined with geographical isolation, discrimination, and discouragement often result in poor employment outcomes for many Roma. In CEE countries, Roma have significantly higher unemployment rates than non-Roma, and when employed, they work largely in informal, low-paying jobs. Public employment services (PES) that orient their financial and human resources toward hard-to-place job seekers could play a useful role in enhancing their employability and work chances, through training programs tailored to job seekers' skills and employers' needs; counseling and orientation schemes for young people; and well-designed modules for skills certification, including those acquired in public work programs.

Limited access to productive employment is often reflected in inadequate living conditions. These outcomes for parents constitute the circumstances in which the next generation of Roma children will grow. The share of Roma who live in inadequate housing and without access to basic utilities and services, such as running water and sanitation, is disproportionately large compared with their non-Roma neighbors in CEE. Given the rich diversity among Roma groups and communities, tailored solutions will be required to adequately address gaps in living conditions, combining supply-side interventions (such as provision of adequate infrastructure) with initiatives that tackle demand-side constraints, including raising awareness about services for users, ensuring eligibility to access (through, for example, the provision of legal documentation), or enhancing affordability.

Implementing interventions that help overcome these interrelated barriers will need strong ownership at the national level, coordinated policies across different ministries and government levels, and an integrated delivery system that develops individual interventions in a participatory manner, using locally customized approaches. The 2014–20 programming cycle for European funds represents a unique opportunity to fund and operationalize these interventions.

Widespread ethnic discrimination continues to undermine the effective implementation of policies for the inclusion of marginalized Roma, and thus effectively tackling its sources and punishing acts of discrimination will be essential moving forward. More and better data, rigorous analysis, and evaluation can also play a significant role in dismantling the many incorrect notions around Roma that persist in the public debate, and can strengthen political support for policies aimed at promoting equal opportunities for a growing share of these countries' population.

Abbreviations

AGI	Adolescent Girls Initiative
AGS	A Good Start
ALMP	Active Labor Market Program
AzRIP	Azerbaijan Rural Investment Project
BLISS	Bulgarian Longitudinal Inclusive Society Survey
BMN	benefit in material need
CEE	Central and Eastern Europe
CESAR	Complementing EU Support for Agricultural Restructuring
CIP	Complex Instruction Program
CLLD	community-led local development
CPTED	Crime Prevention through Environmental Design
EC	European Commission
ECD	early childhood development
ECE	early childhood education
EF	European funds
ESF	European Social Fund
ESIF	European Structural and Investment Funds
EU	European Union
EU-SILC	European Union Statistics on Income and Living Conditions
GMI	guaranteed minimum income
HBS	Household Budget Survey
HOI	Human Opportunity Index
HRD	Human Resources Development
IOP	Integrated Operational Programs
IUDP	Integrated Urban Development Plans
IUP	integrated urban project
JCP	Jobcentre Plus
LAG	local action groups
M&E	monitoring and evaluation

NGO	nongovernmental organization
OECD	Organisation for Economic Co-operation and Development
PARSP	Post-Accession Rural Support Project
PES	public employment services
PISA	Programme for International Student Assessments
REF	Roma Education Fund
RHSP	Roma Health Scholarship Program
RIMIL	Roma Inclusion Mobile Innovation Lab
RRS	Regional Roma Survey
SIIS	Sistema Integrado de Información Social (Integrated Social Information System)
UNDP	United Nations Development Programme
UNICEF	United Nations Children's Fund

PART 1

A Fair Chance for Roma Children

Life Story—"Our Job was to Study"

The story of a young Roma female university grad from Hungary living in an urban nonsegregated area

I grew up in a city in a working class family. At the beginning of the 1980s, my parents, who come from a rural Roma community, moved to the city. My parents worked in a factory in the city, and we lived in a nonsegregated suburb. I don't know what it is like living in a Roma community; this made a big difference for me because I did not go to a segregated school, and I did not grow up in a remote, disadvantaged village.

As a schoolgirl, I liked reading books at home, and together with my parents, we gradually built up a home library. I have a younger brother, who also has a university education. My mother finished primary school, and my father has a secondary vocational education. With the political changes in the late '80s, many factories closed down, and after losing their jobs, my parents made a living by selling clothing. My parents had high expectations for my brother and me and wanted us to go far. Our job was to study.

I went to working-class, nonsegregated primary and secondary schools in my neighborhood, and the education there was good. In primary school, one of my classmates was also a Roma, but she left after two or three years. I had my Roma identity within my family and it was okay, and I had another one as a student who studies well at school. In school, my gypsy identity would sometimes come up when there were conversations about the bad connotations of being a Roma. I had good years in primary school. I had close friends and almost all of my teachers were very supportive and close to me. They would always tell us when we made a mistake and when we did well, and they motivated me to go to secondary school and university.

I had a harder time in secondary school. There, none of my teachers and class-mates were close to me. The teachers never prized the students for their achievements, which made the students more passive and less caring about performing well. My classmates in secondary school, would sometimes use the "gypsy card" when I did something they did not like. But these few cases were not a huge issue for me, espe-cially since I had a strong family and I didn't really care and I never hide my Roma identity. Once, my high school teacher of geography, who belonged to a far-right party, made me stand up for a long time because I was unprepared for class. But I guess that my ethnicity also played a role in his decision to punish me. This experi-ence hurt my dignity and made me work harder. You cannot fail, you cannot make any mistakes because then you are put in a box, and I did not want to belong in that box.

Throughout my university studies, I got a monthly scholarship from a Roma NGO, which covered part of my costs. I also worked to support myself. I became aware of the Roma Education Fund (REF) only toward the end of my studies. Being a beneficiary of the REF scholarship certainly made a difference for me, although it would have been even a bigger difference if I had found out about it earlier. In my free time, I volunteer for a Roma NGO. I can say that I owe 80 percent of my achievements to my parents and 20 percent to my teachers, although my ambition and personality might have also played a role in my educational and professional choices and achievements.

Overview

Roberta Gatti

Introduction

Early Inequalities Amount to Unfair Life Chances for Roma...

Inequalities between Roma and non-Roma in new European Union member countries in Central and Eastern Europe (CEE) with large Roma populations start early and are striking (see figure O.1). Some of these inequalities reflect hard-wired family circumstances. For example, a Roma child is much more likely to grow up in a household at the very bottom of the income distribution. Other inequalities reflect limited access to basic goods and services that are necessary not only for realizing one's potential in life, but also for living with dignity. For example, except for the case of Hungary, Roma children are about half as likely to attend preschool as their non-Roma neighbors. Similarly, Roma children are systematically less likely than non-Roma to live in housing that has running water, a bathroom, or an indoor kitchen.[1]

The circumstances in which Roma children are born and raised shape their lifelong opportunities in ways that perpetuate inequality. For example, data for Romania show that factors such as being born in low-income families or having parents with little education, as well as ethnicity itself, are associated with unequal access to education and basic services such as water and sanitation. The evidence shows that gaps in access are not being bridged over time. For example, while coverage of water supply expanded throughout Romania in the past decade, the difference in coverage between Roma and non-Roma not only failed to shrink, but actually increased slightly (see chapter 1).

and Translate into Deep Inequalities Later in Life...

Skewed opportunities, institutional design, and discrimination and negative stereotyping contribute to deepening these inequalities over the life cycle. For example, an analysis of school testing results of 15-year-olds (Programme for International Student Assessment [PISA]) shows that, in CEE countries, differences in socioeconomic circumstances continue to explain a large share of differences in education outcomes.[2] This suggests that rather than playing the role of the "great equalizer," education systems remain ill-equipped to

Figure O.1 Roma versus Non-Roma Distribution of Income for Families with Children (Ages 0–17), Romania and Bulgaria

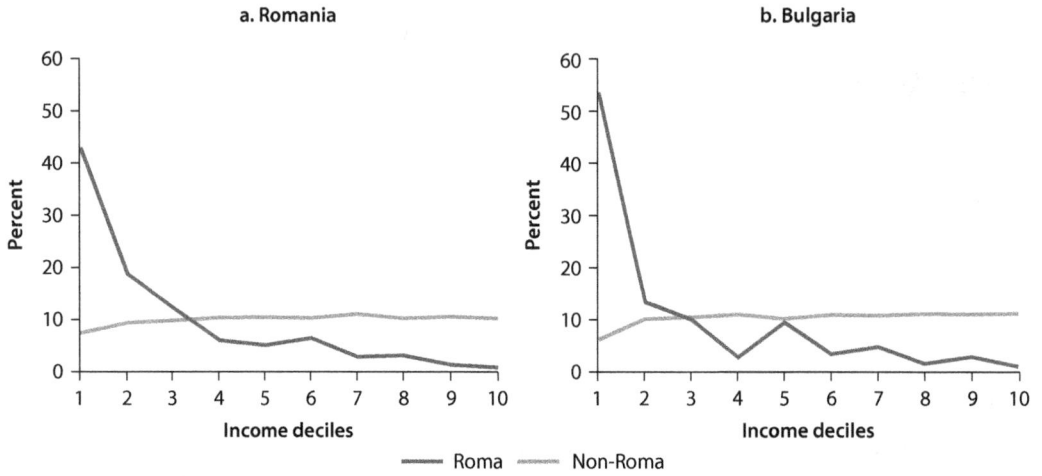

a. Romania

b. Bulgaria

Roma —— Non-Roma ——

Source: World Bank and Open Society Institute 2011.

Figure O.2 Roma versus Non-Roma Rates of Preschool Enrollment (Ages 0–6) and Slum Habitation (Ages 0–17)

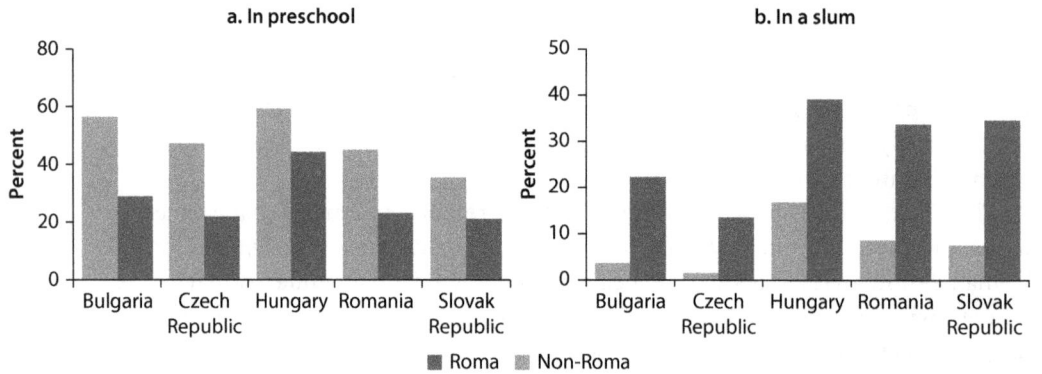

a. In preschool

b. In a slum

Roma ■ Non-Roma ■

Source: UNDP, World Bank, and EC 2011.

overcome the barriers faced by children from marginalized socioeconomic backgrounds, including many Roma (see figure O.2).

Discrimination can also affect how initial circumstances translate into outcomes, as well as how opportunities are redistributed in life transitions after childhood. According to the Regional Roma Survey (RRS), between 27 and 62 percent of Roma report having experienced discrimination while searching for jobs. Moreover, as individuals observe the experiences of others in their group and their disappointing interactions with markets, they may (rationally) draw the conclusion that exerting effort is not rewarded, and may subsequently decrease their own effort. In other words, discrimination can shape not only the returns to effort (say, given a certain level of skills, whether people of different ethnicity are equally likely to find employment or earn a similar wage) but also the incentive to exert that effort, through what is known as the "internalization of exclusion" (a behavior through which individuals, observing the lack of success of their peers in, say, job search, rationally exert lower effort in searching for a job).

Despite No Apparent Differences in Aspirations and Preferences

Contrary to prevalent societal beliefs that gaps between Roma and non-Roma may be largely due to differences in preferences and aspirations, the RRS indicates that Roma and non-Roma have similar preferences for work in as far as they seek lower paid but secure employment (see figure O.3) and for their children's education attainment. These preferences are reflected in behavior. For example, controlling for education and other basic correlates, Roma participate in the labor market as much as non-Roma. However, Roma are on average less successful in finding employment.

Why Equality of Opportunity?

For life chances to be fair, opportunities—that is, access to the basic services that are necessary (yet not sufficient) for anyone to succeed in life—should not be correlated with circumstances over which individuals have no control, such as ethnicity, or how much one's parents earn (de Barros et al. 2009).

While there is debate regarding whether and how much public policies should aim to decrease inequality in outcomes such as consumption or income, there is consensus that societies should strive to decrease inequalities that are due to initial circumstances, and can therefore be deemed unfair. But equality of opportunity matters not only from an ethical perspective. Growing evidence shows it is a central component of long-term economic growth and development, in that it helps ensure that a society makes the most effective use of its human capital resources. The economic rationale for promoting equal opportunities for Roma children is even more compelling in the case of CEE countries, which are

Figure O.3 Employment Aspirations for Roma versus Non-Roma Men and Women

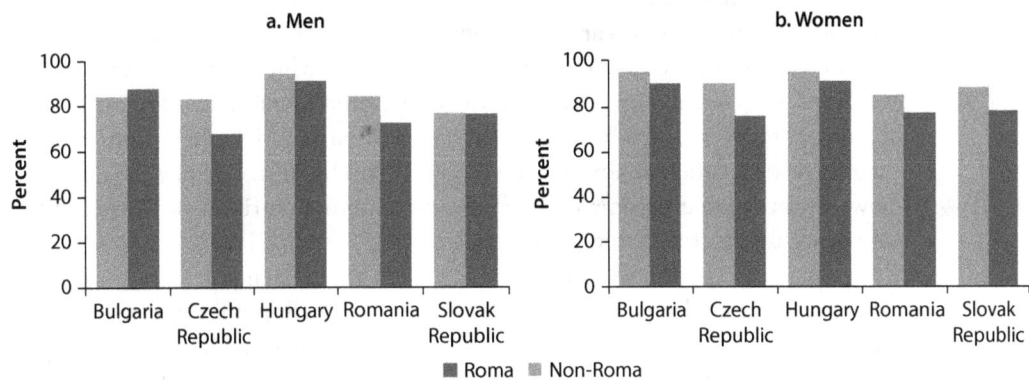

Source: UNDP, World Bank, and EC 2011.

experiencing rapid population aging, and where the young and growing Roma population represents an increasingly large share of new labor market entrants.

This book focuses on identifying pathways to promote fair chances for marginalized Roma in CEE countries and discusses policies that can sever the link between initial circumstances and outcomes later in life. Consistent with international evidence, these policies center on investing in children early on, to improve nutrition and cognitive development, which offer significant long-term benefits, particularly for the most disadvantaged—and later, to ensure that Roma children can access quality and inclusive education. However, the focus on the early stages of life is not exclusive. First, leveling the playing field during childhood might not be enough to secure equal opportunities: Roma might continue to face unfair chances during key life transitions, such as when looking for a job. Equally as important, for returns to education to materialize, a broader set of policies must address some of the disadvantaged circumstances in which a large share of Roma children grow up, including promoting access to productive employment for parents and upgrading living conditions. As adults' outcomes are their children's circumstances, this approach can help break the cycle of poverty for marginalized Roma and bridge a gap that both the international experience and the emerging evidence on the potential impact of early interventions show is all but inevitable (Kertesi and Kézdi 2014).

What follows summarizes key barriers to and good practices in promoting equal access to education for children, to productive employment for adults, and to improved living conditions for families.

Pathways to Equality of Opportunity for Marginalized Roma

Access to Quality and Inclusive Education

Education is a powerful instrument for improving equity, reducing poverty, and promoting economic growth. However, international assessments of education systems in the five CEE countries that have significant Roma populations indicate systemwide inequalities that disproportionately affect Roma students' ability to access quality education (see figure O.4).

Access to education remains a challenge for marginalized Roma children. This is especially the case for early education; anywhere between 55 and 70 percent of Roma children ages 3–6 do not attend preschool, which reflects both a lack of facilities and cost and awareness barriers for Roma families. In addition to preschool enrollment, disadvantaged Roma children could benefit from greater cognitive stimulation at home. Growing up in families in severe poverty and with low education, many Roma children are at risk of malnutrition and have limited exposure to effective parenting practices.

These early childhood education gaps result in unequal access to quality primary education. Entry assessments in the Czech Republic and the Slovak Republic show that Roma children are frequently streamed into special education at an early age. At the same time, even though primary education is compulsory, territorial disparities lead to gaps in enrollment. Just as importantly, school and class segregation—which are driven by the interaction of population dynamics and geographic segregation, as well as discrimination—are on the rise in countries such as Hungary and the Slovak Republic (see chapter 3; World Bank 2012; Kertesi and Kézdi 2014). As segregation affects schools' ability to attract qualified teachers and also weakens peer effects among pupils, it is likely to impact education quality and achievement for Roma children.

Figure O.4 Index of Equality of Learning Opportunities in European and Central Asian Countries

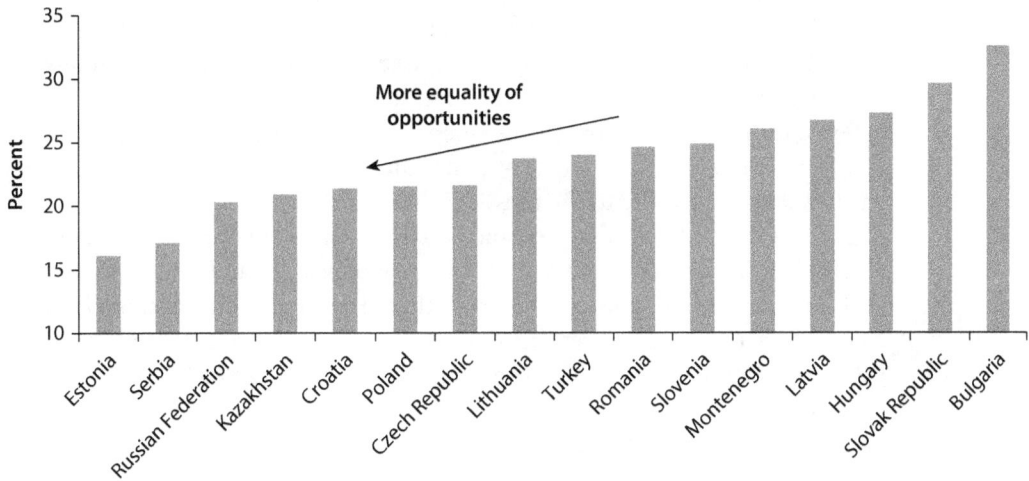

Source: Gortazar et al. 2014.
Note: The index is the percent of the variance in reading scores explained by the main predetermined characteristics (age, gender, and socioeconomic status) in a linear regression (Ferreira and Gignoux 2011).

Figure O.5 Roma Still in School, by Age

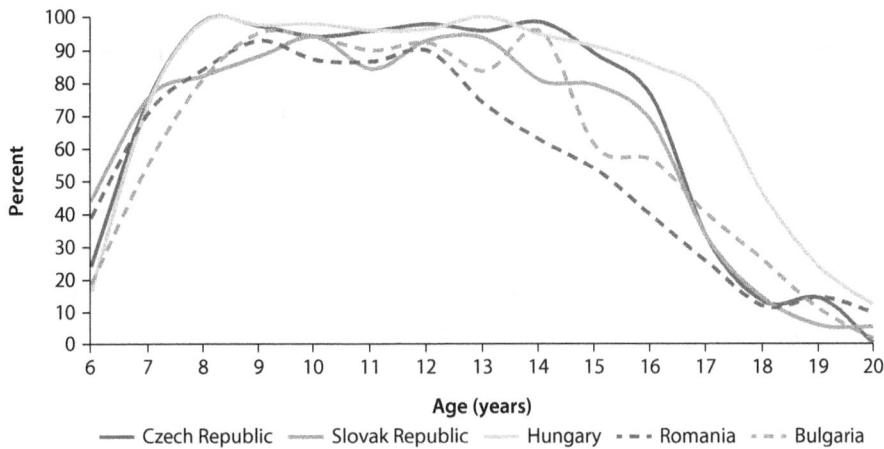

Source: UNDP, World Bank, and EC 2011.
Note: Some data points were unavailable. Percentages shown exclude missing values.

Being Fair, Faring Better • http://dx.doi.org/10.1596/978-1-4648-0598-1

Partly as a result of these factors, increasingly fewer disadvantaged Roma children remain in school as the education cycle progresses (see figure O.5); the majority of them drop out between age 12 (Bulgaria) and 15 (the Czech Republic and Hungary). The share of Roma students who continue their education becomes increasingly smaller with age and declines substantially from age 17; these students are often streamed into low-quality technical and vocational training schools, and few complete the secondary level to transition to college.

Education systems in these countries are still unable to deliver quality learning to the majority of marginalized students largely because their very design—including early tracking, streaming into special schools, and curricula structure—stacks the chances against children from disadvantaged backgrounds. Promoting equal opportunities through education will require rethinking these systems' architecture to feature more inclusive approaches so they can respond to each child's individual needs, and identifying interventions that can overcome the barriers that are specific to the most disadvantaged.

Early interventions that expand quality early childhood development (ECD)—both through more and better early education and via parenting and skills programs—and reduce the barriers that many marginalized Roma families face will have the highest returns in terms of equity and productivity. The private and social benefits of ECD, especially when accompanied by well-designed nutrition interventions, are well established and range from a positive impact on child development to higher test scores and productivity. These benefits are particularly significant for children from disadvantaged backgrounds who often lack a safe and stimulating home environment (see, for example, Burger 2012; Heckman 2006).

Improving Roma children's chances throughout primary and secondary education will require a mix of systemic reforms as well as specific interventions tailored to the most disadvantaged. These will include delaying tracking; enhancing incentives for teachers to work in marginalized areas (for example, experimenting with models such as Teach for America, which provides incentives to attract top graduates to work in marginalized areas); transitioning out of the special schools system (where Roma children are overrepresented); and promoting desegregation. At the same time, remedial educational support, including through scaling up the role of Roma mediators and strengthening teacher training, especially for those in schools with a high share of children at risk of dropping out, will help mitigate differences in performance that are driven by socioeconomic backgrounds.

Finally, promoting access to tertiary education via affirmative action programs that focus on students from marginalized backgrounds would not only contribute to better employment chances for Roma, but also make a positive difference in their community, since young Roma graduates can serve as role models for others.

Relying more systematically on measuring learning outcomes and intervention results can not only serve as the basis for evidence-based policy making but also showcase the benefits of programs geared toward inclusiveness. This is likely to increase overall support for more and better-targeted investments in skills formation for the most marginalized.

Access to Productive Employment

Good jobs are transformational for development. As a key pathway out of poverty, they are a critical factor for improving the circumstances under which the next generation can grow and flourish.

Roma employment rates are lower than those of their non-Roma neighbors (see figure O.6). These outcomes do not reflect Roma preferences for work, but rather important barriers to finding employment. Furthermore, those Roma who do work often have precarious, unstable, and informal jobs.

Limited access to quality education has resulted in important constraints to employability for many Roma. Unemployment and low wages are often driven by mismatches between the specific skills that employers require—both technical and nontechnical—and those usually possessed by the work-able Roma population living in marginalized communities, which is characterized by low levels

Figure O.6 Roma versus Non-Roma Employment Rates for Working-Age Men, Women, and Youth

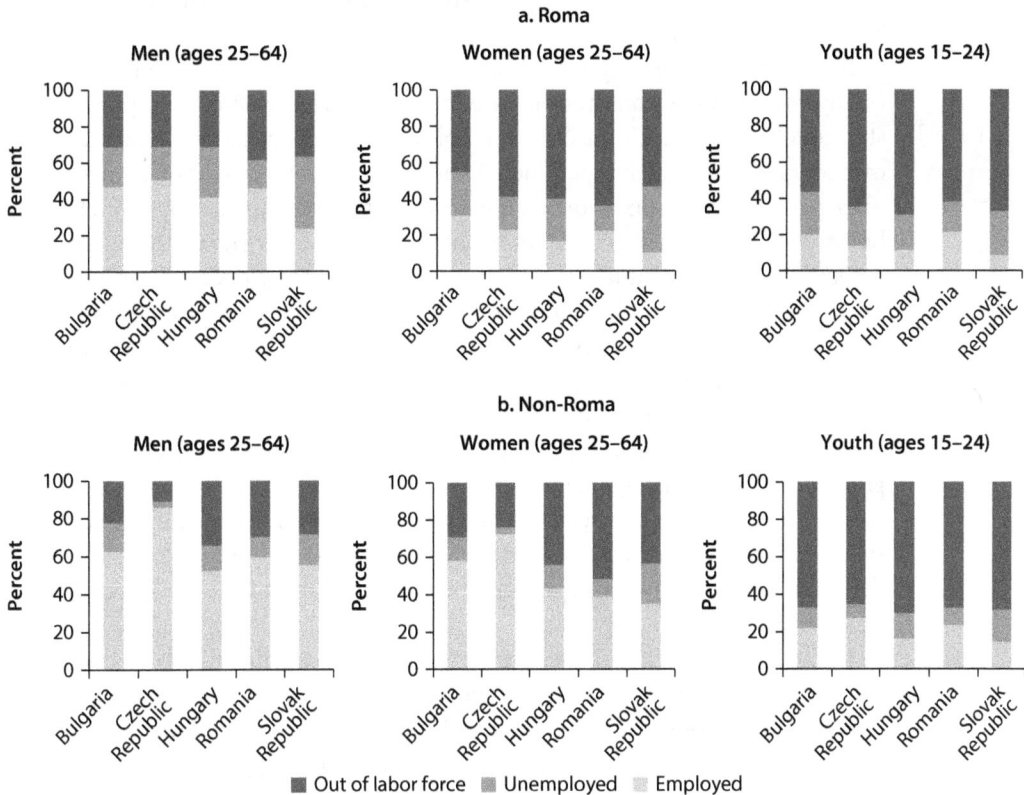

Source: UNDP, World Bank, and EC 2011.
Note: Sample restricted to working-age individuals (ages 15–64).

Being Fair, Faring Better • http://dx.doi.org/10.1596/978-1-4648-0598-1

Figure O.7 Roma versus Non-Roma Skill Levels

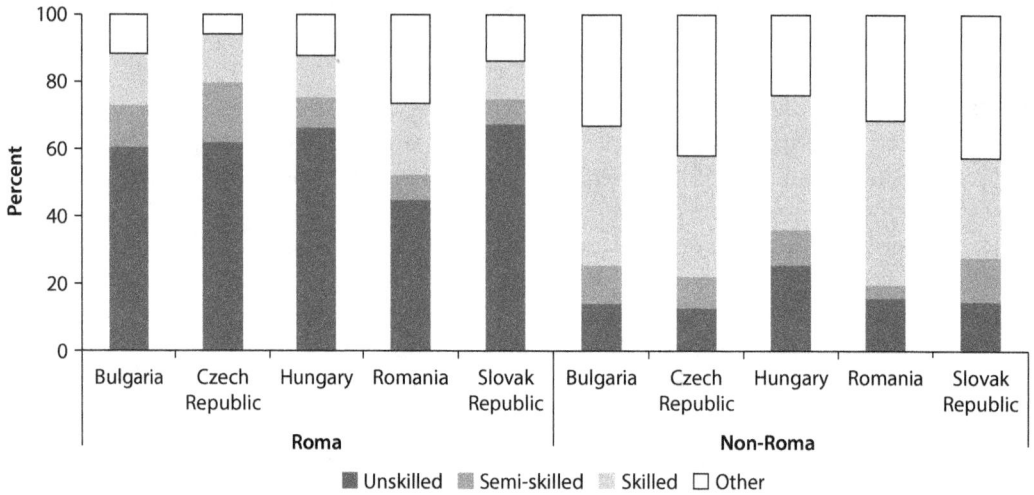

Source: UNDP, World Bank, and EC 2011.
Note: Sample restricted to working-age individuals (ages 15–64).

of education, limited skills and work experience, and long stretches of unemployment (see figure O.7).

At the same time, residential segregation, distance from job opportunities (many marginalized communities are located in areas where unemployment is structurally high), lack of access to employment support services (such as child care services), and the design of benefit and tax systems that do not always "make work pay" for low-skilled workers are important barriers to participation. Ethnic-based discrimination can also contribute to discouragement in the job search, especially when individuals repeatedly observe that their peers are unsuccessful in finding jobs. Many Roma job seekers also lack social networks and information about job and training offers. Last but not least, capital constraints can also be a major impediment for those trying to start a business or become self-employed.

Public employment services (PES) can play an important role in reducing these skill mismatches and information asymmetries. Yet PES in CEE countries grapple with systemic challenges, including limited funding and capacity. There is significant room to reorient their strategic focus away from skilled secondary school and university graduates (often in urban areas) and toward low-skilled and disadvantaged job seekers, especially those in rural areas who are systematically underserved.

In this context, better tailoring interventions and training to job seekers' skills and to employers' needs is likely to significantly improve effectiveness. Given the widespread functional illiteracy among Roma in marginalized localities, second-chance education and literacy programs should become core elements of labor market initiatives focused on improving employability for marginalized Roma, including systems to detect at-risk groups early. In parallel, and as part of an effective school-to-work transition approach, young people could benefit from career counseling and professional orientation programs while at school. At the same time, working closely with local employers will likely build mutual trust between the private sector and PES, and can progressively improve job seekers' placement.

In those areas where labor demand is structurally low, public work programs are likely to remain an important source of livelihood. Linking these programs with well-designed modules for upgrading and certifying skills could facilitate transition to other forms of employment.

Access to Upgraded Living Conditions

Lack of access to basic infrastructure, social services, and markets hamper opportunities to grow, learn, stay healthy, be productive, and participate in social and economic life. The majority of Roma in CEE countries continue to live in poor conditions. For example, a much larger proportion of Roma than non-Roma live in dilapidated houses or slums, while greater shares of Roma households do not have access to improved water sources and sanitation (see figure O.8).

Formal documentation and titling, segregation, and settlement history influence the diverse characteristics of Roma's living conditions, and the challenges associated with these. Common features of disadvantaged Roma communities include low-quality urban blocks of flats or former workers' colonies, urban slum areas, dilapidated urban buildings in historical city areas, rural and periurban informal settlements, as well as traditional rural settlements.

The wide diversity of Roma communities makes tailored solutions necessary. These should be based on an assessment of each community's specific needs and build on broad community involvement and the availability of flexible funding.

Figure O.8 Living Conditions of Roma and Non-Roma Neighbors

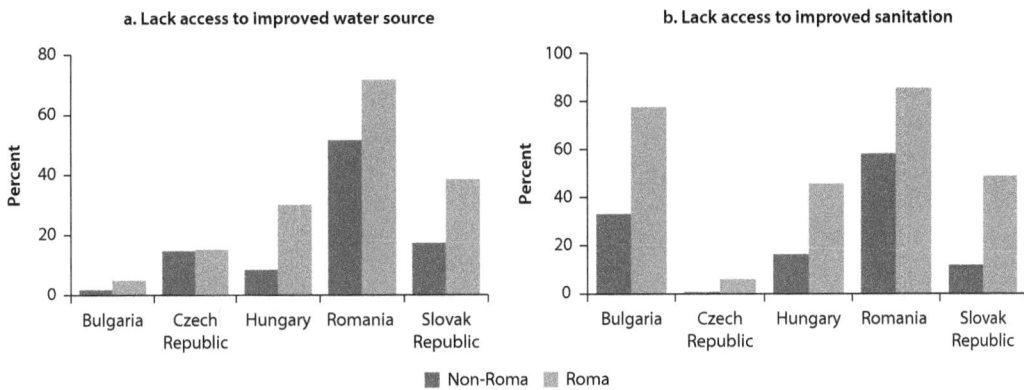

Source: UNDP, World Bank, and EC 2011.
Note: "Improved sanitation" is defined as having a toilet and a shower or bathroom inside the dwelling.

Being Fair, Faring Better • http://dx.doi.org/10.1596/978-1-4648-0598-1

Just as importantly, to achieve sustainable results, interventions that improve physical housing conditions, basic infrastructure, and services need to be coupled with a series of complementary activities that address potential demand-side constraints. These include (a) service users' awareness and capacity; (b) affordability of services; (c) maintenance and operation capacity; (d) eligibility to access the services (such as through civil documentation); and (e) addressing distrust and combating discrimination. A number of good practices in this area suggest that positive results can be obtained with the appropriate ownership and capacity and when interventions are carefully designed.

Implementation Challenges and The Road Ahead

Implementing interventions that help overcome the set of interrelated barriers faced by many Roma will require a delivery system that purposefully coordinates policies—across different ministries and vertically across government levels—with the ultimate common goal of supporting and empowering disadvantaged households. While this is clearly a challenge, examples of programs such as Chile Solidario have shown that these efforts can lead to significant results. To increase the relevance and impact of these interventions and to take into account the diversity of Roma communities, interventions should be developed and implemented in a transparent and participatory manner, using locally customized approaches. The 2014–20 programming cycle for European funds represents a unique opportunity to fund and operationalize these interventions.

Widespread ethnic discrimination continues to hamper the effective implementation of policies aimed at marginalized Roma's inclusion. Tackling its sources and punishing acts of discrimination are essential to combating discrimination. More and better data, rigorous analysis, and evaluation can also play a significant role in debunking the many incorrect notions that persist in the public debate around Roma. The examples of success highlighted in this book demonstrate the potential in these communities that is ready to be unleashed—to the benefit of society at large as well as the Roma themselves—if the appropriate policies can be identified and adopted.

Notes

1. According to the 2011 Regional Roma Survey, a large-scale survey jointly implemented by the United Nations Development Programme (UNDP), the World Bank, and the European Commission (EC)—see description in the preface.

2. It is important to note that PISA data does not allow for analysis by ethnicity.

References

Burger, K. 2012. "Early Childhood Care and Education and Equality of Opportunity: Theoretical and Empirical Perspectives on Current Social Challenges." Springer VS.

de Barros, R. P., F. H. G. Ferreira, J. R. M. Vega, and J. S. Chanduvi. 2009. *Measuring Inequality of Opportunities in Latin America and the Caribbean*. Washington, DC: World Bank and Palgrave Macmillan.

Ferreira, F. H. G., and J. Gignoux. 2011. "The Measurement of Educational Inequality—Achievement and Opportunity." Working Paper 019, Rede de Economia Aplicada, Paris. http://reap.org.br/wp-content/uploads/2011/12/019-The-Measurement-of-Educational-Inequality.pdf.

Gortazar, L., K. Herrera-Sosa, D. Kutner, M. Moreno, and A. Gautam. 2014. "How Can Bulgaria Improve Its Education System? An Analysis of PISA 2012 and Past Results." Working Paper 91321. Washington, DC: World Bank Group. http://documents.world bank.org/curated/en/2014/09/20289139/can-bulgaria-improve-education-system -analysis-pisa-2012-past-results.

Heckman, J. 2006. "Investing in Disadvantaged Young Children Is an Economically Efficient Policy." Paper presented at the Committee for Economic Development/Pew Charitable Trusts/PNC Financial Services Group Forum, "Building the Economics Case for Investments in Preschool," New York, January 10. http://jenni.uchicago.edu /Australia/invest-disadv_2005-12-22_247pm_awb.pdf.

Kertesi, G., and G. Kézdi. 2014. "On the Test Score Gap between Roma and Non-Roma Students in Hungary and Its Potential Causes." Budapest Working Papers on the Labour Market, BWP 2014/1, Institute of Economics, Hungarian Academy of Sciences, Corvinus University of Budapest.

UNDP (United Nations Development Programme), World Bank, and EC (European Commission). 2011. *Regional Roma Survey.* Report, UNDP, World Bank, and EC, New York.

World Bank and Open Society Institute. 2011. Bulgarian Crisis Monitoring Survey, February 2011. World Bank, Washington, DC; Open Society Institute, New York.

World Bank. 2012. *Protecting the Poor and Promoting Employability: An Assessment of the Social Assistance System in the Slovak Republic.* Report, World Bank, Washington, DC.

CHAPTER 1

Being Fair, Faring Better: Promoting Equality of Opportunity for Marginalized Roma

Roberta Gatti, Carmen de Paz Nieves, and Abla Safir, with input from Vlad Grigoras

Summary

Early inequalities for the majority of Roma children in new European Union (EU) member Central and Eastern European (CEE) countries are large and striking, reflecting both hard-wired circumstances—such as being born into poverty or to parents with limited education—and having limited access to those goods and services—such as education, running water, or sanitation—that are necessary for a productive and successful life.

For a society to be fair, such poor contextual conditions should not be allowed to determine how a person progresses in life. However, the evidence shows this is not the case for many Roma across the countries of this study. Roma experience significant inequalities in access to opportunities (housing, education, or basic services such as sanitation) and these inequalities appear to be associated with circumstances such as parental background, residential area, and, to a lesser extent, ethnicity.

This unequal distribution of opportunities appears to lead to marked differences in outcomes over the life cycle, even if Roma in general report similar preferences to those of non-Roma. For example, lack of access to preschool is significantly associated with a lower chance of secondary school attainment for Roma across countries, although Roma parents report the same aspirations for their children's educational attainment as non-Roma parents.

Unequal opportunities can combine with other mechanisms to lead to unequal outcomes for adult Roma. The existing evidence indicates that ethnic-based discrimination is widespread in the region. Discrimination can affect both the set of opportunities available to children—for example, the quality of education via segregation mechanisms—as well as the returns to endowments and effort—for example, if Roma are discriminated in the labor market. Finally, these mechanisms can affect active participation to economic life through what is known as the "internalization of exclusion."

Equality of opportunity is not only a way to promote social justice but also a smart economic choice, especially in rapidly aging societies where young Roma represent a growing share of new labor market entrants. As importantly, the gaps between Roma and non-Roma are not inevitable: emerging evidence and international experience show that it is possible to change the odds faced by marginalized people, including many Roma. Breaking the cycle of exclusion for the next generation of Roma would entail acting early and investing in bridging the gaps in early child development and education, when the returns are highest. However, for those investments to bear fruit, and given that the outcomes of today's Roma families are the next generation's realities, it will also be necessary to address some of the key existing gaps in living conditions and to promote productive employment opportunities for parents through an integrated set of interventions.

Equality of Opportunity: A Fair Start for Marginalized Roma Children

Inequalities between Roma and non-Roma children in new EU member Central and Eastern European (CEE) countries begin early and are striking. Some reflect predetermined circumstances such as poverty and parental education. For example, a Roma child is much more likely than a non-Roma child to grow up in a household with severe material deprivation and to have parents who have little or no education. Other inequalities reflect unfair access to basic goods and services that are necessary for dignified living. As an example, a large majority of Roma children live in households that lack toilets or bathrooms and running water, and, with the exception of Hungary, Roma children in CEE countries are about half as likely to attend preschool as non-Roma children (see figure 1.1).[1] Moreover, for marginalized Roma children, the context in which they are born and raised largely shapes lifelong opportunities and places them at a disadvantage early on. These early differences amount to an unfair start for the next generation of Roma (see figure 1.2).

This book discusses pathways to equal opportunity for Roma children. As such, it focuses on the fairness of the process through which individuals progress in life and meet their full potential, and how society can ensure that circumstances over which individuals have no control (being *born* poor, or to parents with little education) do not predetermine outcomes later in life (*being* poor or acquiring education). While there is debate on whether societies should reduce inequality in outcomes—such as income or consumption—equality of opportunity offers an increasingly accepted concept of social justice for a society that wants to call itself fair (see box 1.1).

Unequal Circumstances and Unfair Opportunities

Unequal Starting Points...

While there is a rich diversity to Roma culture and socioeconomic background across CEE countries, the majority of Roma children continue to live in disadvantaged households (Ivanov and Kagin 2014; World Bank 2010). For example, data from nationally representative household surveys show that in both Bulgaria

Figure 1.1   Roma versus Non-Roma Rates of Child Hunger (Ages 0–6) and Preschool Enrollment (Ages 3–5)

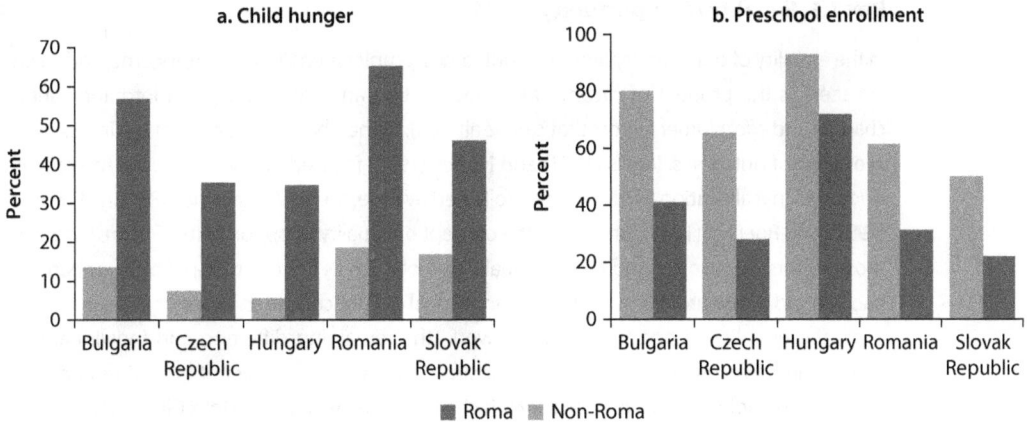

a. Child hunger

b. Preschool enrollment

■ Roma   ■ Non-Roma

Source: UNDP, World Bank, and EC 2011.
Note: Panel a shows the answer to the question, "In the last month, did you or anyone in the household ever go to bed hungry because there was not enough money for food?" among households with children ages 0–6. Panel b shows the preschool enrollment rate for children ages 3–5.

Figure 1.2   Influence of Early Life Circumstances on Equality of Opportunity for Roma Children

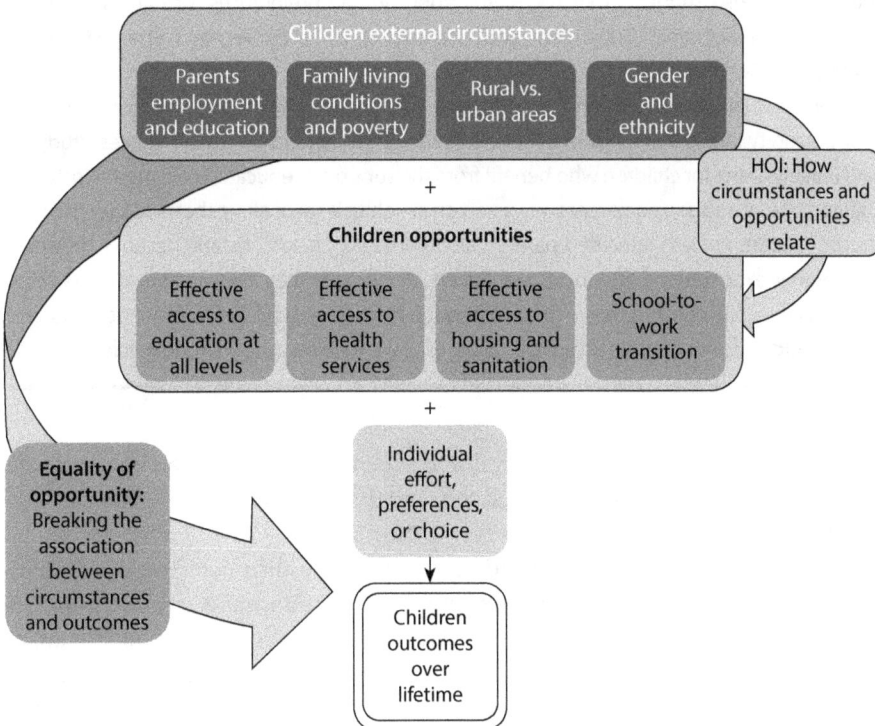

Note: The Human Opportunity Index (HOI) is a statistical tool that provides insights into the extent to which hard-wired circumstances matter for the distribution of opportunities, making the process more or less fair. The HOI is discussed in detail in the spotlight in annex 1A.

Box 1.1 Equality of Opportunity

In the equality of opportunity literature, outcomes (employment, education, income, and so on) are seen as the product of *circumstances* (factors that an individual is born into and cannot change) and *effort* (other factors that can be altered). Rather than only considering fairness in the allocation of outcomes, Rawls (1971) and Nozick (1974) focused on the fairness of the process leading to that allocation. Their work was followed by Arneson (1989), Cohen (1989), and Dworkin (1981), and Roemer (1993) formalized the concept of equality of opportunity. *Circumstances* are those factors that are beyond an individual's control, such as gender, place of birth, or parental background. These are attributes that the individual did not choose and cannot change.

In the equality of opportunity framework, the remaining differences in individual outcomes should be regarded as the result of *effort*, which is the product of behaviors and decisions that an individual chooses and for which she can be held responsible. Circumstances and effort are the two determinants of outcomes, although other authors argue that luck is a third additional aspect that must be included separately (Trannoy et al. 2010).

Behavioral economics shows that individuals differentiate between those inequalities that are due to effort and those that are due to circumstances, deeming those due to the latter as unfair. Experimental studies in behavioral economics and survey evidence show that, when examining outcome distributions, participants distinguish factors depending on whether individuals can be held responsible for them (Cappelen, Sorenson, and Tungodden 2010). The evidence also suggests that there are strong human preferences for fairness (Alesina, Di Tella, and MacCulloch 2004; Fehr and Fischbacher 2003; Osberg and Smeeding 2004; World Values Survey 2008).

While inequality shaped by effort can be more tolerable because it is less unfair, the equality of opportunity literature recognizes that effort can often depend on circumstances; studying hard is likely easier for children who benefit from the support of educated parents, for instance. Children of more educated parents may exert an absolute level of effort that is higher than the effort of children of less educated parents, all other factors held constant, because they may have higher expectations of educational returns or because they benefit from their parents' help with their studies. As a person moves through infancy into childhood, teenage years, and finally adulthood, her effort in shaping outcomes plays an increasingly stronger role.

and Romania, about half of Roma children live in households in the lowest decile of the income distribution, compared to fewer than one in ten non-Roma children (see figure 1.3).

Roma are significantly poorer and more vulnerable than non-Roma, including their own non-Roma neighbors (see box 1.2). In disadvantaged communities across the five new member states, on average 85 percent of Roma children are at risk of poverty, compared to an average of 42 percent of non-Roma children living in the same neighborhood (see figure 1.4). The proportion of Roma children living in households with severe material deprivation is between 73 percent and 93 percent, much higher than among non-Roma children (which varies between 27 percent and 72 percent) living in the same neighborhood. Finally, in contrast

Figure 1.3 Roma versus Non-Roma Family Distribution of Income for Children (Ages 0–17) across Income Deciles, Romania and Bulgaria

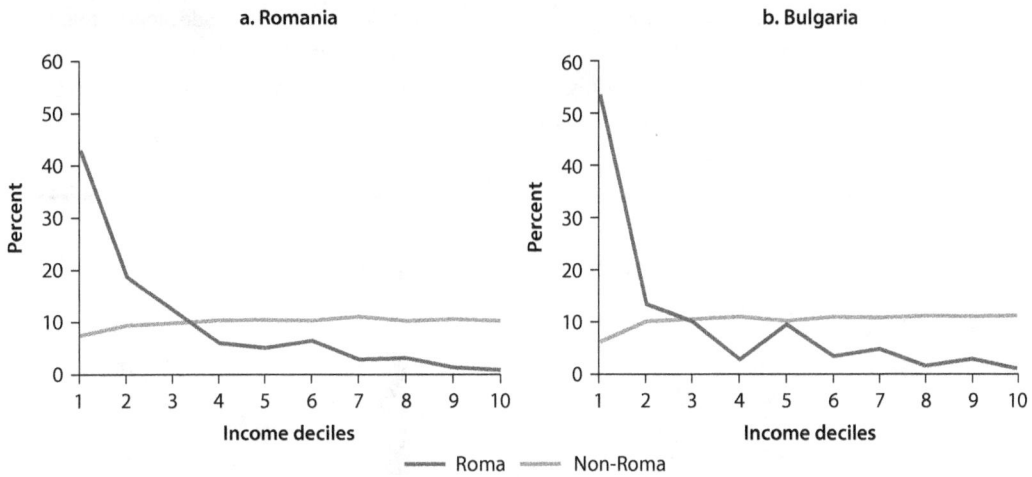

a. Romania   b. Bulgaria

Roma   Non-Roma

Source: Romania, 2013 Household Budget Survey, Bulgaria; World Bank and Open Society Institute 2011.

Box 1.2 Did Poverty among Roma Increase over Time?

Data allowing comparisons of gaps between Roma and non-Roma over time are limited. A recent report published by UNDP (Ivanov and Kagin 2014) analyzes the difference in outcomes between the Regional Roma Survey (RRS) and the UNDP vulnerable group survey of 2004 and shows a mixed picture. The report takes a multidimensional approach to poverty and shows that while the multidimensional poverty rate of Roma decreased substantially between 2004 and 2011 in Bulgaria and Romania (from 57 percent to 42 percent and from 73 percent to 59 percent, respectively), this is primarily the result of a decline in the number of Roma in the "poor" category (5–7 deprivations). However, "severe poverty" (more than 7 deprivations) decreased significantly only in Romania. A closer look at the six indicators underlying the multidimensional poverty index suggests that between 2004 and 2011 the contribution of shortcomings in education and living conditions to multidimensional poverty has declined, while that of shortcomings in fundamental rights and labor activity has increased. The analysis of multidimensional versus monetary poverty metrics also reveals that the decline is similar in both metrics in Bulgaria, while the decline in monetary poverty in Romania is stronger than in multidimensional poverty.

Looking at changes in other outcomes of Roma households, the UNDP analysis finds that the share of Roma with at least lower secondary education increased in all CEE countries (but continues to remain under national averages, as discussed in chapter 2 of this book). Moreover, a statistically significant decline (from 25 percent to 17 percent) in the share of Roma children attending special schools in the Czech Republic (ages 7–15) is notable.

box continues next page

Box 1.2 Did Poverty among Roma Increase over Time? *(continued)*

Reported access to primary health services (insurance and access to general practitioners) significantly improved among the non-Roma during 2004–11 but declined for Roma in Romania and Bulgaria. Access to improved sanitation for Roma households increased between 2004 and 2011; progress in both improved water sources and improved sanitation has occurred only in Bulgaria and Hungary.

Source: Ivanov and Kagin 2014.

Figure 1.4 Roma versus Non-Roma Children (Ages 0–14) at Risk of Poverty

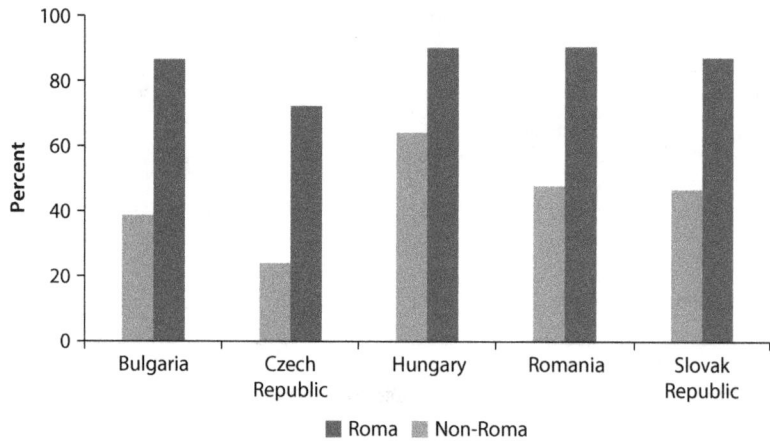

Sources: Eurostat 2014; UNDP, World Bank, and EC 2011.
Note: Figure presents at-risk-of-poverty rate falling below 60 percent of the median income level in a certain country.

Figure 1.5 Roma versus Non-Roma Households with at Least One Child (Ages 0–6) Where at Least One Household Adult (Ages 25+) Has Completed Secondary Education

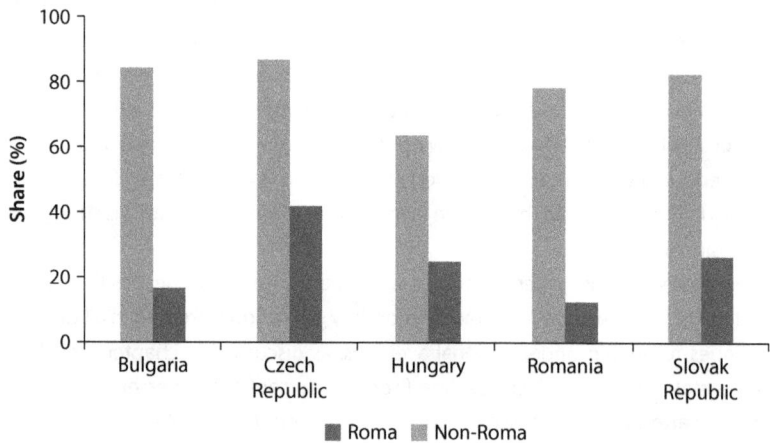

Source: UNDP, World Bank, and EC 2011.

to their non-Roma peers, the majority of Roma children live in households where adults did not attain upper secondary education, thus continuing to have poor employment outcomes (see figure 1.5).

Affect Access to Opportunities...

For life chances to be fair, opportunities—that is, access to basic services that are necessary (yet not sufficient) for success—should not be correlated with circumstances over which individuals have no control, such as ethnicity, race, or parents' earnings (see, for example, the discussion in Molinas et al. 2010).[2] The large differences in access to sanitation, running water, or early schooling for Roma and non-Roma documented by the RRS point to a strong correlation between coverage for these key goods and services and the specific circumstances associated with being Roma (see, for example, figure 1.6 and the discussion in chapter 4).

The Human Opportunity Index (HOI) is a statistical tool that provides further insights into the extent to which hard-wired circumstances matter for the distribution of opportunities, making the process more or less fair. More precisely, the HOI measures access to opportunities (*coverage*), discounting it by how unequally these opportunities are distributed across circumstances such as gender, income, household characteristics, and ethnicity (captured by the *dissimilarity index*). Annex 1A describes the HOI in more detail and showcases its application to Romania. The findings of this analysis confirm the evidence drawn from the RRS—lower opportunities, as measured by access to basic housing services (water supply, bathrooms, flush toilets, sewage disposal) and education are associated with the adverse circumstances in which many Roma children are born. Moreover, differences between opportunities for Roma and non-Roma (and within Roma communities) have not decreased over the past 12 years in Romania.

However, once circumstances such as where a family lives, parental income and education, or being a single-parent household are accounted for, ethnicity (that is,

Figure 1.6 Roma versus Non-Roma Rates of Preschool Enrollment for Children (Ages 3–5) and Slum Habitation for Children (Ages 0–17)

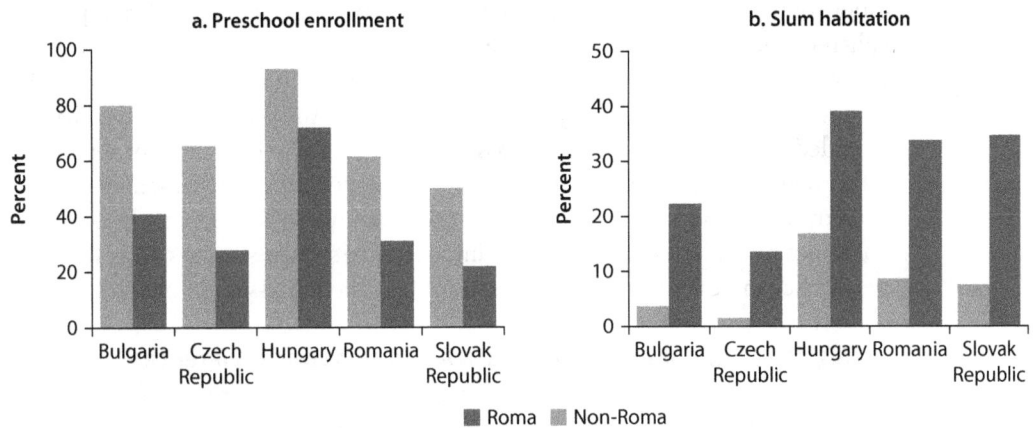

Source: UNDP, World Bank, and EC 2011.

being Roma) seems to play only a marginal *additional* role in explaining access to opportunities. This limited role is explained by the fact that ethnicity itself is associated with initial circumstances: Roma children have higher probabilities of living in rural areas, of having parents with low levels of education, and of being distributed in the lowest consumption quintiles. Therefore, the estimated contributions of ethnicity to the HOI should be understood as lower bounds.[3]

Recent quantitative studies investigating the school performance of eighth graders in Hungary also indicate that circumstances matter significantly. These findings suggest an overwhelming role of parental education and poverty as circumstances that explain child health and parenting, and through those, inequalities for Roma adolescents (Kertesi and Kézdi 2011, 2014). In particular, these works show that the gap between Roma and non-Roma scores decreases dramatically once other socioeconomic characteristics are controlled for, becoming insignificant for reading and decreasing by 85 percent for mathematics.

and Result in Unequal Outcomes…

If a child starts her life with limited access to early education or to decent housing and sanitation, it will be more difficult for her to grow healthy, become a successful student, and find a good job. Today, we observe significant differences in outcomes in educational attainment, employment rates, quality of employment, and wages, all of which vary systematically with being Roma.

Compared to their non-Roma peers, Roma suffer poor health and have much lower life expectancy—in some countries up to 15 years lower (UNDP, World Bank, and EC 2011). Roma face a vicious cycle of poor health throughout life. The poor living conditions they are born into contribute to infectious disease, diarrhea, and respiratory disease, especially among children. Growing up they are more likely to suffer a higher burden of chronic disease, which is consistent with high-risk behaviors such as smoking, poor dietary habits, low levels of physical activity, and teen pregnancy.

While the lack of data does not allow a full-fledged estimation of how early circumstances and opportunities have translated into employment or living condition outcomes for today's Roma adults, different pieces of evidence paint a coherent picture of persistent disadvantage. In the one instance where we can measure the association between access to an opportunity (preschool) and outcomes later in life (secondary school attainment), the RRS shows that having attended preschool is significantly associated with a higher chance of secondary attainment, which is consistent with international evidence on preschool's effect. Moreover, analysis of PISA data[4] shows that a family's socioeconomic background continues to explain a large share of differences in students' scores, thus signaling persistence in outcomes across generations (see the discussion in chapter 2).

…Despite No Apparent Differences in Aspirations and Preferences

Contrary to widely held beliefs (World Bank 2010), differences in outcomes between Roma and their non-Roma neighbors do not seem driven by differences in reported preferences or lifestyle. Among both Roma men and women,

Figure 1.7 Roma versus Non-Roma Employment Aspirations for Men and Women

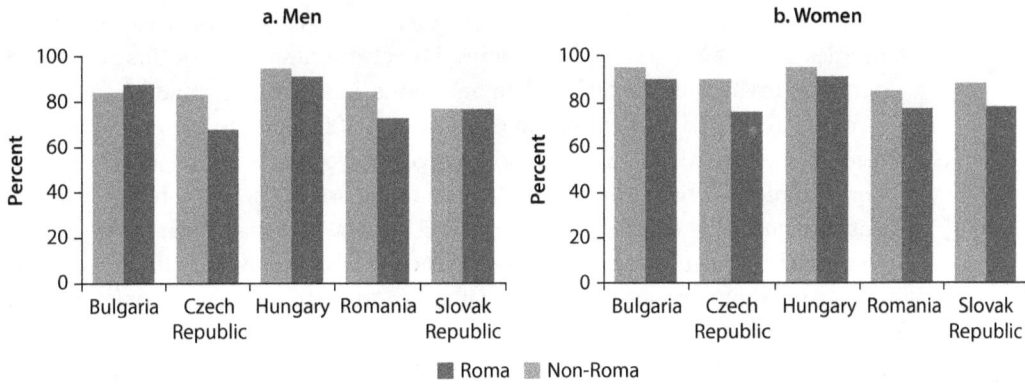

a. Men

b. Women

Roma Non-Roma

Source: UNDP, World Bank, and EC 2011.

Figure 1.8 Similarity of Roma and Non-Roma Parental Goals for Their Male and Female Children to Complete Upper Secondary Education

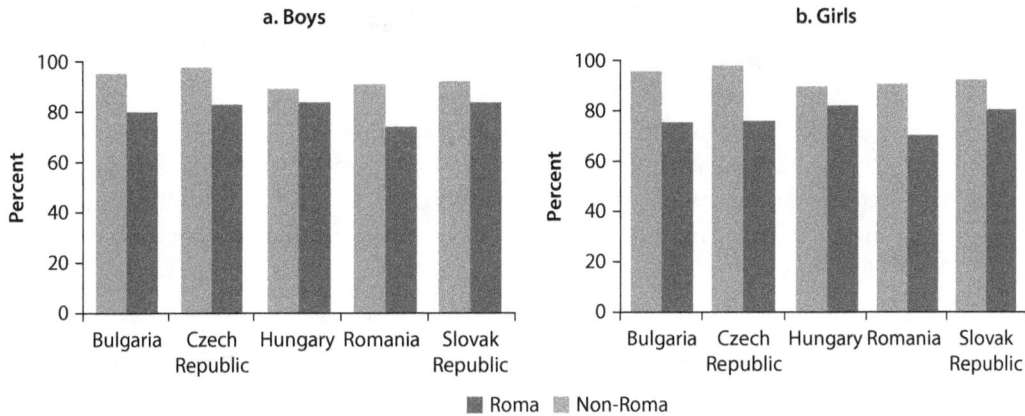

a. Boys

b. Girls

Roma Non-Roma

Source: UNDP, World Bank, and EC 2011.
Note: The panels show the percentage of individuals who answered "secondary vocational/technical/arts, general secondary, associate (2 years) college or university and higher" to the question "What do you believe is a sufficient level of education for a boy?"

significant majorities report preferring "secure ... but low paid" employment over "having higher income but insecure and irregular" employment (see figure 1.7). These responses are very similar to those of non-Roma neighbors' respondents. Comparable majorities of Roma and non-Roma similarly prefer "having secure employment but having to be at work 8 hours a day 5 days a week and not having the freedom to manage your time" compared with "having irregular employment but being free to manage your time."

In addition, Roma and non-Roma parents report the same educational aspirations for their children. When asked, "What do you believe is a sufficient level of education for a child?" Roma parents display similar preferences as non-Roma parents (see figure 1.8). Remarkably, the preferences are similar for sons and for daughters.

Other Mechanisms That Contribute to Unequal Outcomes

Other mechanisms, such as ethnic-based discrimination, can further skew opportunities to generate unequal outcomes. Direct discrimination occurs when one person is treated less favorably than another is, has been or would be treated in a comparable situation (European Commission 2008) on the grounds of gender, race, ethnicity, national origin, disability, age, religion or belief, or sexual orientation. Indirect discrimination occurs where an apparently neutral provision would put persons of a specific racial or ethnic origin at a particular disadvantage compared with others, unless that provision is objectively justified by a legitimate aim and the means of achieving it are appropriate and necessary (European Commission 2008). Because of the subtle and covert nature of discrimination, it is often very difficult to measure and determine its extent and influence.[5]

Data from the RRS (where participants self-report discrimination) indicate discrimination is widespread in the region. For example, 32 percent of those Roma in the Slovak Republic who have been in contact with educational institutions report enduring ethnic-based discrimination. In addition, there is evidence that the general public distrusts Roma populations, with respondents largely declaring that they do not want to have Roma as neighbors compared to other ethnic minorities (see figures 1.9 and 1.10).

Data on school and classroom segregation of Roma in new EU countries also point to underlying discrimination in education. For example, 12 percent of Roma children in the Slovak Republic and 18 percent in the Czech Republic are streamed into special schools for children with mental disabilities, although they can perform on par with their peers in an integrated school environment (Asenov et al. 2014).

Figure 1.9 Roma Self-Reported Perception of Neighbor Ethnic Discrimination against Roma Population

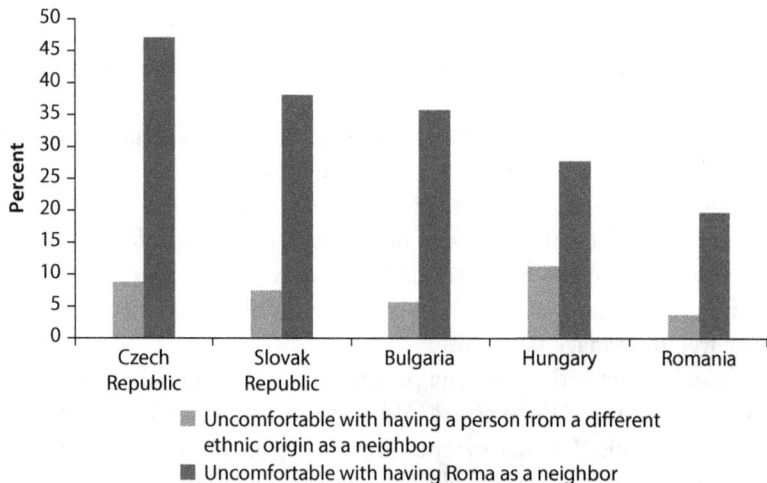

Uncomfortable with having a person from a different ethnic origin as a neighbor

Uncomfortable with having Roma as a neighbor

Sources: European Commission 2008; Eurobarometer Survey 2012.

Figure 1.10 Roma Self-Reported Ethnic Discrimination during the Job Search Process

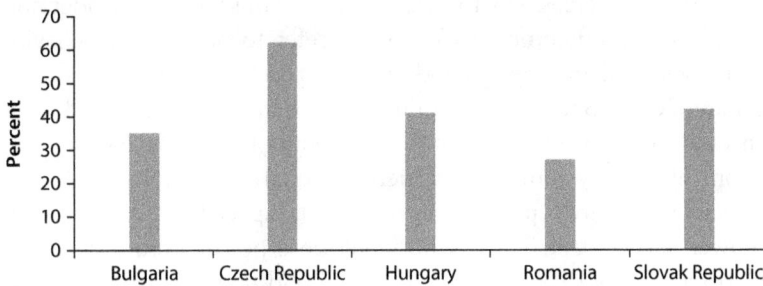

Source: FRA 2011 (FRA Roma Pilot Survey).

Although discrimination and segregation seem clearly linked with "being Roma," the emerging evidence on the role of ethnicity in explaining inequalities for Roma paints a complex picture. The evidence from the HOI decomposition in Romania suggests a direct, albeit small, contribution of ethnicity to shaping opportunities. Similarly, estimates computed from the RRS data indicate that unexplained factors linked to ethnicity might explain outcome gaps between Roma and non-Roma. For example, Roma secondary students' attainment is lower than their non-Roma neighbors, even after a rich set of socioeconomic covariates are controlled for. In the same vein, a large share of the earnings gap between Roma and non-Roma remains unexplained by differences in observed background characteristics (such as education and experience). In both cases, these unexplained gaps could be associated with discrimination or other elements of "being Roma" (see also World Bank 2010). Conversely, the aforementioned analysis of test scores in Hungary seems to indicate that gaps are overwhelmingly due to socioeconomic differences.

The way in which circumstances and opportunities translate into outcomes later in life might also be affected by how individuals internalize negative stereotypes. Those who identify with a group may mimic the group's behavior, which can lead to a vicious cycle of exclusion (World Bank 2013b). As individuals observe the outcomes of others in their group and their interactions with markets, they may conclude—rationally—that effort is not rewarded and therefore decrease it (Loury 1999). For example, in the context of a game with children from different castes in India, children from lower castes showed a poorer performance when each player's caste was made salient than when they were unknown (Hoff and Pandey 2006). These "aspiration traps" that discourage individuals from investing in their capabilities are observed across countries and sectors (see box 1.3). Research shows that if individuals think they will experience discrimination, they tend to give up. An actual episode of discrimination can lead to a decrease in learning ability (Elmslie and Sedo 1996). Moreover, with anti-school attitudes developing over time, the influence of their environment may lead adolescents to regard dropping out as a success (see the discussion on Roma in Spain in Martínez, Enguita, and Gómez 2010).

Recent research increasingly focuses on the role of social and gender norms in explaining unequal outcomes. Social norms refer to patterns of behavior that flow from socially shared beliefs and are enforced by informal social sanctions (World Bank 2014). Social norms influence expectations, values, and behaviors. As such they can prevent interventions (including laws or access to better services) from effectively removing barriers to equal opportunities (World Bank 2011). Social norms are typically very persistent, especially in areas that directly affect power and control. Those who would lose power from a change in the social norm are likely to actively resist change, and those who would gain often are too weak to impose change (see box 1.4).

Pathways to Promoting Equal Opportunities for Roma Children

Why Equality of Opportunity?

This book focuses on pathways to promoting equal opportunities for Roma children on the basis of the idea that in a fair society, outcomes should not depend on circumstances such as gender, ethnicity, or parental background, since an individual cannot be held responsible for these. In the case of children, including Roma, all inequalities can be deemed unfair since a child cannot exert any control over them.

Around the world, the discussion on equality of opportunity has become more prominent in the public debate in developing and high-income countries alike.[6] Leveling the playing field to ensure that individual outcomes do not depend on circumstances is essential both from a moral perspective—minimizing "unfair" inequality due to circumstances—and an economic one—not letting

---

Box 1.3 The Internalization of Exclusion Debate

There is increasing evidence that exclusion can affect performance. For example, perceived discrimination can alter both job seekers' expectations from the labor market and their future labor supply decisions. Members of excluded groups may therefore become discouraged and drop out of the labor force (Goldsmith et al. 2004). For example, "women and minority groups frequently underinvest in their human capital because they have been brought up to believe that they cannot do certain things that other people can do. [They] internalize their second class status in ways that cause them to make choices that perpetuate their disempowered status" (Alsop, Bertelsen, and Holland 2006).

An analysis of Afrobarometer data from 18 countries concludes that citizens use ethnicity as a "heuristic for judging their own life chances" and that "the overall well-being of the group affects an individual's own self-esteem" (Lieberman and McClendon 2012). The differences in preferences are larger where wealth disparities between groups are high, for instance.

Source: World Bank 2013b.

Box 1.4 The Role of Social and Gender Norms: A Case Study from Bulgaria

Recent qualitative research in four Roma communities in Bulgaria investigated and confirmed the role social norms play in the context of the socioeconomic inclusion of marginalized Roma.

The research found that while traditional social and gender norms are largely intact and similar across the four communities, one can observe a disconnect between proclaimed values and what is practiced. The extent of change varies across communities and norms, including the notion that men are superior to women; the association of manhood with the role of family provider; and women's virginity before marriage. The research found that Roma men in the four communities are increasingly failing to live up to the role of family provider as persistent poverty, unemployment, and the inability to generate steady income takes its toll. As a consequence, men's authority inside the family and in the community often declines. Despite traditional gender roles being formally upheld, de facto male authority in the family seems to be increasingly challenged by women, particularly in the absence of income that originates from men. Women's virginity prior to marriage was found to be a defining social norm for women in the four communities. Public discussions relating to virginity typically cause a lot of friction between traditional and nontraditional Roma girls, reflecting the changing views on the gender values of virginity and womanhood. The discussions revealed that young Roma women are increasingly feeling torn between adhering to traditional values versus modern attitudes and lifestyles.

Intrahousehold and intergenerational relationships are also in a state of flux as social norms and gender roles continue to evolve. As traditional gender roles increasingly break down, family relationships are affected. A household's senior members—including parents and grandparents—are increasingly feeling the erosion of their influence on younger generations. They feel powerless against the new norms and values that younger generations adopt from mainstream society. Overall, the research found that the four Roma communities are caught between traditional values and social norms; contrasted with the imperatives of their economic situation, as well as the aspirations and practices of modern Bulgarian society. Women's higher education, for example, offers their employment new value and is changing their role in family life. They increasingly view employment as a form of self-expression and expect more involvement from their partners in household and child care duties. The renegotiation of social and gender norms can be witnessed across all surveyed communities, albeit to varying degrees. This renegotiation process creates considerable levels of stress between the sexes, inside families, and in communities. These findings confirm the need for policies to acknowledge and respond to challenges emerging from shifting social norms.

Sources: Das 2013; World Bank 2014b.

---

adverse circumstances prevent individuals and society from developing talent and skills. The evidence shows that early inequalities have significant impacts on outcomes later in life and can perpetuate over generations (World Bank 2005). For example, if children from disadvantaged families do not have the same opportunities as children from those that are wealthier to receive quality education, they can expect to earn less as adults.[7]

A long-standing tenet in economics points to a trade-off between efficiency and equity. However, a growing body of evidence finds that, in the presence of imperfect markets, unequal opportunities often lead to wasted productive human potential and to inefficient allocations of limited resources, therefore undermining economic efficiency (World Bank 2005). This conclusion has been supported by further evidence across countries in different development stages, suggesting that equality of opportunity is an important ingredient in promoting and sustaining growth (Grimm et al. 2010; Berg and Ostry 2011; Berg, Ostry, and Zettelmeyer 2011; Dunnzlaff et al. 2011; Marrero and Rodríguez 2013; Molina, Saavedra, and Narayan 2013).

Equalizing opportunities for Roma children is a particularly smart economic choice in rapidly aging countries such as those in CEE (see box 1.5). Roma are a young and growing population, while the non-Roma majority is rapidly aging due to low fertility, longer life expectancy, and emigration (see figure 1.11 and World Bank 2013a). Promoting education and skills upgrading for Roma—a key pathway for equal opportunity—would therefore amount to investing in higher productivity for a growing segment of the population.

Box 1.5 Equality of Opportunity and the Smart Economics Framework

In recent years, the World Bank has produced evidence and analysis that indicates that investing in efforts to reduce the existing gaps between Roma and non-Roma populations would deliver economic gains. These investments would yield not only individual benefits for the Roma but also substantial aggregate gains, mostly stemming from the higher productivity of this minority through upgraded skills. In other words, these policies would be *smart economics*.

The smart economics approach answers the following question: How much larger would economies be, and how much higher would government revenue be, if Roma enjoyed the same labor market opportunities as the majority populations? For that purpose, a lower and an upper bound of these benefits are calculated using official Roma population estimates and the commonly accepted estimates by Roma experts. Productivity differences are proxied by calculating the average earnings gap between Roma and non-Roma.

Using data on the labor share of total economic output and comparing the labor profile of the average working-age Roma with that of the average working age non-Roma from the majority population, the total productivity loss per individual is calculated. Multiplying this by the number of working-age Roma gives the aggregate productivity loss for the economy as a whole. To calculate the foregone government revenues and savings, information on employment probabilities and income tax conditional on having a job is used, as well as estimates on the difference between the social protection payments toward Roma and toward majority non-Roma.

This economic approach is aligned with the equality of opportunity framework. Both approaches identify important economic arguments for why bridging the gaps between Roma and non-Roma benefits society. At the same time, the equality of opportunity approach stresses that a society that wants to call itself fair would not tolerate such large differences between the mainstream population and minority groups.

Source: World Bank 2010.

Operationalizing Equality of Opportunity for Roma Children

By identifying policies that help break the link between circumstances and outcomes, the equality of opportunity framework used in this work offers a lens through which to prioritize interventions that can help level the playing field for Roma children.[8]

Access to inclusive and quality education is one such policy (World Bank 2005). There is rich evidence of the crucial impact of education, especially in

Figure 1.11 Roma versus Non-Roma Distribution of Male and Female Population by Age, Bulgaria, Hungary, and Romania

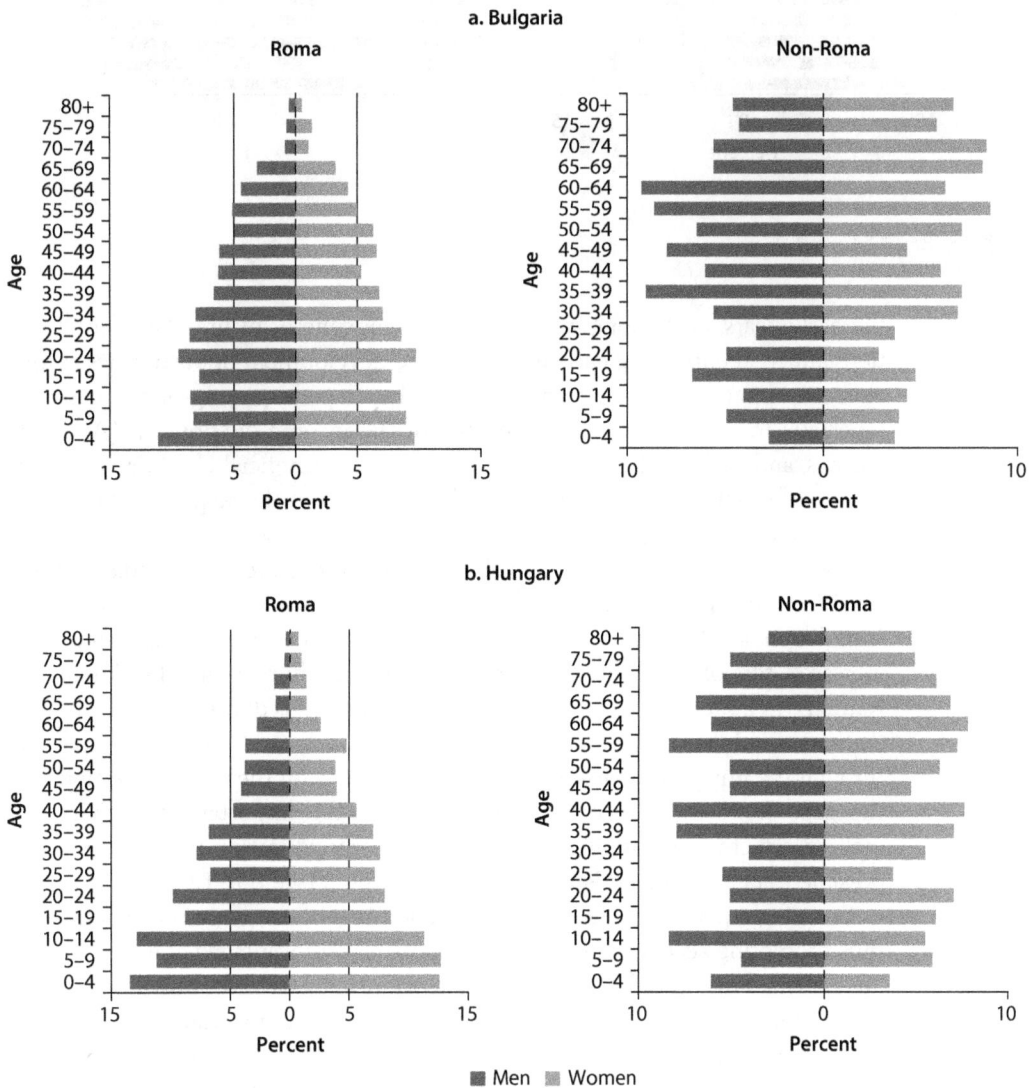

a. Bulgaria

b. Hungary

■ Men ■ Women

figure continues next page

Figure 1.11 Roma versus Non-Roma Distribution of Male and Female Population by Age, Bulgaria, Hungary, and Romania *(continued)*

c. Romania

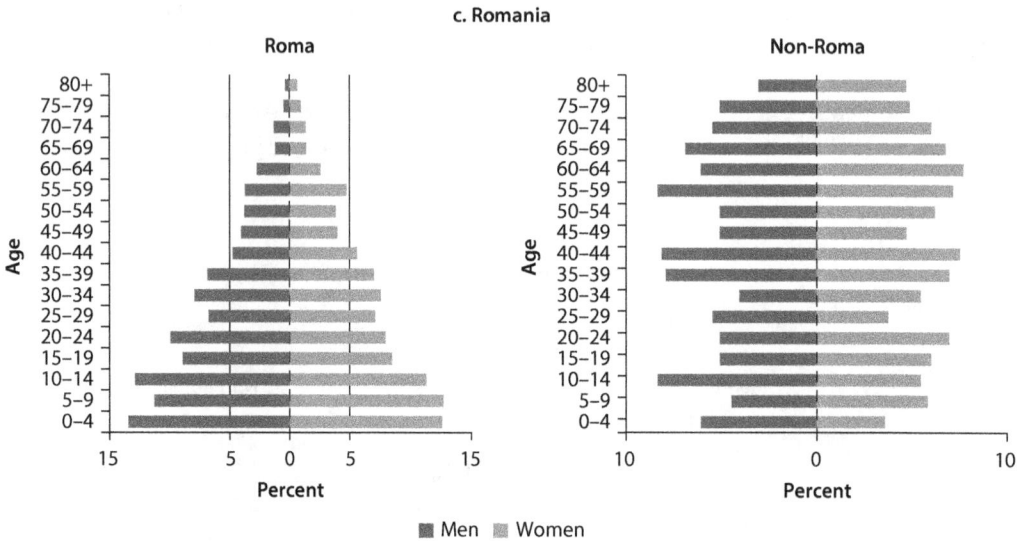

Source: UN, World Bank, and EC 2011.

the early years, on lifelong outcomes across all spheres of life. Policy interventions aimed at equalizing early education and development opportunities among children appear to have a significant positive impact on long-term outcomes, especially for children at the lower end of the income distribution (Andreoli, Havnes, and Lefranc 2014), as they "can promote beneficial child development where informal learning environments do not support the acquisition of important capabilities" (Burger 2012).[9]

Investing in early childhood development has proven to be particularly effective in leveling opportunities for disadvantaged children, as appropriate cognitive stimulation and nutrition in the first 1,000 days of life are associated with increased school attainment and productivity in future years (Heckman and Kautz 2014). Inequality in opportunities in childhood is detrimental to intragenerational mobility (from childhood to adulthood) and can self-perpetuate through the impact of worse parental circumstances on the next generation. Yet, the gaps Roma now face are not inevitable—the important role that such malleable factors as parenting practices and early education play suggests it is possible to change life odds for marginalized Roma (see box 1.6).

Ensuring equal access to quality education regardless of circumstances—and thus promoting access and designing support for disadvantaged children, including many Roma—should be considered a priority for CEE countries. Yet returns to promoting early school access are unlikely to fully materialize unless other complementary investments accompany this effort.[10] In the case of marginalized Roma, educational inequalities, differences in living conditions, and related health outcomes all combine to make the playing field uneven for the next

Box 1.6 The Role of Family Background for Equal Educational Opportunity

Based on the initial work of Allmendinger (1989), further research has discussed how in modern societies, the time an individual spends in the school system (vertical stratification) and the type of institution in which they study (horizontal stratification) are central "processes governing the allocation of individuals to social positions" (Bernardi and Ballarino 2011).

The empirical literature (from the 1967 Coleman report to the recent OECD PISA reports) has documented that one important reason for within-country differences in educational attainment is family background. Initial differences in individual achievement at school due to parental education are likely to widen over time (Carneiro and Heckman 2003). Carneiro (2006) finds that although adolescent student achievement is strongly affected by home and school environments, the most important dimension of school environments is students' family background.

Early tracking and educational segregation appear to reinforce the family background impact on educational outcomes (Ammermuller 2005; Hanushek and Wößmann 2005; Schütz, Ursprung, and Wößmann 2005). For example, it has been observed that "as school desegregation was largely halted in the late 1980s [in the United States], the black-white achievement gap stopped declining" (Gamoran and Long 2006).

generations. How can a child learn and thrive if in poor health and when living in deteriorated housing?

Since parental outcomes are their children's circumstances, an integrated approach to improve equality of opportunity also means that parents' outcomes—particularly with regards to employment and living conditions—need to be addressed. For example, poor earnings of parents make a large share of Roma children more likely to go to bed hungry, which undoubtedly impacts their developmental outcomes. Therefore, interventions that sustain equal opportunities for children—better nutrition, early cognitive stimulation and schooling, access to key services such as water and sanitation—are entry points for an integrated set of policies that can sustain marginalized households, especially at key nodes.

Just as important, opportunities change over the life cycle (World Bank 2013b). There are critical transitions—such as from adolescence to adulthood, from school to work, or during a job search—when opportunities are reallocated and affected by shocks, discrimination, and social norms. For example, data from the RRS suggest that the positive impact of preschooling on educational attainment for Roma children may weaken over time, probably in connection with the increasing role played by other factors related to the family background and environment.

In addition, at all such key nodes it will be necessary to identify the most effective balance between policies targeted toward all disadvantaged groups

Figure 1.12 Operationalizing Equality of Opportunity for Roma Children and Addressing Mediating Factors for Future Outcomes

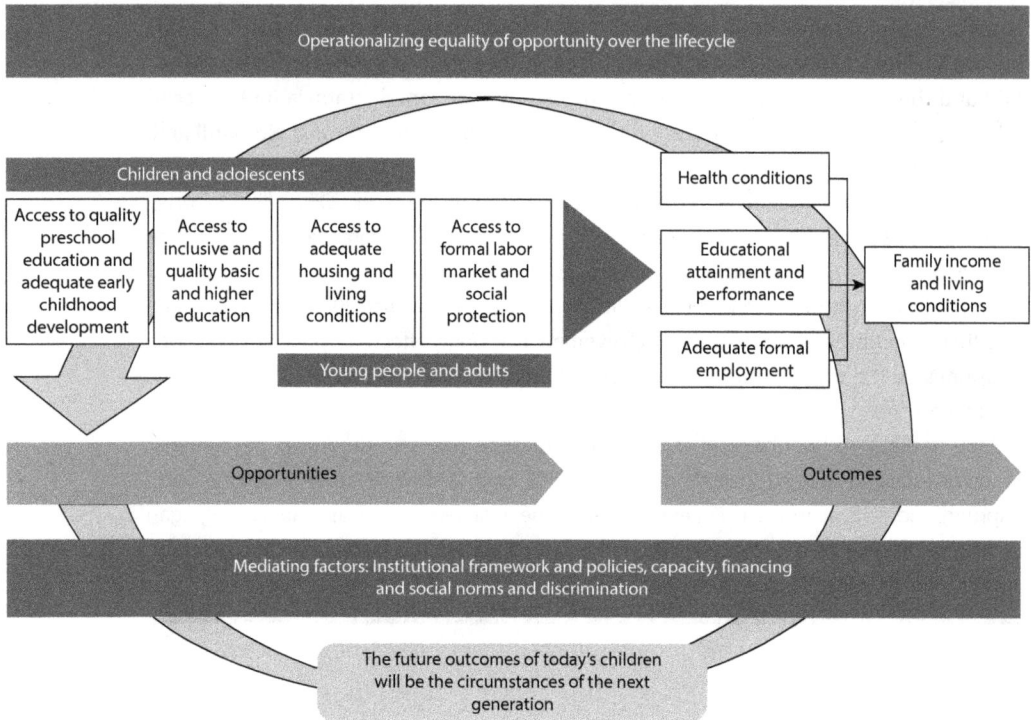

vis-à-vis those specifically tailored to Roma. It may well be that at some of those central transitions, an initiative aimed at all vulnerable populations (such as neighborhood improvements in a deprived area) would suffice, be politically acceptable, and equally benefit the Roma populations within the broader group, as long as inclusion or exclusion errors are small and/or do not disproportionately affect Roma.[11] However, specific challenges faced by the Roma minority might require tailored measures that adequately address these constraints, such as hiring Roma mediators to promote and facilitate access to educational or social services.

Figure 1.12 summarizes how factors such as discrimination and social norms can trigger unequal opportunities later in life for marginalized Roma and thus compound initial inequalities.

Structure of the Report

The remainder of this book focuses on three key pillars: healthy development for children and access to inclusive and high-quality education (chapter 2); access to productive employment (chapter 3); and improved living conditions (chapter 4). After presenting key diagnostics, the chapters have a strong focus on directions for policy and offer examples of good practices from within the region and around the world. Considerations of stigma and gender inequalities are woven into each chapter, based on available quantitative and qualitative evidence. A final chapter (chapter 5) brings together cross-cutting issues to effectively implement an agenda for promoting equal opportunities for marginalized Roma, as well as areas for future research.

Annex 1A: Spotlight on the Human Opportunity Index

This spotlight uses data from the Romania household budget surveys and census to compute the HOI for various opportunities for Roma and non-Roma. The exercise shows that the distribution of opportunities is influenced by initial circumstances. As a result, Roma children—who are more likely to be born in marginalized families, living in rural areas, or with parents with low education—are at a disadvantage. Once these circumstances are accounted for, ethnicity seems to play only a marginal additional role in explaining access to basic services in Romania. However, and given that ethnicity is associated with adverse initial circumstances, estimated contributions of the overall role of ethnicity to the HOI should be understood as lower bounds for the overall role of ethnicity.

The Logic of the Index

Measuring how *circumstances*—those hard-wired characteristics over which an individual has no control—shape *opportunities*—such as access to key goods and services—provides important insights into how far a society is from an equitable development process and, in turn, into what measures could progressively level the playing field across all individuals.

The HOI is a statistical tool that allows such measurement: In practice, it is calculated as a coverage rate discounted by how differently goods and services are allocated for the population of interest (here children ages 0–17) across different circumstance groups (such as parents' education, gender, ethnicity and religion) (see box 1A.1 and Molina et al. 2010). The HOI runs from 0 to 100, with 100 being universal coverage (in which case, individual circumstances have no impact on one's opportunities and society is perfectly equitable) and zero being no coverage at all. The HOI can change as the result of changes in people's circumstances (the composition effect), in overall service coverage (the scale effect), or in how equitably services are distributed (the equalization effect).

On the basis of household budget surveys and census data (see box 1A.2), this exercise allows a discussion of (a) the extent to which inequalities of opportunity exist at the national level in Romania, and what the drivers of these inequalities are; (b) how opportunities for Romanian Roma and non-Roma children have changed during recent years; (c) the extent to which Roma and non-Roma children are different in terms of key circumstances in the country; and (d) whether these circumstances matter to an equal extent for Roma and for non-Roma.

Box 1A.1 The Human Opportunity Index

"**The Human Opportunity Index** [is] a composite indicator that combines two elements: (a) the level of coverage of basic opportunities necessary for human development, such as primary education, water and sanitation, and electricity and (b) the degree to which the distribution of those opportunities is conditional on circumstances exogenous to children, such as gender, income, or household characteristics. This index assesses the importance of both improving overall access to basic opportunities and ensuring its equitable allocation" (de Barros et al. 2009, p. 55).

HOI = Coverage of basic opportunity * (1—Dissimilarity Index)

The D-index is a measure of inequality of opportunity that "measures dissimilar access rates to a given basic opportunity for groups of children defined by circumstance characteristics (specifically, children's area of residence, gender, parent's level of education, per capita family income, number of siblings, and presence of two parents at home) compared with the average access rate to the same service for the population of children as a whole. The D-index ranges from 0 to 100, in percentage terms, and in a situation of perfect equality of opportunity, D will be zero. The D-index has an interesting interpretation as the fraction of all available opportunities that need to be reallocated from children of better-off groups to children of worse-off groups to restore equal opportunity" (de Barros et al. 2009, p. 56).

Source: de Barros et al. 2009.

What Accounts for Unequal Opportunity in Romania?

In Romania, access to opportunities (understood as access to basic services such as water supply, bathrooms, flush toilets, and sewage disposal) expanded substantially between 2001 and 2013. The HOI analysis shows that this happened mainly through an increase in overall coverage rather than through a more equitable distribution. For example, the HOI for access to water supply, computed with ethnicity as the sole circumstance, increased by 13 percentage points. However, this improvement was solely due to an increase in coverage across the board, which however benefitted non-Roma more so than Roma. Indeed, the difference between Roma and non-Roma (captured by the dissimilarity index) not only failed to diminish but actually increased slightly.

As shown in box 1A.1, the dissimilarity index captures the variation in coverage between circumstance groups. In practical terms, the score can be interpreted as the share of opportunities that need to be redistributed across children with different characteristics in order to ensure equality of opportunities. In 2013, the dissimilarity index including only the ethnicity variable, was 3.1 percent—which means that to have equal access among Roma and non-Roma children, 3.1 percent of the access to water supply should be redistributed from non-Roma children to Roma children.

It is important to note that the size of the dissimilarity index is influenced by the size of the groups: The smaller the disadvantaged group—in this case the Roma—the fewer resources need to be reallocated to ensure an equitable distribution. A dissimilarity index of 3.1 percent is significant when we consider that, in the sample, Roma represent only 5.2 percent of the total number of children. The figures are of similar magnitude for other basic services (see table 1B.1).

The HOI can be computed to account for a variety of circumstances at the same time—not only ethnicity but also children's birthplaces and parental

---

Box 1A.2 Data Used to Estimate the Human Opportunity Index for Romania

The HOI estimates are based on the Romania Household Budget Survey (HBS) for 2001, 2007, and 2013, and on the 2011 census data.

The HBS is a nationally representative survey conducted on approximately 30,000 households/70,000 individuals each year (when using sampling weights, 2.1 percent were Roma in 2001; 2.6 percent in 2007; and 2.4 percent in 2013). Because of the high total number of respondents, the Roma children subsample is large enough to allow us to perform analyses on those services relevant to the total population of children (in 2001, 697 Roma ages 0–17 were in the sample; this was 710 in 2007, and 448 in 2013). The survey reports information about income levels/consumption, parents' level of education, whether the parents live in the same household as the child, access to different types of utilities (such as water, sewage, flush toilets, electricity, bath), residential area, and type of family (single-parent or both parents present).

The HBS subsamples for children belonging to some specific age groups (such as 10–14 years old or 16–17 years old) are too small to reliably estimate the inequality of opportunity in accessing education. To specifically compensate for this issue, data from the 2011 census were analyzed. The census has all the information available in the HBS (residential area, type of family, and so on) except for income/consumption. In the census data, 3.1 percent of the population declared themselves Roma (among children, the percentage of Roma is 6.4). Of 16–17-year-olds living with at least one parent, 17,168 children declared themselves Roma and 378,129 as non-Roma.

Even if the advantages of using census data are hard to ignore, there are some drawbacks. There seems to be consensus among stakeholders that the Roma population is underestimated in the census. On the other hand, no rigorous estimation of this group is available, although other unofficial estimations report that it could be as large as 3 million people. Another critical disadvantage refers to the potential bias due to the difference between the composition of the Roma interviewees captured by the census and the actual structure of Roma population. Unfortunately, there is no systematic evaluation of the direction of this bias. Anecdotal evidence suggests that Roma living in extreme poverty might not have been interviewed (one reason being that the areas that the census tracks were defined well in advance and did not always include dwellings not owned by the household members and/or informally occupied).

---

background—and disentangle their effect. Computing the HOI for basic housing services in Romania in this way and comparing it over time shows that the HOI increased by about 15 percentage points between 2001 and 2013 both because of an increase in coverage and because over time, opportunities have been redistributed more equitably across socioeconomic groups (see figure 1A.1 and table 1B.1 for detailed information). However, when looking specifically at Roma and non-Roma, as the earlier discussion pointed out, equity has not been reduced but, if anything, slightly increased.

Which circumstances had a stronger impact on inequality of opportunity in Romania? The Shapley decomposition of the dissimilarity index[12] allows us to isolate the role of each circumstance in children's inequality of opportunity (see table 1B.2). For example, in part because water supply coverage was not extensive across the country in the early 2000s, the largest degree of inequality was initially explained by residential area (64 percent of the dissimilarity), followed by income (18 percent). Once these factors are accounted for, ethnicity contributes only marginally to the overall level of dissimilarity. Between 2001 and 2013, coverage jumped by approximately 15 percentage points, and the dissimilarity index decreased approximately by the same extent. Because the improvement

Figure 1A.1 Coverage, Human Opportunity Index, and Dissimilarity Index for Water Supply Considering Various Sociodemographic Circumstances, Romania, 2001 and 2013

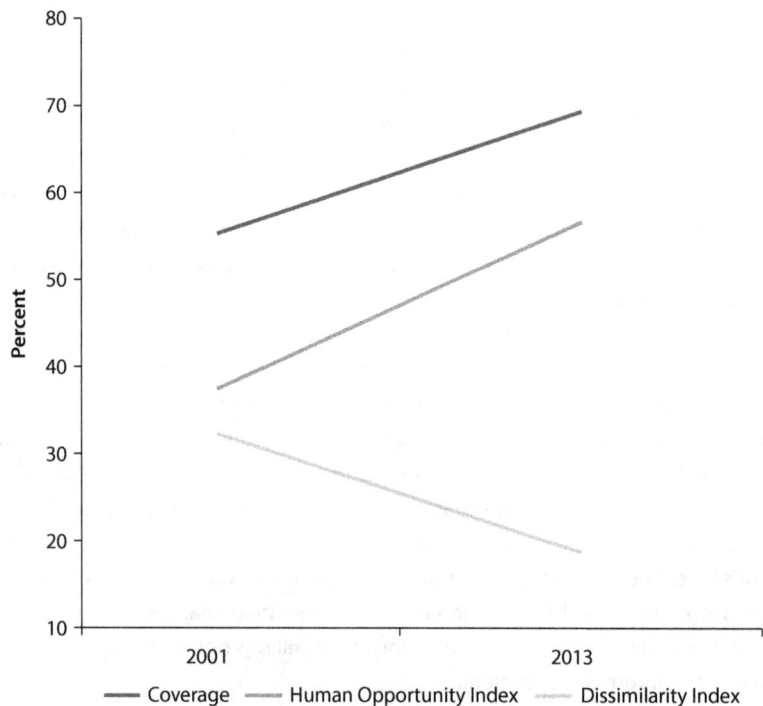

Source: Estimates based on HBS 2001/2013.

was mainly in rural areas, residential area started to matter less in explaining inequalities, and the role of the other circumstances becomes more prominent. Nevertheless, because of the small percentage of Roma out of the whole population, and because differences in access between Roma and non-Roma can be explained by other socioeconomic differences (such as parental education and income, which are highly correlated with ethnicity), only a small share of the dissimilarity index continued to be explained by ethnicity (4 percent).

When looking at the HOI for education opportunities (measured by the school attendance rate of children ages 16–17), parental education is instead the most significant explaining factor (contributing to 60 percent of the dissimilarity index), followed by residential area (contributing to 25 percent). Ethnicity contributes relatively more significantly than for water supply coverage—11 percent—although this might be due to the fact that family income could not be included in the model because of data restrictions (table 1B.3).[13]

What Are the Factors That Explain the Differences between Roma and Non-Roma in Terms of Opportunity in Romania?

Difference in opportunities between Roma and non-Roma might be driven by a variety of factors (a) structural differences in circumstances; (b) hard to quantify, unobserved characteristics that may be associated with ethnicity (including discrimination, stigma, and social norms);[14] and (c) an interaction between circumstances and ethnicity—which would differentiate the role of circumstances for Roma and non-Roma.

Estimations reported in the previous section indicated that, after considering other circumstances (such as location, parental income, and living with a single parent), ethnicity seems to play only a marginal additional role in explaining access to basic services. The roles of residential area and income in unequal access to housing services may reflect the "territoriality" of these services (one cannot have access to such services if one does not live in an area where such services exist). However, ethnicity is associated with adverse initial circumstances: Roma have higher probabilities of living in rural areas (62 percent compared to 51 percent of non-Roma), of having parents with low levels of education, and of being distributed in the lowest consumption quintiles (see table 1B.5 and figure 1A.3). Therefore, these estimated contributions to the HOI should be understood as lower bounds for the overall role of ethnicity.

Given the strong correlation between ethnicity and other circumstances that increase inequality of opportunity, it is useful to understand to what extent Roma children are among the individuals with the lowest probabilities of having access to key services. The characteristics used to compute the HOI are good predictors of the probability that children have access to services such as water and education (see tables 1B.6 and 1B.7). Given their ethnicity and also other observed characteristics (parents' education, income, residential area, and so on), 60 percent of Roma are among the lowest quintile of children in terms of access to piped water.

How Did the Gap between Roma and Non-Roma Opportunities Change over Time?

The HOIs estimated separately for Roma and non-Roma provide a snapshot of how access to key services changed for Roma and non-Roma in Romania over the past decade. In 2013, the HOI for water supply[15] estimated for Roma was approximately one-third of the HOI for non-Roma (21 percent against 59 percent)—see figure 1A.2 and table 1B.4 for detailed data. When looking at the data over time, the HOI for Roma barely increased, from 17 percent to only 21 percent, while for non-Roma the increase was significant. The major increase in the HOI for non-Roma is due to both a significant improvement in coverage and a decrease in inequality (which is captured by a lower dissimilarity index in 2013 than in 2001). Instead, the high level of inequality among the Roma did not decrease significantly over time (in 2013, it was higher than the inequality among non-Roma). The HOI for other basic services shows similar patterns, suggesting that Roma children continue to suffer from limited access to multiple basic services and that, within the Roma population, certain groups continue to be marginalized.

Concluding Remarks

Access to basic services has increased significantly in Romania during the past 15 years. This improvement is due in equal measure to an overall improvement in the coverage of these services and to a decrease in inequality among people.

The decomposition of the dissimilarity index indicates that residential area and income are key determinants of children's inequality of opportunity of access to housing services. Although ethnicity has an increasing role over time, it appears to account overall for a relatively low share of inequality in the allocation of opportunities. This happens for two main reasons. First, the Roma population is

Figure 1A.2 Roma versus Non-Roma Human Opportunity Index, Coverage, and Dissimilarity Index for Water Supply, Computed Separately, Romania, 2001 and 2013

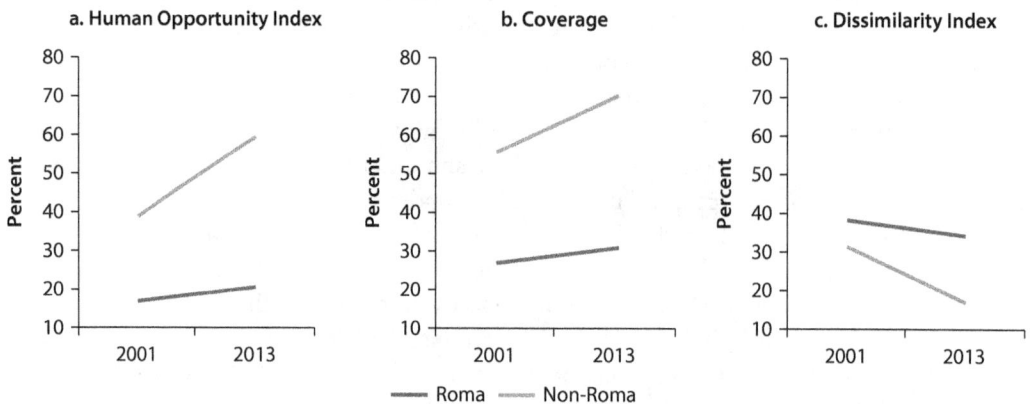

Source: Estimates based on HBS 2001/2013.

Figure 1A.3 Roma versus Non-Roma Distribution of Children by Quintile, Urbanicity, and Parental Education, Romania, 2013

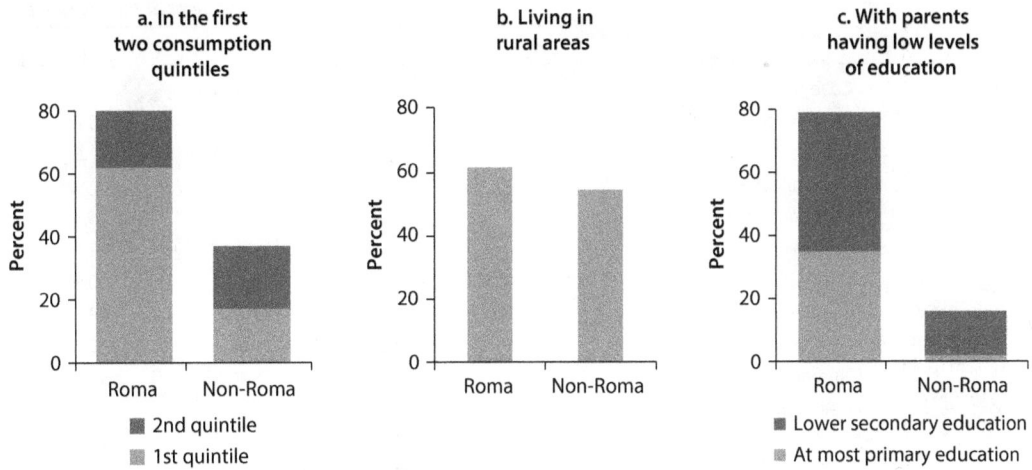

a. In the first two consumption quintiles

b. Living in rural areas

c. With parents having low levels of education

■ 2nd quintile
▨ 1st quintile

■ Lower secondary education
▨ At most primary education

Source: Estimates based on HBS 2013.

relatively small out of the total, and therefore its influence on the overall index is essentially limited; second, ethnicity is associated with adverse initial circumstances: Roma have a higher probability of living in rural areas, of having parents with low levels of education, and/or of earning low incomes.

Separate analyses of the HOI for Roma and non-Roma, respectively, show that the level of opportunity is much lower for Roma than for non-Roma. Moreover, while access to basic services barely increased and inequality showed only a slight reduction for Roma, it soared for non-Roma because of both an improvement in the coverage of basic services and a decrease in access inequality.

Annex 1B: Additional Tables

Table 1B.1 Human Opportunity Index Estimate with "Roma" Ethnicity and Defined Sociodemographic Variables Used as Circumstances, Romania, 2001 and 2013

		Ethnicity		Set of sociodemographic variables*	
		2001	*2013*	*2001*	*2013*
Water supply system—within the building	Coverage (C)	55.2	69.4	55.2	69.4
	Dissimilarity (D) Index	2.4	3.1	32.1	18.49
	Human Opportunity Index	53.9	67.3	37.5	56.6
	Decomposition				
	Change (p.p.)		13.4		19.1
	Scale (%)		104		50.6
	Equalization (p.p.)		−4		49.4

table continues next page

Table 1B.1 Human Opportunity Index Estimate with "Roma" Ethnicity and Defined Sociodemographic Variables Used as Circumstances, Romania, 2001 and 2013 *(continued)*

		Ethnicity		Set of sociodemographic variables*	
		2001	*2013*	*2001*	*2013*
Existence of bathroom with bathtub and/or shower (within or outside the dwelling)	Coverage (C)	50.5	62.3	50.5	62.3
	Dissimilarity (D) Index	3.2	3.9	36.2	23.7
	Human Opportunity Index	48.9	59.9	32.2	47.5
	Decomposition				
	Change (p.p.)		11		15.3
	Scale (%)		104		49.2
	Equalization (p.p.)		−4		50.8
Existence of sewage disposal system (public or private)	Coverage (C)	56.3	68.7	56.3	68.7
	Dissimilarity (D) Index	2.6	2.9	28.1	19.2
	Human Opportunity Index	54.8	66.6	40.5	55.5
	Decomposition				
	Change (p.p.)		12		15.0
	Scale (%)		102		59.2
	Equalization (p.p.)		−2		40.8
Flush toilet (within or outside the dwelling)	Coverage (C)	51.6	63.5	51.6	63.5
	Dissimilarity (D) Index	3.0	3.5	32.3	22.5
	Human Opportunity Index	50.1	61.2	35.0	49.2
	Decomposition				
	Change (p.p.)		11		14.2
	Scale (%)		103		56.3
	Equalization (p.p.)		−3		43.7

Source: Estimates based on HBS 2001/2013.
Note: p.p. = percentage points.
* Residential area, parental education level, ethnicity, quintiles of income per authors' estimates, and type of family (single parent or both parents).

Table 1B.2 Coverage of Water Supply and Shapley Decomposition of Dissimilarity Index, 2001 and 2013

	2001	*2013*
Water supply coverage	55.2	69.7
Water supply coverage in rural areas	18.9	47.7
Water supply coverage in urban areas	89.7	91.3
Dissimilarity index	32.1	18.6
Shapley decomposition of the D-index		
Roma versus non-Roma	1.5	4.1
Apprenticeship/vocational training versus lower secondary education, at most	2.0	4.0
Secondary education versus lower secondary education, at most	5.6	8.2
Tertiary education versus lower secondary education, at most	8.4	14.9
Quintiles of income per authors' estimates	18.5	30.0
Rural versus urban	64.0	37.6
Single-parent versus dual-parent household	0.1	1

Source: Estimates based on HBS 2001/2013.

Table 1B.3 Children (Ages 16–17) in School and Shapley Decomposition of Dissimilarity Index, 2011

	2011
Percentage of children ages 16–17 attending school	
Dissimilarity (D) Index	4.3
Shapley decomposition of the D-index	
Roma versus non-Roma	11.8
Rural versus urban	24.1
Single-parent versus dual-parent household	1.1
Girls versus boys	3.2
Primary education versus upper secondary education, or higher	18.2
Lower secondary education (gymnasium) versus upper secondary education, or higher	41.6

Source: Estimates based on 2011 census data.

Table 1B.4 Human Opportunity Index for Water Supply for Roma versus Non-Roma, 2001 and 2013

	Roma		Non-Roma	
	2001	2013	2001	2013
Coverage (C)	27.3	31.4	56.6	71.7
Dissimilarity (D) Index	38.5	34.5	31.6	17.1
Human Opportunity Index (HOI)	16.8	20.6	38.7	59.5
Change of HOI (p.p.)		3.8		20.8
Decomposition of HOI change				
Composition (p.p.)		1.8		−0.8
Scale (p.p.)		0.8		10.8
Equalization (p.p.)		1.1		10.8

Source: HBS 2001/2013. Circumstances used included the maximum levels of parents' education; quintiles of consumption per estimates; residential area; and being raised by a single parent.
Note: Water supply system in the house. p.p. = percentage points.

Table 1B.5 Distribution of Roma versus Non-Roma, by Consumption Quintiles, Residential Area, and Parental Education, Romania, 2001 and 2013

	2001			2013		
	Non-Roma	Roma	Total	Non-Roma	Roma	Total
Quintiles of consumption per authors' estimates						
First	17	65	19	17	62	19
Second	20	21	20	20	18	20
Third	21	7	20	21	12	20
Fourth	21	3	21	21	6	20
Fifth	21	3	20	21	2	20
Total	100	100	100	100	100	100

table continues next page

Table 1B.5 Distribution of Roma versus Non-Roma, by Consumption Quintiles, Residential Area, and Parental Education, Romania, 2001 and 2013 (continued)

	2001			2013		
	Non-Roma	Roma	Total	Non-Roma	Roma	Total
Residential area						
Urban	49	38	48	46	39	46
Rural	51	62	52	54	61	54
Total	100	100	100	100	100	100
Parents' education						
Primary education at most	3	47	5	2	35	4
Lower secondary education	13	33	14	14	44	15
Apprenticeship/vocational	23	7	23	22	8	21
High school	44	8	42	38	8	37
Tertiary education	17	4	16	24	5	23
Total	100	100	100	100	100	100

Note: Consumption quintiles are computed for children only.

Table 1B.6 Distribution of Access to Piped Water for Roma versus Non-Roma Children (Ages 0–17), by Quintiles/Deciles of Probability, 2013

Quintiles/deciles	Probability of access to piped water	% of Non-Roma	% of Roma
First	0.24	20	59
First	0.16	9	47
Second	0.34	11	12
Second	0.54	17	29
Third	0.80	23	11
Fourth	0.95	20	1
Fifth	0.99	20	0
Total	0.69	100	100

Source: Estimates based on HBS 2013.
Note: Data presented are based on children's characteristics (ethnicity, parents' education, household income, residential area, and family type).

Table 1B.7 Distribution of Access to Education for Roma versus Non-Roma Children (Ages 16–17), by Quintiles/Deciles of Probabilities

Quintiles/deciles	Probability of attending school	% of Non-Roma	% of Roma
First	0.7	16.5	99.4
First	0.6	7.6	82.8
Second	0.8	9.0	16.6
Second	0.9	21.4	0.6
Third	0.96	37.6	0
Fourth	0.98	3.8	0
Fifth	0.98	20.8	0
Total	0.9	100	100

Source: Estimates based on the 2011 census.
Note: Data presented are based on children's characteristics (ethnicity, parents' education, household income, residential area, and family type).

Notes

1. Data are from the 2011 Regional Roma Survey (RRS), a large-scale United Nations Development Programme (UNDP), World Bank, and European Commission (EC) survey conducted in communities with large Roma populations in Bulgaria, the Czech Republic, Hungary, Romania, and the Slovak Republic. The sample focused on those communities where the share of the Roma population is greater or equal to the national share of the Roma population. This approach covers around 80–90 percent of the Roma population in each country. Summary findings were presented in "Roma at a Glance" (UNDP/FRA 2012). See full description in the preface.

2. Opportunities can best be understood as the possibility to effectively choose among available options, or to "take advantage" of some combination of events to enhance a person's life achievement potential. Opportunities require the existence of "functionings" (that is, being healthy, as opposed to accessing good nutrition; see Sen 1979, 1985). Access to goods and services is a necessary, but not sufficient, condition for these functionings to materialize. Since functionings are hard to measure, "access" is considered here to be synonymous with opportunities (see World Bank 2014).

3. Based on the Romania census data, annex 3A presents a complementary take on the interplay between ethnicity and marginalization at the community level.

4. PISA data does not allow for analysis by ethnicity.

5. Theorists have tried to measure discrimination concretely using statistical techniques, especially in relation to labor market discrimination. The two best-known models are the (a) "taste model" (Becker 1957), whereby discrimination arises because employers and workers have a "distaste" for working with people from different ethnic backgrounds and the (b) "ignorance model" (Arrow 1971), in which discrimination arises when the employer, through ignorance or prejudice, assumes that certain groups of workers are less productive than others and is thus less willing to employ them.

6. See, for example, Janet Yellen's remarks on the problem with decreased equality of opportunity in the United States due to rising education costs (October 2014) and the recent analysis on the United States by Chetty et al. (n.d.) at http://www.equality -of-opportunity.org/.

7. Other important impacts of being disadvantaged are linked to voice. Because the poor have less voice in the political process, they are less able to influence spending decisions to improve public schools for their children, hence reinforcing exclusion (World Bank 2005). While important, these effects are outside the scope of this book.

8. For an in-depth discussion see, for example, Brunori et al. (2013).

9. Conversely, research shows that individuals who had low levels of cognitive development at preschool age achieve lower levels of education later and have lower wages (Currie and Duncan 1999; Case and Paxson 2006).

10. As put by Escobal (2012): "Children who share a certain set of circumstances may be simultaneously deprived in several well-being dimensions, and inequality in accessing one particular opportunity may be correlated with inequality in accessing several other opportunities."

11. See spotlight on territorial targeting (in annex 4A) and evidence from Romania on potential exclusion errors when using geographic targeting.

12. The Shapley decomposition of the dissimilarity index estimates the marginal contribution of each circumstance to inequality in access to opportunities, "net" of other

circumstances. It calculates the dissimilarity index with all combinations of circumstances and calculates an average of each circumstance's contribution to each combination.

13. Because of the very small number of cases, it was not possible to compute the HOI for school attendance from the Household Budget Survey (which had information on household income), hence the 2011 census data was used.

14. This unobserved component is basically captured by the 4 percent contribution of ethnicity to explaining the inequalities of opportunity in the Shapley decomposition described above.

15. The same patterns can be observed when looking at other basic housing services/facilities: sewage disposal system, flush toilet or bath.

References

Alesina, A., R. Di Tella, and R. MacCulloch. 2004. "Inequality and Happiness: Are Europeans and Americans Different?" *Journal of Public Economics* 88 (2004): 2009–42.

Allmendinger, J. 1989. "Educational Systems and Labour Market Outcomes." *European Sociological Review* 5: 231–50.

Alsop, R., M. F. Bertelsen, and J. Holland. 2006. *Empowerment in Practice: From Analysis to Implementation*. Washington, DC: World Bank.

Ammermuller, A. 2005. "Educational Opportunities and the Role of Institutions." ZEW Discussion Paper 05–44, Centre for European Economic Research, Mannheim, Germany.

Andreoli, F., T. Havnes, and A. Lefranc. 2014. "Equalization of Opportunity: Definitions, Implementable Conditions and Application to Early-Childhood Policy Evaluation." IZA Discussion Paper 8503, Institute for the Study of Labor, Bonn.

Arneson, R. 1989. "Equality of Opportunity for Welfare." *Philosophical Studies: An International Journal for Philosophy in the Analytic Tradition* 56 (1): 77–93.

Arrow, K. 1971. "The Theory of Discrimination." Working Paper 403, Department of Economics, Industrial Relations Section, Princeton University, Princeton, NJ.

Asenov, R., I. Tomova, S. Cherkezova, and L. Stoychev. 2014. "Drivers of Labor Market Discrimination of Roma in Bulgaria." Fieldwork, Bulgaria.

Becker, G. S. 1957. *The Economics of Discrimination*. Chicago, IL: University of Chicago Press.

Berg, A., and J. D. Ostry. 2011. "Inequality and Unsustainable Growth: Two Sides of the Same Coin?" IMF Staff Discussion Note 11/08, International Monetary Fund, Washington, DC.

Berg, A., J. D. Ostry, and J. Zettelmeyer. 2011. "What Makes Growth Sustained?" *Journal of Development Economics* 98 (2): 149–66.

Bernardi, F., and G. Ballarino. 2011. "Participation, Equality of Opportunity and Returns to Tertiary Education in Contemporary Europe." AlmaLaurea Working Paper 10, AlmaLaurea Inter-University Consortium, Bologna, Italy.

Brunori, G., D. Barjolle, A.-C. Dockes, S. Helmle, J. Ingram, L. Klerkx, H. Moschitz, G. Nemes, and T. Tisenkopfs. 2013. "CAP Reform and Innovation: The Role of Learning and Innovation Networks." *Eurochoices* 12 (2): 27–33.

Burger, K. 2012. "Early Childhood Care and Education and Equality of Opportunity: Theoretical and Empirical Perspectives on Current Social Challenges." Springer VS.

Cappelen, A. W., E. O. Sorenson, and B. Tungodden. 2010. "Responsibility for What? Fairness and Individual Responsibility." *European Economic Review* 54: 429–41.

Carneiro, P. 2006. "Equality of Opportunity and Educational Achievement in Portugal." Paper prepared for the 2006 Conference on Economic Development in Portugal organized by the Bank of Portugal, Lisbon.

Carneiro, P., and J. Heckman. 2003. "Human Capital Policy." NBER Working Paper 9495, National Bureau of Economic Research, Cambridge, MA.

Case, A., and C. Paxson. 2006. "Stature and Status: Height, Ability, and Labor Market Outcomes." NBER Working Paper 12466, National Bureau of Economic Research, Cambridge, MA.

Chetty, R., N. Hendren, P. Kline, E. Saez, and N. Turner. n.d. "The Equality of Opportunity Project." http://www.equality-of-opportunity.org.

Cohen, G. A. 1989. "On the Currency of Egalitarian Justice." *Ethics* 99 (4): 906–44.

Currie, J., and Duncan, T. 1999. "Does Head Start Help Hispanic Children?" *Journal of Public Economics* 74 (2): 235–62.

Das, M. 2013. "Exclusion and Discrimination in the Labor Market." Background paper for the *World Development Report*, World Bank, Washington, DC.

de Barros, Ricardo Paes, F. H. G. Ferreira, J. R. Molinas Vega, and J. Saavedra-Chanduvi. 2009. "Measuring Inequality of Opportunities in Latin America and the Caribbean." World Bank, Washington, DC.

Dunnzlaff, L., D. Neumann, J. Niehues, and A. Peichl. 2011. "Equality of Opportunity and Redistribution in Europe." *Research on Economic Inequality* 19: 99–129.

Dworkin, R. 1981. "What Is Equality? Part 2: Equality of Resources." *Philosophy and Public Affairs* 10 (4): 283–345.

Elmslie, B., and S. Sedo. 1996. "Discrimination, Social Psychology, and Hysteresis in Labor Markets." *Journal of Economic Psychology* 17 (4): 465–78.

Escobal, J. 2012. "Multidimensional Poverty and Inequality of Opportunity in Peru: Taking Advantage of the Longitudinal Dimension of Young Lives." Young Lives Working Paper 79, University of Oxford.

European Commission. 2008. "Proposal for a Council Directive on Implementing the Principle of Equal Treatment between Persons Irrespective of Religion or Belief, Disability, Age or Sexual Orientation." Publications Office of the European Union, Luxembourg.

FRA (European Union Agency for Fundamental Rights). 2011. FRA Roma Pilot Survey.

Fehr, E., and U. Fischbacher. 2003. "The Nature of Human Altruism." *Nature* 425 (6960): 785–91.

Gamoran, A., and D. A. Long. 2006. "Equality of Educational Opportunity: A 40-Year Retrospective." Working Paper 2006-9, Wisconsin Center for Education Research, University of Wisconsin–Madison.

Goldsmith, A. H., S. Sedo, W. Darity Jr., and D. Hamilton. 2004. "The Labor Supply Consequences of Perceptions of Employer Discrimination During Search and On-the-Job: Integrating Neoclassical Theory, and Cognitive Dissonance." *Journal of Economic Psychology* 25: 15–39.

Grimm, M., K. Harttgen, S. Klasen, M. Misselhorn, T. Munzi, and T. Smeeding. 2010. "Inequality in Human Development: An Empirical Assessment of 32 Countries." *Social Indicators Research* 97 (2): 191–211.

Hanushek, E. A., and L. Wößmann. 2005. "Does Educational Tracking Affect Performance and Inequality? Differences-in-Differences Evidence across Countries." NBER Working Paper 11124, National Bureau of Economic Research, Cambridge, MA.

Heckman, J. J., and T. Kautz. 2014. "Fostering and Measuring Skills: Interventions That Improve Character and Cognition." In *The Myth of Achievement Tests: The GED and the Role of Character in American Life*, edited by J. J. Heckman, J. E. Humphries, and T. Kautz, 341–430. Chicago, IL: University of Chicago Press.

Hoff, K., and P. Pandey. 2006. "Discrimination, Social Identity, and Durable Inequalities." *American Economic Review* 96 (2): 206–11.

Ivanov, A., and J. Kagin. 2014. "Roma Poverty from a Human Development Perspective." Roma Inclusion Working Papers, UNDP, Istanbul.

Kertesi, G., and G. Kézdi. 2011. "The Roma/Non-Roma Test Score Gap in Hungary." *American Economic Review: Papers and Proceedings* 101 (3): 519–25.

———. 2014. "On the Test Score Gap between Roma and Non-Roma Students in Hungary and Its Potential Causes." Budapest Working Papers on the Labour Market, BWP 2014/1, Institute of Economics, Hungarian Academy of Sciences, Corvinus University of Budapest.

Lieberman, E. S., and G. H. McClendon. 2012. "The Ethnicity–Policy Preference Link in Sub-Saharan Africa." *Comparative Political Studies* 46 (5): 574–602.

Loury, G. 1999. "Social Exclusion and Ethnic Groups: The Challenge to Economics." Paper presented at the Annual World Bank Conference on Development Economics, Washington, DC, April 28–30.

Marrero, G. A., and J. G. Rodríguez. 2013. "Inequality of Opportunity and Growth." *Journal of Development Economics* 104 (C): 107–22.

Martínez, L. M., M. F. Enguita, and J. R. Gómez. 2010. "Disengaged from Education: Processes, Experiences, Motivations and Strategies of Early School Dropout and School Failure." Revista de Educación, Número Extraordinario de 2010, 119–45. http://www.mecd.gob.es/dctm/revista-de-educacion/articulosre2010/re201005.pdf?documentId=0901e72b81203eb3.

Molina, E., A. Narayan, and J. Saavedra-Chanduvi. 2013. "Outcomes, Opportunity and Development: Why Unequal Opportunities and Not Outcomes Hinder Economic Development." Policy Research Working Paper 6735, World Bank, Washington, DC.

Molinas, J., R. Paes de Barros, J. Saavedra, and M. Giugale. 2010. *Do Our Children Have a Chance?* Human Opportunity Report for Latin America and the Caribbean, World Bank, Washington, DC.

National Institute of Statistics (Romania). 2013. Household Budget Survey.

Nozick, R. 1974. *Anarchy, State and Utopia.* New York: Basic Books.

Osberg, L., and T. Smeeding. 2004. "'Fair' Inequality? Attitudes toward Pay Differentials: The United States in Comparative Perspective." *American Sociological Review* 71 (June): 450–73.

Rawls, J. 1971. *A Theory of Justice.* Cambridge, MA: Harvard University Press.

Roemer, J. 1993. "A Pragmatic Theory of Responsibility for the Egalitarian Planner." *Philosophy and Public Affairs* 22: 146–66.

Schütz, G., H. Ursprung, and L. Wößmann. 2005. "Education Policy and Equality of Opportunity." IZA Discussion Paper 1906, Institute for the Study of Labor, Bonn.

Sen, A. 1979. "Equality of What?" Paper presented at the Tanner Lecture on Human Values, Stanford University, Stanford, CA.

———. 1985. *Commodities and Capabilities*. Amsterdam: North-Holland.

Trannoy, A., T. Sandy, F. Jusot, and M. Devaux. 2010. "Inequality of Opportunities in Health in France: A First Pass." *Health Economics* 19: 921–38.

UNDP/FRA (United Nations Development Programme/Fundamental Rights Agency). 2012. "The Situation of Roma in 11 EU Member States—Survey Results at a Glance." Publications Office of the European Union, Luxembourg.

UNDP, World Bank, and EC (European Commission). 2011. *Regional Roma Survey*. Report, UNDP, World Bank, and EC, New York.

World Bank. 2005. *World Development Report 2006: Equity and Development*. Washington, DC: World Bank.

———. 2010. "Roma Inclusion: An Economic Opportunity for Bulgaria, Czech Republic, Romania and Serbia." Policy Note, World Bank, Washington, DC.

———. 2011. *World Development Report 2012: Gender Equality and Development*. Washington, DC: World Bank.

———. 2013a. *Mitigating the Economic Impact of an Aging Population: Options for Bulgaria*. Washington DC: World Bank.

———. 2013b. *Inclusion Matters: The Foundation for Shared Prosperity*. Washington, DC: World Bank.

———. 2014. *Human Opportunity Report for Sub-Saharan Africa*. Washington, DC: World Bank.

World Bank and Open Society Institute. 2011. Bulgarian Crisis Monitoring Survey, February 2011. World Bank, Washington, DC; Open Society Institute, New York.

World Values Survey Database. 2008. World Values Survey (accessed March 11, 2015), http://www.worldvaluessurvey.org/wvs.jsp.

PART 2

Equality of Opportunity in Education, Labor Markets, and Living Conditions

Life Story—Breaking the Rule: Going to High School and On

The story of a young female Roma university graduate from a rural settlement in Romania

I grew up in a poor Roma family in a segregated settlement situated between two villages in southwest Romania. My father was one of the most brilliant students in his school. He graduated from high school, but he couldn't continue his education because his family had no money and his parents forced him to get married. My mother never finished primary school.

My family keeps the Roma traditions and culture, and we all communicate in Romani. Since Romania joined the EU, many people from my community have gone abroad to search for jobs and a better life. People used to travel around the country and make mud bricks for a living. Entire families were involved in brickmaking. They would leave their settlements in early spring and come back in late autumn. Because of that, many children dropped out of school. The girls in my community quit school more often than the boys, because they have to take care of the house. But I was lucky. Although my parents were also traveling and selling bricks, my grandparents stayed at home so we could go to school. My grandfather was a blacksmith, and he was making horseshoes and combers, which my grandmother was selling or exchanging for food. And this is how we survived until my parents returned.

In primary school, I was in a segregated Roma class. There was not enough space for all the students in the main school building, so us Roma studied in an abandoned building, about a kilometer from the main school. In the first grade, we were 35 in my class. But by the time we reached the eighth grade, the girls had gotten married and the boys had dropped out.

The education in that school was really bad. We never had the same teacher. We never had books. We never attended events held in the main school building. We were treated as "handicapped," as the requirements for our class were lower than average. When it was very cold, we didn't go to school because we had no good shoes.

But my parents helped. When my father was home, he helped me with my homework. My mother always told me, "Do not be in a hurry to get married, be independent in your life." I was the first girl from my community to attend high school. I broke the "rule" that Roma girls are not allowed to go to high school. My grandfather warned me, "Once you step out of this house, it will be hard to come back. You have to be really strong and clear on what you want to do with your life. And don't forget, my child, that you will suffer a lot outside of the Roma settlement."

I didn't know the difference between Roma and non-Roma. I asked him, "Why?" And he told me, "You have to be strong once you face the Romanians. You have to be three times smarter than they are. Because they have put a name on us, that we are stupid, that we are thieves, and that we are dirty, and you have to prove that that they are wrong about us."

I went to a secondary boarding school in a village about 30 kilometers from home. Around the time I went to high school, my parents left for Germany to search for work. Despite their unstable lives there, they would send me their last penny to pay for school.

I wasn't ready for high school because I had a lot of gaps in my knowledge. I couldn't speak proper Romanian. I was the only Roma in my high school class, and everyone treated me like a person with a contagious disease. During the first year, I wanted to drop out many times, but I heard my grandfather's words in my mind. They gave me the strength to show my classmates that I could do better. I started to study hard, and soon I was the best student in my class. The teachers in the high school were generally indifferent to me, although sometimes they would use me as an example to push the other students to study, because, they said, if the Roma girl could do it, then they could do it too.

I knew I couldn't achieve much with only a high school education, so I went to university. I was exempt from paying tuition fees because of my strong academics. I tried to find a job while I studied, but I was always turned down because of being Roma. Once I saw an advertisement that a bakery was hiring a shop assistant. I went there and asked the woman behind the window if the vacancy was open and the woman, who was writing something, didn't even look at me and said the job was still available. But then, when she saw me, she apologized and said that she was confused and the job had actually been given to someone else.

So to raise money for my studies, I worked as a cleaner in Germany during summer breaks. Right now I'm getting a second master's degree abroad. When I graduate, I'm going to go back to Romania and search for a job in the local administration.

Life Story—"I Read All the Books at Home"

The story of a young Roma man from Bulgaria, living in a rural nonsegregated area

I grew up in a traditional Roma family in a village in north Bulgaria. I have been in contact with Bulgarians from an early age, because my house is next to a Bulgarian apartment building. I have an older sister and a younger brother. I am the only one with a university degree in my family and in my community.

My mother works on a dairy farm. She went to elementary school, but never finished. My father is a farmer, and he is among the few Roma in my community with a secondary education. In my home village, there are equal parts Bulgarians, Roma, and Turkish. The government jobs in the village are usually taken by Bulgarians. The Turkish run small family businesses, like cafes and restaurants, or migrate abroad. The majority of Roma cannot find decent jobs because they have low education and skills. Many migrate, or they work in the gray economy, and some resort to petty crimes for a living. There are few Roma families who make a living from agriculture and from breeding livestock. My community does not value education, and girls are not allowed to study; the argument is that education doesn't get you anywhere: "Why should Roma study when even many Bulgarians are unemployed?"

When I was a child we didn't have enough toys, but we had a lot of books at home. My father liked buying books because they were cheap. The first thing I did when I learned to read was to read all the books at home. I think this is the difference between my family and the other families in the village; the other children that I was playing with didn't have many books at home.

I went to nonsegregated primary and secondary schools. All my teachers in primary school were very supportive and never differentiated among us children. In fifth grade, I had a teacher of Bulgarian literature and language who was my classmate's mother. This was a big plus for me, we had a competition going, her son and me, and we were always asking her for additional exercises. I was going to afterschool classes because my parents did not help me with my homework. I attended the local secondary school, where the quality of education was poor. The school is among the worst in Bulgaria. In all the measurements you can imagine it is very far down on the list, but it still exists. We were only nine students in my class. Nobody would believe that someone from that school would go on to graduate from university.

In tenth grade, I got married. It was an arranged marriage. But I really wanted to continue my education. I realized that beyond the village there are many other opportunities, and I wanted a different life from my parents. I told my literature teacher that I wanted to continue my studies. One day, I went with her and with my driving *instructor from high school to the university in the city and they helped me register for the entry exams.*

My parents were against me going to university. They did not have money to support me, but they also insisted that because I was married I had to get a job and take care of my family. But when they saw that they couldn't stop me, they told me, "Okay, if you really want to do it, go for it, but we cannot support you financially." In the summer, I worked in construction. I saved some money, I passed the exams and I got accepted to the university. In the first months of my studies, I went home only for the weekends. During the winter break, I did not spend the holidays with my family because I worked in a bakery in the city to earn much needed money.

The work in the bakery was hard, I worked in the night and slept during the day, and I had no social life. Later, I got a scholarship from the university for my good grades and a little financial support from my parents. Around that time, my wife moved to the city. She decided to continue her education and enrolled in a secondary school and worked at the same time. In my first year at the university, I was not aware of the Roma Education Fund scholarship. In the second year, I volunteered in a local Roma NGO and there I learned about the REF scholarship. I applied for it. The REF scholarship was the biggest financial support I got during my studies, and without it I would not have finished university. I earned additional money for my studies from a part-time job at the NGO where I had volunteered.

CHAPTER 2

Equality of Opportunity for Marginalized Roma Children: Starting Right

Sandor Karacsony

Summary

Education is a powerful instrument for improving equity, reducing poverty, and promoting economic growth. International assessments of education systems in the five new member Central and Eastern European (CEE) countries that have significant Roma populations indicate systemwide inequalities that disproportionately affect Roma students' ability to access quality education. Inequality starts early in life for marginalized Roma children, often by the time they are in kindergarten. Driven by further barriers to quality education, this early learning gap widens later in life and eventually hampers a Roma child's chances of succeeding on par with the non-Roma population as an adult (figure 2.1 presents some of the most salient facts about education for Roma in marginalized communities).

Approximately 37 percent of children in Roma households across CEE countries grow up in poverty, which severely impairs their lifelong cognitive and socioemotional development potential and hinders their ability to attend school and socialize with their peers. Few Roma children have access to quality preschool education, which undermines their school readiness, their chances of achieving higher educational levels, and of obtaining necessary employment skills. Supply- and demand-side investments in adequate child development in the first 1,000 days of life are necessary to address these early learning gaps, as well as more and better investments in kindergartens and preschools.

While primary school enrollment levels are generally similar between the Roma and their non-Roma neighbors, only 6 percent of Roma adults in CEE report completing upper secondary education, in stark contrast with 40 percent of non-Roma neighbors and the even higher completion rate among the general population. Completion rates are particularly low among Roma women. This cannot be explained by different educational aspirations, as the Regional Roma Survey (RRS) finds that most Roma parents across the region prefer their children to complete secondary or tertiary education. However, Roma pupils are disproportionately affected by repeats, dropouts, and school segregation. Investments in both education access and education quality throughout all grades, coupled with targeted measures, can reduce Roma students' dropout rates and early school leaving. In conjunction, it is also critical to improve marginalized Roma's access to tertiary education through merit-based scholarships, targeted affirmative action measures, and transportation subsidies.

Promoting Roma's access to and completion of quality education will benefit not only Roma individuals but also wider society, as population dynamics make education interventions a necessity: between 7 and 20 percent of the new labor market entrants in these countries are Roma (World Bank 2012c), who enter the labor market largely unprepared. The EU's goal of achieving smart and inclusive growth, together with the new CEE states' increasing need for their workforce to survive in a challenging global skills competition, demand further investments in more inclusive education systems. Along with targeted measures to help the Roma overcome a variety of learning gaps, these investments would not only contribute to reducing unemployment and poverty among the Roma population, but would also translate into considerable economic benefits in the form of productivity gains and fiscal contributions (World Bank 2013).

The group to which the policy or scientific discourse commonly refers as "the Roma community" is not at all homogenous; Roma families, like non-Roma ones, present a broad variety of socioeconomic backgrounds and profiles. Education systems have a crucial role to play in acknowledging diversity and cultivating the ethnic identity and self-esteem of Roma students, for example, by teaching Roma history or the Romani language; strengthening the next generation's sense of identity and empowerment; and instilling in them a sense of confidence and pride.

Figure 2.1 Notable Facts about School Enrollment among Roma

Fewer than 50% of Roma children are enrolled in preschool.

School systems largely sort children based on their social status and abilities.

Only 11% to 31% of young Roma reach upper secondary education.

The share of Roma among tertiary education graduates does not exceed 1%.

Yet Roma and non-Roma parents have similar aspirations for their children's education.

Source: UNDP, World Bank and EC 2011.

Being Fair, Faring Better • http://dx.doi.org/10.1596/978-1-4648-0598-1

Education, the Key Driver of Development

Education is a powerful driver of development, and one of the strongest instruments for reducing poverty, raising incomes, and promoting economic growth. Policies that aim to end poverty and boost shared prosperity depend on more and better investments in quality education and learning. However, international assessments of the education systems in the five CEE countries that have significant Roma populations produce sobering results: In the 2012 Programme for International Student Assessments (PISA), all five countries rank below the OECD average in terms of equity in education opportunities—the Slovak Republic, Hungary, and Bulgaria are among the worst performers in this dimension. Students from four of the five countries also perform significantly below OECD countries' average, with students from the Czech Republic being the only ones to perform at average levels. These findings indicate that all of these countries have selective school systems that are unable to overcome the learning gaps driven by children's socioeconomic background. In other words, instead of acting in line with their historic role and development mandate of being a socioeconomic "equalizer," these school systems appear to be a source of further inequality.

Inequality in educational outcomes starts early in life for marginalized Roma children. In 2011, approximately 85.5 percent of children in CEE and Roma households were at risk of poverty or social exclusion, which is expected to severely impact their lifelong cognitive and socioemotional development potential and hinder their ability to attend school, learn, and socialize with their peers. Few Roma children have access to quality preschool education. In CEE, 43 percent of Roma children between three and six years of age are enrolled in preschool, compared to 56 percent of their non-Roma neighbors (see figure 2.2). This undermines Roma children's school readiness and their chances of achieving higher educational levels and obtaining the necessary skills for employment later in life. Evidence in and outside of the EU (World Bank 2012e) demonstrates that early intellectual stimulation at home and in preschool develops the foundations of cognitive and socio-emotional skills, which improves adults' chances of socioeconomic success, especially for vulnerable groups and marginalized Roma communities. Many factors underlie the lack of access to quality education for Roma. For example, in the case of Hungary and the Slovak Republic, constraints to accessing early child education appear to be related to limited availability in the geographical areas where Roma tend to concentrate (Kertesi and Kézdi 2012; World Bank 2012a). Overall, resources of schools that serve more disadvantaged communities, or are mainly attended by Roma children (such as in Hungary or Romania), are often inadequate (Csapó et al. 2009).

Despite their families' intentions, most Roma students drop out of school before completing upper secondary education. While primary school enrollment levels are generally similar between the Roma and their non-Roma neighbors, only 6 percent of Roma adults (ages 25–64) report completing upper

Figure 2.2 Roma and Non-Roma Gross Preschool Enrollment Rate for Boys and Girls (Ages 3–5)

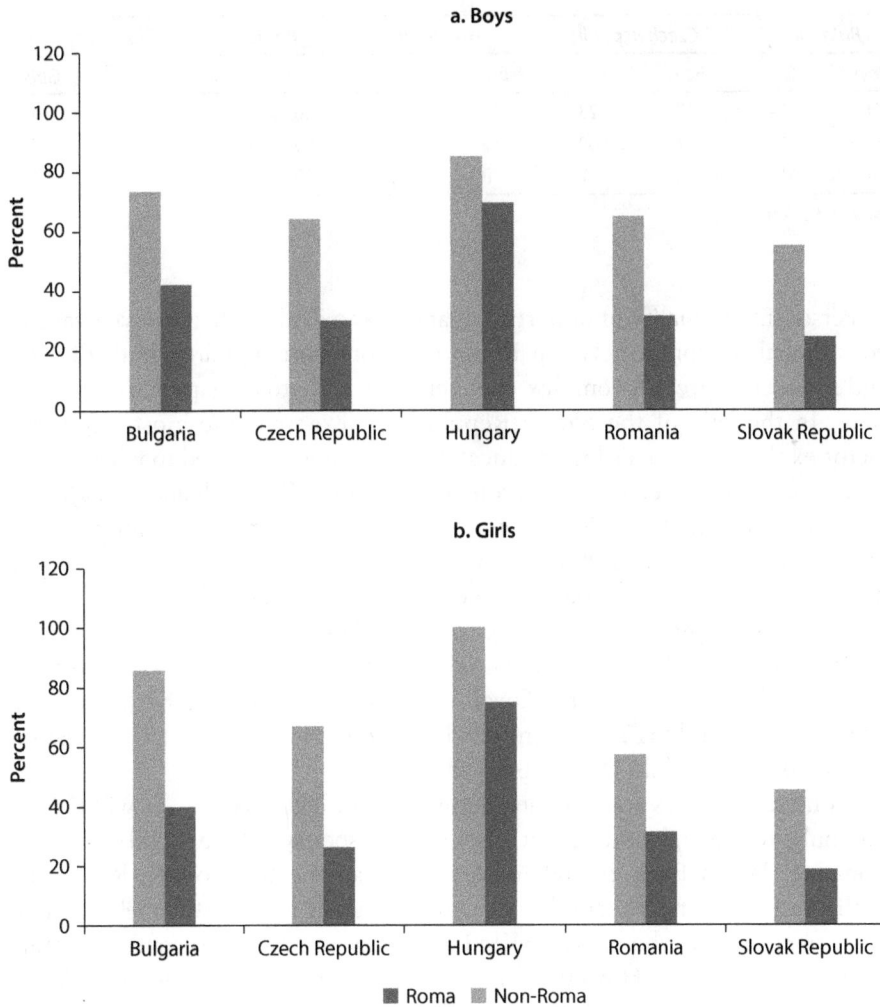

a. Boys

b. Girls

■ Roma ■ Non-Roma

Sources: UNDP, World Bank, and EC 2011.

secondary education in CEE; this is in stark contrast with 40 percent of non-Roma who live nearby and the even higher completion rate among the general population. Completion rates are particularly low among Roma women. This phenomenon, however, cannot be explained by lower educational aspirations; the RRS finds that most Roma parents across the region prefer their children to complete secondary or tertiary education (see table 2.1). According to the RRS, there are various reasons why students leave school early. In Bulgaria and Romania, for example, dropout rates are driven by education-related costs; meanwhile, in the Czech Republic and Hungary, "being sufficiently educated" is the most frequently cited reason for leaving school.

Being Fair, Faring Better • http://dx.doi.org/10.1596/978-1-4648-0598-1

Table 2.1 Roma Parent Self-Reported Preferences for Their Male and Female Children's Educational Level Attainment

Percent

	Bulgaria		Czech Republic		Hungary		Romania		Slovak Republic	
	Boys	Girls	Boys	Girls	Boys	Girls	Boys	Girls	Boys	Girls
Basic	20	24	17	23	16	17	26	29	16	19
Secondary	65	62	77	69	82	80	55	53	68	67
Tertiary	16	14	6	7	3	3	19	18	16	14

Source: UNDP, World Bank, and EC 2011.

Persistent inequality of opportunity appears to explain the observed gaps in educational outcomes between Roma and non-Roma children both directly and indirectly through complex channels that perpetuate gaps across generations. In the case of the Slovak Republic, for example, the most important factor explaining Roma's lower educational outcomes is related to whether the household head has completed secondary education (World Bank 2012a). This is further confirmed by evidence from Hungary suggesting that home environment and parenting skills, together with health, explain most of the observed differences in Roma and non-Roma students' performance (Kertesi and Kézdi 2011). On the other hand, evidence from the RRS suggests that factors linked to ethnicity—discrimination potentially among them—seem to matter for educational differences in the Slovak Republic; provided all other factors are equal, a Roma child is 26 percent less likely to complete secondary education than a non-Roma child (World Bank 2012a).

Promoting Roma's access to and completion of higher education will benefit not only Roma individuals, but also greater society. Recent evidence from Romania (World Bank 2014a) indicates that among the working Roma, the probability of being an employee increases significantly with one's level of education; a Roma who has completed university has the same chance of getting a job as a non-Roma. However, for the majority of Roma, the aforementioned education gap leads to a significant skills gap, which, further compounded by labor market discrimination, will grow into large employment differentials (see chapter 3).

Population dynamics make education interventions a necessity. Because of the aging general populations and young and growing Roma minorities, 7–20 percent of the new labor market entrants in Bulgaria, the Czech Republic, Hungary, Romania, and the Slovak Republic are Roma (World Bank 2012c), who arrive to the labor market largely unprepared. The EU's goal of achieving smart and inclusive growth is coupled with the new member CEE states' increasing need for their workforce to survive in a challenging global skills competition. This makes investments in more inclusive education systems, along with targeted measures to help the Roma overcome a variety of learning gaps, a pressing demand.

Doing so will not only contribute to reducing unemployment and poverty among the Roma population, but will also herald considerable economic benefits in the form of productivity gains and fiscal contributions (World Bank 2013). As an example, a simulation exercise in the Slovak Republic found potential high rates of return on further investments in Roma education ranging from 63 to 105 percent (depending on the specific scenario) (World Bank 2012a). A similar exercise conducted in Hungary also found that an investment that helps a young Roma successfully complete secondary school would yield significant direct long-term benefits to the national budget; discounted to age four, the present value of the future benefits is about HUF 19 million (a70,000 in 2006) relative to the value the government would gain in case an individual dropped out after primary school (Kertesi and Kézdi 2006).

It is important to acknowledge that the group to which the policy or scientific discourse commonly refers as "the Roma community" is not at all homogenous: Roma families, like non-Roma ones, present a broad variety of socioeconomic backgrounds and profiles. In turn, there is no "one size fits all" solution in education policies that address gaps for the marginalized Roma—families or pupils in different communities face different challenges, and education policy measures and programs need to reflect and adjust to the existing diversity. It is equally important to realize that education systems have a crucial role to play in acknowledging diversity and cultivating the ethnic identity and self-esteem of Roma students. This could be done by teaching Roma history or the Romani language; strengthening the next generation's sense of identity and empowerment; and instilling in them a sense of confidence and pride. Such measures can draw on promising NGO-led programs (see box 2.1) and can help lay the foundation for core leadership skills and competencies among the next generation of Roma.

Box 2.1 Barvalipe—Building Roma Pride[a]

Since 2011, the Roma Initiatives Office from the Open Society Foundation has been developing a concept called *Barvalipe*—which means "richness" or "pride" in some Roma dialects—that aims to support the emergence of a confident new generation of Roma advocates who are capable of leading Roma organizations or working in EU institutions, international organizations, and national public services to improve the situation of the Roma communities in Europe. Barvalipe combines three critical elements: (a) strengthening pride in belonging to Roma communities; (b) building the confidence and courage to push for change; and (c) creating a sense of community among those Roma who have the potential to become leaders in public life. From 2011 to 2013, the Barvalipe concept was addressed during yearly summer camps, where about 30 young Roma, ages 18–30,

box continues next page

Being Fair, Faring Better • http://dx.doi.org/10.1596/978-1-4648-0598-1

Box 2.1 Barvalipe—Building Roma Pride[a] *(continued)*

came together to learn about their culture, language, history, and achievements, with the goal of encouraging their sense of civic duty and social responsibility. In addition to the age and ethnicity requirements, the participants needed to be proficient in English and to come from countries participating in the Decade of Roma Inclusion 2005–15 (Albania; Bosnia and Herzegovina; Bulgaria; Croatia; the Czech Republic; Hungary; Macedonia, former Yugoslav Republic of; Moldova; Montenegro; Romania; Serbia; the Slovak Republic; and Spain) or from Kosovo, Moldova, Russian Federation, Turkey, or the Ukraine. The main activities conducted during the 10-day long camps were lessons on the basics of Romani language and history and participation in debates and talks with prominent Roma. In addition, participants learned about the history of Roma during the Holocaust through a one-day trip to a concentration camp where about 20,000 Roma were killed. Starting in 2014, the Barvalipe concept was reoriented and expanded to strengthen its impact around the country; Barvalipe programs were adjusted to the local environments, drawing on the knowledge and experience of Roma intellectuals, linguists, artists, and civic and political leaders.

a. Unless otherwise noted, the discussion of results is not based on experimental or quasi-experimental methods. Hence, inferences about the causal impact of the interventions are not warranted in principle.

Early Investments Produce the Highest Returns

The Case for Investing in Education Early...

International evidence shows that attending preschool increases an individual's chance of achieving socioeconomic inclusion later in life. Early childhood development (ECD) programs are particularly beneficial to children from disadvantaged backgrounds. As Nobel laureate economist James Heckman (2006) argues, investing in disadvantaged young children is a rare public policy with no equity-efficiency trade off. A review of the scientific literature published in *The Lancet* similarly concludes that "unless governments allocate more resources to quality early child development programs for the poorest people in the population, economic disparities will continue and widen" (Engle 2011, p. 1339).

A PISA study (OECD 2010) reports that in most countries, students who have attended at least one year of preprimary education tend to perform better than those who have not, even when controlling for socioeconomic background. PISA research also shows that the relationship between preprimary attendance and performance tends to be greater in school systems with a longer duration of preprimary education, smaller pupil-to-teacher ratios, and higher public expenditure per child at the preprimary level (OECD 2013). An analysis of PISA results in Bulgaria (Gortazar et al. 2014) demonstrates that among children of low socioeconomic status, attending at least a two-year preprimary education program is correlated with a 10-point increase in PISA math scores, relative to having attended one year or none at all.

In addition, research evidence from Hungary indicates that longer preschool attendance effectively reduces cognitive and school achievement gaps later in life, especially for children from disadvantaged backgrounds (Kertesi and Kézdi 2014).

Indeed, econometric work based on the RRS finds a strong correlation between Roma children's preschool enrollment and positive educational outcomes. The World Bank (2012e) reports a positive correlation between preschool attendance[1] and children's self-perceived cognitive skills and self-confidence; a lower chance of special school attendance in the Czech Republic and the Slovak Republic; a lower chance of receiving social benefits in the Czech Republic, the Slovak Republic, and Romania; and a higher probability of achieving education at a secondary school (International Standard Classification of Education [ISCED] 3) in all five countries. The study also finds that Roma children enrolled in preschool are much more likely to recognize numbers, the alphabet, and understand simple sentences in the Slovak Republic, while Roma adults who attended preschool as children were much less likely to be enrolled in a special school (by more than half); much more likely to complete secondary school (by more than half); and less likely to be on social assistance (by 20 percent).

Where Romani is prominently used as the primary language at home (as is the case in all five countries except Hungary), preschool participation provides a unique opportunity for Roma children to learn the language of instruction in primary school. Preschool education also provides an opportunity for Roma and non-Roma children to interact with each other from the early educational stages, which may mitigate prejudice and stereotypes later on. Nevertheless, the enrollment levels of kindergarten-age Roma remain very low throughout the region. With Hungary being a notable exception, Roma children from vulnerable families are left unprepared for school entry (see figure 2.2).

The level of preschool attendance varies across the region. Hungary has a wide network of kindergartens, low associated costs (there are no tuition fees, and children pay only for meals and extracurricular activities; meals are free for disadvantaged children), and conditional cash transfers for families with multiple disadvantages who enroll their child in preschool before age four and maintain stable attendance during the school year.[2,3] Since 2014, preschool education in Hungary has been compulsory from age three (this rule enters into de facto force in the 2015–16 school year due to capacity constraints), and since 2008, local governments have been required to offer free kindergarten placements to children from families with multiple disadvantages from such age (Eurydice 2012).

On the other end of the spectrum stand the Czech Republic and the Slovak Republic, where Roma preschool participation is very low; only one in four Roma children ages 3–6 years are enrolled in preschool education, while among non-Roma neighbors the participation rate is 65 percent for the Czech Republic and 53 percent for the Slovak Republic. In Romania and

Bulgaria, preschool enrollment has generally increased over the past decade, and enrollment of Roma children stands at 37 percent and 45 percent, respectively.

Barriers to kindergarten attendance vary across countries. Whereas the majority of Roma parents wish their children to complete secondary education, when asked why they did not enroll their children in preschool, many stated a desire to raise children at home in their early years. Cost was an additional consideration, but almost half of parents reported being willing to reconsider enrollment if a Roma teaching assistant was present. More than half of parents reported they would reconsider if there were no fees or if they received food coupons (World Bank 2012e). Language barriers may be a common challenge for Roma children in preprimary (and also primary) education; the share of Roma households that speak Romani at home is high in all countries (with the exception of Hungary; see table 2.2), while the language of instruction in schools is the official national language. Since the mainstream curriculum is not taught in Romani, early exposure to the country's official language is critical for Roma children's later success in school.[4]

...and the Case for Investing in the Family

Poverty and deprivation at home create an uneven playing field for Roma children even before they reach preschool age. Child development depends not just on schooling but also on the home environment. Roma children face multiple disadvantages in this regard. The RRS reports that the Roma infant mortality rate (35 cases per 1,000) is twice as high as for non-Roma neighbors (16 per 1,000). The vaccination rate of Roma children is also low; 9 percent of Roma children in the Slovak Republic and Romania, and 5 percent in the Czech Republic and Bulgaria have never been vaccinated at all. With so many children growing up in deep poverty, infants are at a higher risk of malnutrition, and families lack the means to purchase books and other learning tools. For example, in Romania, UNICEF has drawn attention to the risk of child malnutrition, estimating that 72 percent of those suffering from malnutrition are children under age three.

Improving early child health and nutrition has particularly significant benefits. A child born with a healthy birth weight (more than 3,000 grams), who is

Table 2.2 Share of Roma Households That Primarily Speak the Romani Language at Home

Country	%
Bulgaria	64.6
Czech Republic	44.6
Hungary	6.7
Romania	41.0
Slovak Republic	71.6

Source: UNDP, World Bank, and EC 2011.

Table 2.3 Evidence of Roma Parental Support for Cognitive Development of Their Children (Ages 3–5)

	Bulgaria	Czech Republic	Hungary	Romania	Slovak Republic
Number of books at home					
Mean	1.8	7.0	7.2	1.2	2.6
Median	0	5	4	0	1
Activities with children, past 3 days (%)					
Looked at picture books or read books	23	50	57	17	44
Drew or painted	21	51	42	19	45
Taught letters or counted	15	21	29	12	22

Source: UNDP, World Bank, and EC 2011. Limited to households with children ages 3–5.

exclusively breastfed for the first six months of life, and who grows well during the first years, has a much better chance of having a healthy childhood, higher educational achievement, and greater labor productivity as an adult. Recent evidence also shows that breastfed children are less likely to develop chronic disease later in life; for example, a 4 percent reduction in obesity risk is associated with every month of breastfeeding (Singhal and Lanigan 2007). On the contrary, children born with low birth weight (less than 2,500 grams) are at a higher risk of childhood stunting, more prone to infectious disease, and show lower educational achievement and adult productivity.

In addition to a healthy start, many young Roma children could benefit from greater cognitive stimulation at home. The importance of learning at home is further underscored by evidence that effective parental support for cognitive development can bear significant impacts on children's educational outcomes (Kertesi and Kézdi 2011). In Romania, a typical Roma child ages 3–5 has only one book at home, and this situation is similar in Bulgaria and the Slovak Republic (Roma families in the Czech Republic and in Hungary have more books—five and four, for a typical family, respectively). In Romania, only 1 in 8 Roma children ages 3–5 were taught letters or counting by their caregivers in the three days before the interview, and fewer than one-fifth looked at picture books or read, drew, or painted with their caregivers (see table 2.3).

Directions for Policy

Support Adequate Child Development in the First 1,000 Days of Life

Evidence from Hungary suggests that health is one of the key mediating factors for different educational outcomes between Roma children and their non-Roma peers (Kertesi and Kézdi 2011). Policy makers should therefore first focus on developing and rolling out both supply- (provider) and demand- (household) side interventions that target poor families to receive regular maternal and child health checkups. For example, smart incentives for paying providers tied to results (such as through completing the vaccination protocol of Roma infants) can help address the child mortality rate; in addition, kindergartens or community centers may host events that provide parents with information and knowledge on healthy nutrition, feeding practices, the importance of checkups, and learning stimulation in the home. Investments in expanding the capacity of crèches and nurseries may ensure that children whose families live in extreme poverty and whose home environment is not conducive to cognitive stimulation and healthy life can also access quality early education and care. Home visiting nurses in the first postnatal year could additionally contribute to adequate child development in this very early phase. Box 2.2 provides a good practice example of a complex intervention supporting child development from Hungary.

Roma children are more likely to be born at lower births weights, are less likely to be exclusively breastfed, and tend to eat less healthy diets (FDG 2009). Counseling young mothers and their families on the benefits of breastfeeding and healthy dietary habits is key to achieving better outcomes. Practically all Roma women give birth in a hospital (according to the 2011 RRS), which offers an excellent opportunity to counsel them on breastfeeding and young child feeding practices.

Four main policy measures can help to increase the enrollment of Roma children in preschools and support early learning at home: (a) better informing parents of the benefits of a formal preschool education; (b) using Roma teaching assistants to more directly involve parents in preschools; (c) eliminating existing cost barriers and considering conditional cash transfers based on attendance; and (d) supporting parenting at home (World Bank 2012e). Bennett (2012) further recommends a multidimensional concept of early childhood services for Roma

---

Box 2.2 Biztos Kezdet: Hungary's Success with a Variation on the United Kingdom's Sure Start Program

Inspired by the United Kingdom's Sure Start model[a] launched in 1999, the Biztos Kezdet program started in 2003 and currently operates Children's Centers in more than 110 localities in the most disadvantaged regions with large Roma populations.[b] The program provides integrated social services to children ages 0–6 (early childhood education and care) and their parents (parental training, employability support). The program does not create a new parallel child care provision system, but rather complements the existing system with a clear focus on the most vulnerable communities. Biztos Kezdet Children's Centers were originally set up with funding from Norway Grants and the European Union, and since 2012 they have been funded from the national budget. In 2006, three years after its launch, the program provided services to 400 families and 700 children, adding to the current number of 4,000 that use its services.

a. For a comprehensive peer review of the UK's Sure Start model and other country pilots (including Hungary in 2006), see the peer review synthesis report "Sure Start" by Fred Deven at http://ec.europa.eu/employment_social/social_inclusion /docs/2006/pr_uk_en.pdf. For a recent evaluation of the Sure Start project, see "The impact of Sure Start Local Programmes on Five-Year-Olds and Their Families" at http://www.ness.bbk.ac.uk/impact/documents/RR067.pdf.
b. Detailed information about the program (in Hungarian) is available at http://www.biztoskezdet.eu.

---

who live in extreme poverty and exclusion, based on preparing Roma children first in the family and community before they enter formal early childhood education and care programs. Recommended interventions range from "pre- and postnatal health, parenting and adult education, play and stimulation programs for toddlers conducted in the relevant Roma dialect," with Roma communities, NGOs, and Roma health and education assistants ensuring the success of such services (Bennett 2012, p. 14).

ECD programs outside the EU may also offer EU policy makers good examples regarding what to do and how to make progress in this area. For example, in Jamaica—where gross enrollment in preschool stands at 99 percent—the government has developed a robust ECD framework that articulates around a National Parenting Strategy, providing preventive health care for children ages 0–6, and conducting screening and early intervention for at-risk households and children. The government is also investing in the continuous inspection of ECD facilities, the effective delivery of the curriculum through trained early childhood practitioners and teachers, and—with World Bank support—aims to establish a national early childhood management information system to support evidence-based policy making.

Invest in Kindergartens and Preschools

Given kindergarten capacity constraints throughout the region, all CEE governments need to invest in the expansion of quality preschool education and promote the benefits of kindergarten attendance in communities that have a large share of marginalized Roma. Additional investments should target adequate staffing (including diversity training for preschool teachers), resources, and curricula that pay proper attention to the development of cognitive and socio-emotional skills and are culturally relevant.

In Bulgaria, the Czech Republic, Romania, and the Slovak Republic, compulsory preschool education may be considered for at least two years prior to enrolling in primary school. In all CEE countries, an extra year of (free) preschool education may be considered to help improve the school readiness of children who are not yet ready to enter first grade. In addition, appropriately designed financial incentives may help increase early childhood education attendance rates among vulnerable families—for example, disadvantaged families could receive social assistance benefits that are conditional on preschool attendance.

At the program level, local municipalities should make efforts to raise awareness of the benefits of quality early education through, for example, kindergarten-community liaisons (World Bank 2012a). They should also involve parents in early childhood education partnerships, including by developing community-based preschool systems where appropriate. Such activities may include organizing parent support groups in Roma communities; creating opportunities for Roma parents to participate in school activities (in school or after school hours), such as supporting the teacher in preparing activities or supervising children during activities; and supporting parent-led educational activities for children. These initiatives would also help to respectfully integrate the Romani and mainstream language diversity into the preschool environment. In regions where preschool infrastructure and facilities are limited, EU funds are an important opportunity to develop infrastructure. Future investments in infrastructure should be planned in line with evolving needs at the local level, taking into consideration demographic trends in the school population (see box 2.3).

Box 2.3 A Good Start by the Roma Education Fund

The pilot project titled A Good Start (AGS), supported by European Commission DG Regional Policy, was launched in 16 localities across CEE. It involved a complex set of center-, community-, and home-based interventions that were customized to the local community. Certain activities were common to all localities. For example, the local partner organizations employed community mediators, predominantly of Roma ethnic origin, whose role was to conduct intensive outreach work and liaise between the local communities and the institutions. They also conducted regular home visits and helped families enroll their children in preschool.

The basic structure was complemented with country-specific activities. For example, as part of Hungary's Your Story program, mothers attended regular sessions where they received children's books and learned to read and tell stories to their children. The sessions were led by Your Story facilitators, who often were Roma women from the local community. The participants were taught a variety of skills ranging from reading, writing, role playing, and parenting, and were individually counseled on a wide range of issues and concerns. Following the completion of this first phase, Your Story clubs evolved into reading clubs, building on the skills obtained.

Similarly, the Home Preschool Community Liaison Program encouraged Roma mothers, fathers, and/or grandparents to participate in the school experience by leading one kindergarten session alone or in pairs. The mothers were trained along with the teachers and were given skills to conduct a session on a subject of their choice. The participation of the College of Nyíregyháza, a higher education institution, was also linked to the whole AGS portfolio in Hungary. Pedagogy and andragogy students participated in Your Story sessions and home visits as part of their required practical training and to gain experience with socially disadvantaged Roma children.

In Romania, similar reading activities were designed in the project's framework; these involved the participation of local AGS partners and parents. In the Slovak Republic, AGS activities included afterschool instruction/tutoring that was provided in the first year of primary education. To facilitate preschool attendance, material support was distributed that addressed differing needs (such as clothes, shoes, school supplies, and hygiene packages). In some cases, children were also transported and accompanied to and from school.

In addition to these projectwide and country-specific activities, each locality within the AGS project received assistance to conduct additional locality-specific activities; for example, certain localities were given help vaccinating children, or assisting parents and children obtain official identification documents. In Macedonia, former Yugoslav Republic of, the

---

box continues next page

Box 2.3 A Good Start by the Roma Education Fund *(continued)*

Roma Education Fund used its small grants scheme to finance construction (or adapt existing buildings) to increase kindergarten capacity. Further activities included parenting education, diversity training for teaching staff, training on child-centered pedagogy, preparing community mediators for home visits, and community motivation events.

Attending and Finishing School Is Critical for Roma Pupils

Unequal Access to Good Schooling

Following the gaps in early childhood education participation, the first major challenge many Roma children face is when enrolling in primary education. In the Czech Republic and the Slovak Republic, where compulsory education starts at age six, children undergo an initial assessment of their skills at the primary school[5] or by a specialist from a center for pedagogical and psychological counseling. This may result in either a recommendation that the child be enrolled in the first year of primary school or spend an extra year in preschool/at home (based on parental preference),[6] or enter the preparatory year in the primary school or enter some form of special needs education. Roma children tend to perform poorly in the initial skills assessment more often than non-Roma, likely due to low preschool attendance rates (28 percent in the Czech Republic and 24 percent in the Slovak Republic),[7] disadvantaged background, and widespread use of Romani language at home (45 percent and 65 percent, respectively;[8] the official language is used during testing).[9] This often leads Roma children to be streamed early to the so-called 0th grades (preparatory grades within primary school) and to special education.

Despite the fact that children between 7 and 15 years of age should be enrolled in compulsory education throughout the region, in all countries but Romania, both Roma and their non-Roma neighbors lag behind the national averages in terms of primary school enrollment, likely driven by territorial disparities (see figure 2.3).[10]

In terms of educational quality and student performance, an analysis of 2012 PISA results reveals that CEE countries' school systems are quite selective, and tend to sort children based on their social status and ability (see figure 2.4). For example, in Bulgaria, peer characteristics explain more of the differences in PISA test scores than do individual characteristics; a child's performance on the PISA test depends more on her type of classmates than on her own individual qualities.

This systemwide segregation of pupils based on social skills and ability has already had a major impact on the performance of pupils of lower socioeconomic status. In areas with higher concentration of marginalized Roma population, this leads to school stratification with a strong ethnic dimension. Because of the lack of reliable ethnic identification, PISA data does not allow for the analysis of possible gaps in test scores between Roma and non-Roma; however, an analysis of standardized national test scores of Hungarian eighth graders shows that factors such as differences in health, parenting, school, and class assignment account

Figure 2.3 Roma versus Non-Roma Rate of Gross Enrollment in Compulsory Education for Boys and Girls (Ages 7–15)

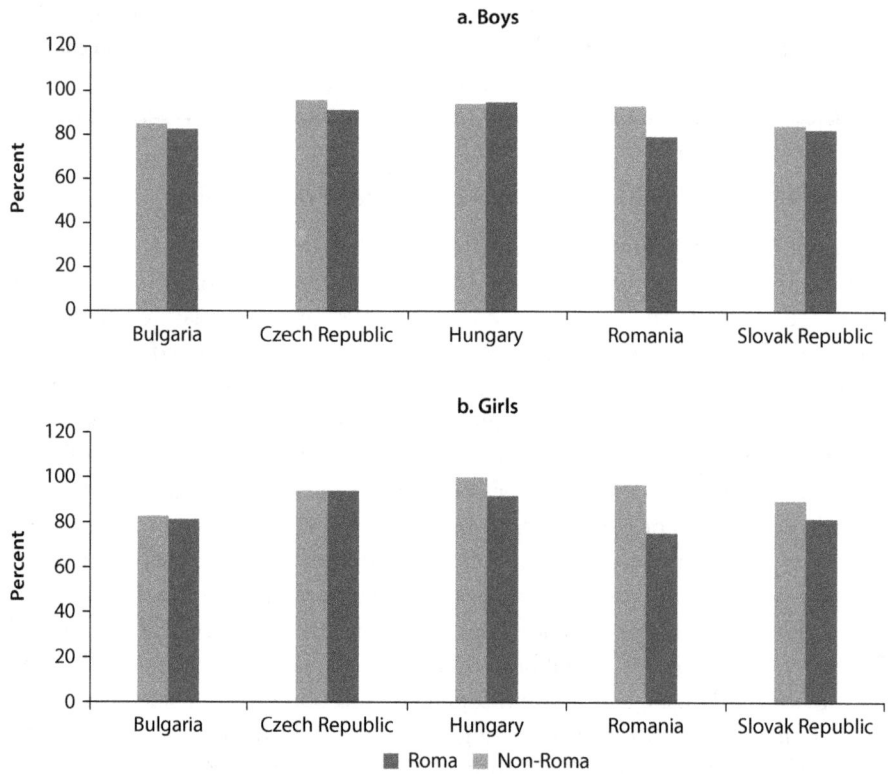

a. Boys

b. Girls

■ Roma ■ Non-Roma

Sources: UNDP, World Bank; EC 2011; UNECSO Institute for Statistics 2012 (only for national means).

Figure 2.4 Index of Equality of Learning Opportunities in European and Central Asian Countries

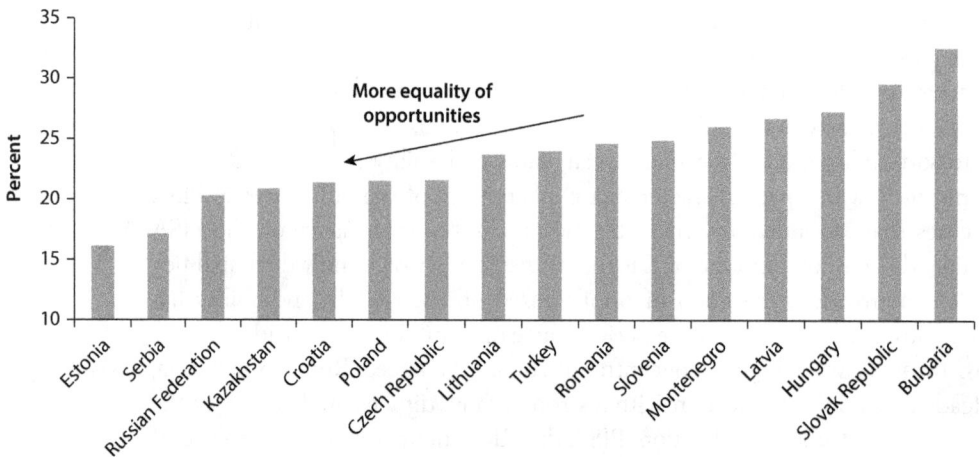

More equality of opportunities

Source: Gortazar et al. 2014.
Note: The index is the percent of the variance in reading scores explained by the main predetermined characteristics (age, gender, and socioeconomic status) in a linear regression (Ferreira and Gignoux 2011).

Being Fair, Faring Better • http://dx.doi.org/10.1596/978-1-4648-0598-1

for much of the score gap between Roma and non-Roma in reading and math (Kertesi and Kézdi 2011).

It is almost universal for young Roma in the Czech Republic, the Slovak Republic, and Hungary to complete primary education (ISCED 1). Completion rates in Bulgaria and Romania are still low, but improved in the past decade to 86 and 83 percent, respectively. However, problems already start to arise in these grades, such as the rising share of grade repeaters (especially in the Slovak Republic and Hungary) and children who are streamed to special education, both of which lead to dropping out. Most young Roma in the Czech Republic, Hungary, and the Slovak Republic complete lower secondary education, while this is true only for approximately half of them in Bulgaria and Romania (see figure 2.5). In all countries, Roma remain to have difficulties reaching the upper secondary education level, with shares of those who succeed ranging from 31 percent of young Roma in the Czech Republic to 11 percent in Romania.[11] Data from the Hungary Life Course survey provide a considerably better picture: the upper secondary school completion rate in Hungary by age 20–21 is 46 percent of those who started the first grade of primary school and 52 percent of those who started upper secondary school (Hajdu, Kertesi, and Kézdi 2014). These differences may be attributed to the different characteristics of survey samples.

Roma Children Face Barriers to Accessing Education Services

According to the RRS, almost all Roma children in Romania have primary schools within "walking distance," that is, less than 3 kilometers; this is the case for between 85 and 93 percent of Roma children in Bulgaria, Hungary, and the Slovak Republic, and 79 percent in the Czech Republic (see table 2.4). Nevertheless, a more detailed analysis using the 2013 Atlas of Roma Communities in the Slovak Republic[12] highlights that many Roma live at the outskirts of villages or towns (24 percent) or in segregated settlements (17 percent), often without easy access to a school due to missing roads, a lack of safe pavement, and longer walking distances. In fact, there is no primary school (ISCED 1) in almost one-third of the 1,035 Slovak villages and towns with Roma populations covered by the Atlas, and the nearest primary school is located on average 5 kilometers away. The state reimburses the cost of public transportation for children who attend primary schools or for special needs children, but in cases where there is no public transportation, or the school catchment areas set by municipalities are too large, getting to and from school remains a problem.

In addition, costs associated with school attendance can present a significant barrier for poor students. Although compulsory education is free in all five countries, there are various costs associated with schooling—such as textbooks, clothing, school dining, transportation, parents' association fees, and so on—that poor Roma are unable to afford. For example, in the Czech Republic, there are no systemic measures in place to decrease the direct financial costs of education. As a result, children from disadvantaged families are unable to access extracurricular

Figure 2.5 Level of Educational Attainment for Young Roma Men and Women, 2011

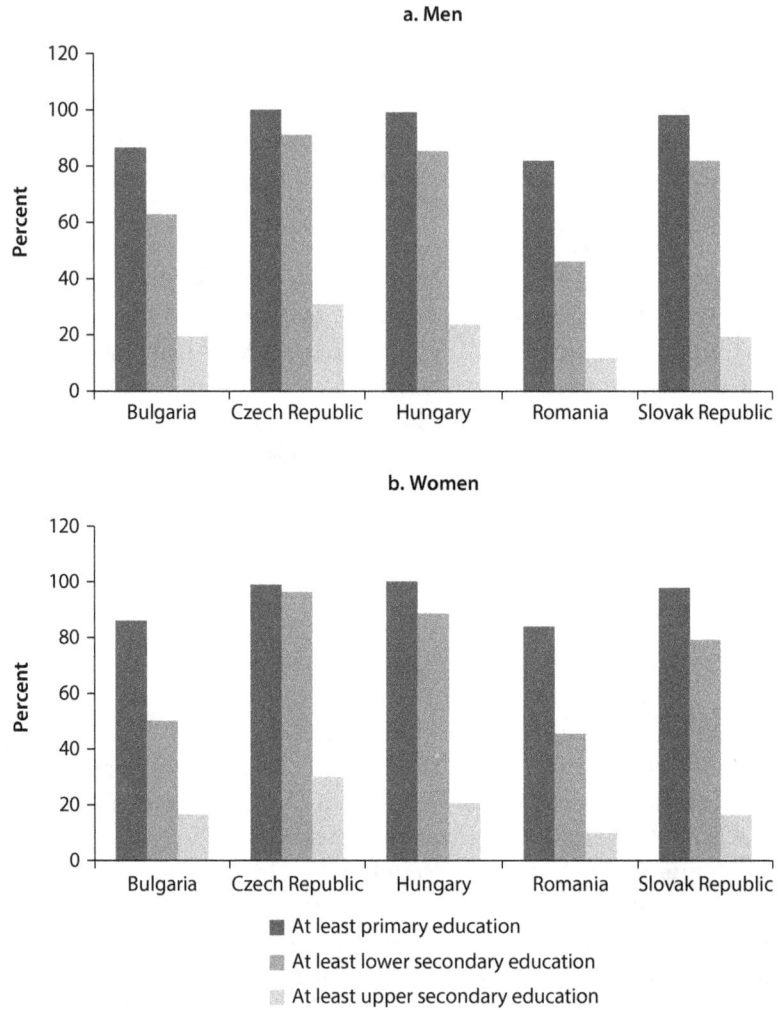

a. Men

b. Women

■ At least primary education
■ At least lower secondary education
▧ At least upper secondary education

Source: UNDP, World Bank, and EC 2011.
Note: Share of Roma ages 14–20 who completed at least primary education; share of Roma ages 17–23 who completed at least lower secondary education; share of Roma ages 20–26 who completed at least upper secondary education.

Table 2.4 Distance of Roma Households to Nearest Primary School
Percent

	Bulgaria	Czech Republic	Hungary	Romania	Slovak Republic
Less than 1 km	57.4	46.5	42.7	68.7	44.9
1–3 km	31.7	32.2	42.7	28.5	48.2
3–5 km	5.6	16.6	9.1	1.3	4.3
5–10 km	2.9	4.4	2.8	0.1	1.8
More than 10 km	2.3	0.2	2.8	1.5	0.8

Source: UNDP, World Bank, and EC 2011.

activities and school trips, and some cannot pay for school dining or aids. Some schools try to solve these problems in an ad hoc manner; some cooperate with the local social affairs office, which pays an extra one-off social benefit to cover school aids for needy families recommended by the school, while others do not charge children from poor families' fees for afternoon activities (Baslová and Homrová 2012).

In addition, and as highlighted throughout this chapter, inequalities in performance appear to be common across countries. Roma typically have class peers who come from similar socioeconomic backgrounds, and so peer effects also play a role; international evidence suggests that high-performance peer groups enhance, and low-performance peer groups inhibit, individual learning performance. According to the RRS, even when they attend schools with peers from the majority population, Roma children do not tend to benefit from such peers, which suggests that they may suffer social exclusion in the school environment if they speak Romani (World Bank 2012b). Hungarian research finds that Roma students are 40 percentage points more likely than non-Roma ones to study in classrooms in which the majority of their peers have inadequate reading skills. This increased likelihood is in large part due to residential and social disadvantages, but ethnicity remains a significant factor in the school system's selection mechanisms (Kertesi and Kézdi 2014).

In some countries, the high share of children with postponed entry (either at parental request or expert recommendation) into compulsory education may further exacerbate the education challenges Roma pupils face. Such children make up 15 percent of all children enrolled in the Czech Republic, and 9 percent in the Slovak Republic. Children with a postponed educational start can either stay in kindergarten[13] or not enroll at all. In the Czech Republic, the share of children with postponed enrollment where the families choose to keep the child at home reaches approximately 50 percent; in the Slovak Republic, it is as high as three-quarters of the total number of non-enrolled.

Little information is available on the share of Roma children who are among those who postponed entering compulsory education, and there indeed may be children (Roma and non-Roma alike) who are not prepared for school and whose entry into education may have negative consequences for their long-term development. Nevertheless, using this option beyond its intended purpose—that is, allowing extra preparation time for those children who are not yet ready for school—also amounts to a wasted opportunity for children who would be prepared for school. It will be increasingly difficult for these children, particularly the ones from marginalized communities, to catch up with peers.

Delayed school entry may also contribute to less total time spent in school. Moreover, if a student is required to repeat grades, he or she will complete the period of mandatory attendance without completing lower secondary education; environmental factors—such as families' financial need for the child to enter the workforce early—may prevent the student from enrolling in upper secondary education programs and obtaining skills and work qualifications.

Roma Pupils Often Repeat Grades and Drop Out Early

Roma children are much more likely than non-Roma to repeat grades. According to ROCEPO (2011), as many as 30 percent of children from marginalized backgrounds in the Slovak Republic repeat the grade after their first year in primary school, compared to a national average of 9 percent. The second big wave of repetitions comes in the fifth grade, right after transitioning to lower secondary education. Here, 19 percent of children from marginalized backgrounds repeat the fifth grade compared to the national average of 4 percent, and figures remain greater than 15 percent in the subsequent grades for children from marginalized backgrounds. In the Czech Republic, 15 percent of Roma children do not stay with their peers after the first grade, either because they have to repeat this year or are transferred to special education (GAC 2009).

Although the share of children who repeat a grade is negligible in Bulgaria (0.2 percent) and low in Romania (1.5 percent), both countries have a high share of primary education dropouts. In the case of young marginalized Roma, this translates to 14 percent in Bulgaria and 17 percent in Romania failing to complete primary education (according to the RRS). Based on data from the National Statistical Institute of Bulgaria, the share of repetitions in 2013–14 was at 0.1 percent in primary education, but increased to 2.5 percent in lower secondary education (grades 5–8). This increase in repetitions goes hand-in-hand with an increase in dropouts driven by the interplay of two factors: (a) unaddressed knowledge and learning gaps accumulated in elementary school and (b) a shift to a more complex upper primary/lower secondary curriculum that is taught by subject-specific teachers. This likely presents more learning challenges to Roma children from disadvantaged families compared to their non-Roma peers, especially considering the lower attendance rates in early childhood education, upon which the foundations of successful subsequent school years are built.

For many Roma children, the learning experience ends with dropping out of school. A recent longitudinal study (Ivan and Rostas 2013) by REF Romania shows that a Romanian Roma student in lower secondary education is six times more likely than a non-Roma student with a comparable socioeconomic status to drop out of school. Indeed, in Romania, RRS data shows a steady decline in the share of Roma children in school starting as early as age 12; in Bulgaria, a steep drop occurs in the share of Roma children in school after age 14. Similarly, in the Slovak Republic, a steady decline starts at age 13. The Czech Republic and Hungary manage to keep more than 90 percent of Roma children in school until they are 15 years old. The significant drop to less than 50 percent of Roma in school occurs after age 16 in the Czech Republic and at age 18 in Hungary (figure 2.6). However, it is important to note that recent changes in the Hungarian education system lower the age for which education is compulsory from 18 to 16, a change that is not yet captured by the 2011 data but that may further negatively affect the dropout rate.

Completing secondary education remains a challenge for most Roma students. As discussed previously, almost all the young Roma in CEE complete

Figure 2.6 Decline in Roma Youth School Attendance, by Age

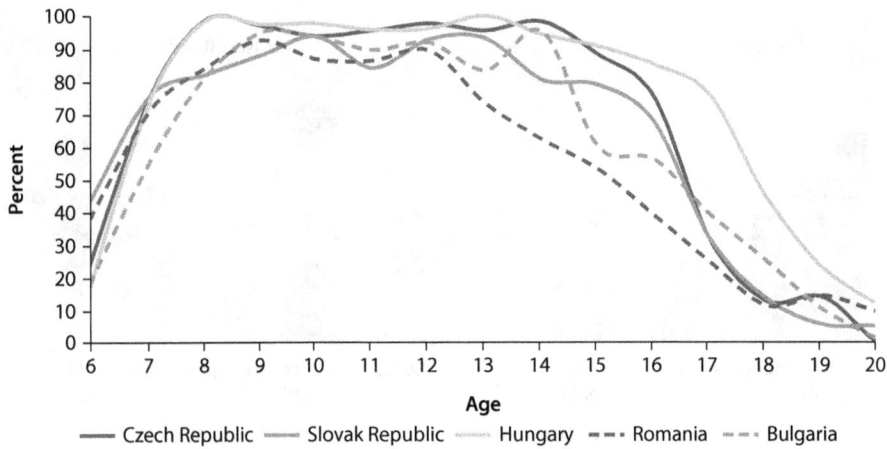

Source: UNDP, World Bank, and EC 2011.
Note: Some data points were unavailable. Percentages shown exclude missing values.

primary education. While most of the Roma pupils in the Czech Republic, Hungary, and the Slovak Republic, and roughly half in Bulgaria and Romania, also complete lower secondary education, Roma children often complete the period of compulsory education before the final grade of the lower secondary (ISCED 2) level, as a result of entering preparatory grades and of repeating grades more often than non-Roma.

For example, in the case of the Slovak Republic, ROCEPO (2011) reports that 11 percent of children from socially disadvantaged backgrounds end compulsory education in grade 7, and 19 percent in grade 8, compared to approximately 2 percent at the national level. Moreover, upper secondary education (ISCED 3) remains a challenge for Roma (see figure 2.7); the difference compared to their non-Roma peers is very significant in each of the five countries. This means that a very large share of Roma students in CEE lose the opportunity to obtain professional skills and to contribute to the increased demand for skills in the modern economy, as well as receive the necessary training for tertiary education.

The reasons why Roma pupils drop out of school vary from country to country (see table 2.5). When asked in the RRS, "other reasons" are cited among the most frequent responses. In Bulgaria[14] and Romania, most respondents point to the high costs of education (these are often the "hidden costs" associated with schooling, discussed earlier in this chapter). In each country, a significant number of dropouts consider themselves sufficiently educated, and in Hungary, the Czech Republic, and Romania, many respondents indicate they dropped out either because they need to work or they found a job.

Recent survey evidence from Romania indicates that Roma are especially vulnerable to early school leaving, usually in connection with poverty, special segregation, and cultural factors (World Bank 2014b). Similarly, a 2008 study

Figure 2.7 Roma versus Non-Roma Upper Secondary School Completion Rates for Men and Women (Ages 25–64)

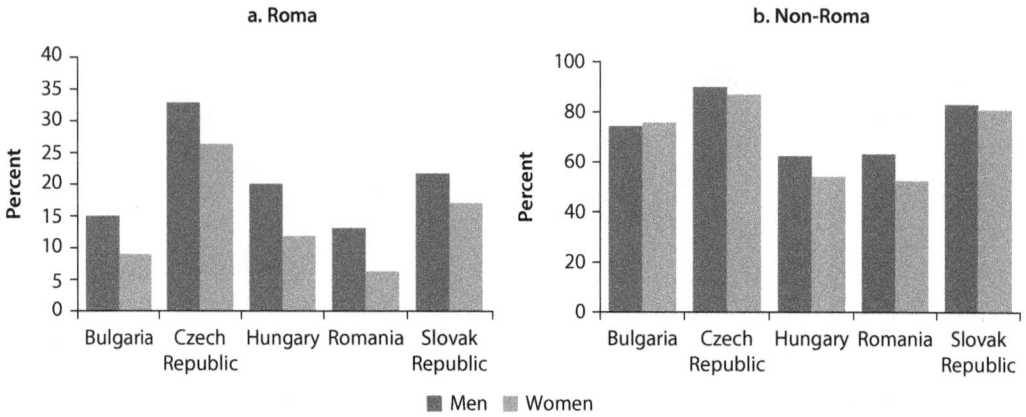

a. Roma

b. Non-Roma

■ Men ■ Women

Source: UNDP, World Bank, and EC 2011. "Secondary school completion" is defined as having completed either a vocational/technical or a general secondary school program, or a higher level of education. Sample restricted to individuals ages 25–64.

Table 2.5 Factors Determining Why Roma Children Do Not Attend or Drop Out of School
Percent

	Costs of education too high (for example, fees, transport, and books)	Need to work for income/ found job	Did not pass entry exam or did poorly in last level	Feel sufficiently educated	Marriage	Pregnancy	Other
Bulgaria	32.14	5.24	0.00	14.76	10.00	3.81	16.67
Czech Republic	7.04	12.90	6.16	16.72	0.29	9.97	23.17
Hungary	10.77	11.60	4.70	21.82	5.52	9.67	25.41
Romania	27.34	9.86	1.38	19.03	10.38	1.04	14.19
Slovak Republic	17.01	2.35	3.52	24.63	0.29	3.52	10.26

Source: UNDP, World Bank, and EC 2011.

finds that child labor—the combination of a (limited) school attendance with work activities—has a considerable effect on school performance, eventually leading to dropout (Pantea 2008).

In a survey of Roma girls in Serbia (CARE 2011), the hostility of the school environment and teachers' prejudices were ranked as the most common reasons why girls leave school early (69 percent of respondents); the teachers often ignore or fail to take measures to end bullying and harassment against Roma students by their non-Roma peers.

A recent study from Hungary (Hajdu, Kertesi, and Kézdi 2014) finds that while the gaps in high school attainment and college attendance between Roma and non-Roma are strongly related to the skills gap that emerges before high school, almost half of the ethnic difference in the high school dropout rate remains unexplained. This residual difference in dropout rate is influenced by social isolation; the dropout gap observed between Roma and non-Roma students with one or more close contacts with high-status peers shrinks considerably, and disappears between those with three or more such contacts. Further cross-country studies indicate that the process leading to early exit from the education system, in which external factors interact with sociological and psychological ones, is complex and gradual. Over this process, influenced by their peers, many children develop "anti-school" attitudes that eventually translate into early school abandonment, often despite their parents' will (Martínez, Enguita, and Gómez 2010).

Providing information about the costs and expected returns of education is a crucial component of curbing dropouts. The aforementioned "hidden costs" may not pose actual impediments to school attendance for disadvantaged families. For example, in Bulgaria, textbooks, transportation, snacks, and lunches are all free in the educational cycle where most dropouts occur (grades 5–8); nevertheless, these costs are the most frequently cited reason in the RRS for not going to school or dropping out, suggesting that households may not have correct information about what it actually costs to attend school. This highlights the need to provide information to families about free services, any fees associated with education, opportunities to request support through assistance programs, as well as the expected returns on education and skill acquisition, such as higher earnings and better job quality.

Furthermore, dropouts and grade repetition, which disproportionately affect Roma children, indicate the need for an academic assistance support system. Some promising models (including the ones discussed in boxes 2.4 and 2.5) that have been considered successful in various contexts include:

- Extensive involvement of Roma teaching assistants to help overcome cultural and language barriers, as well as mistrust between schools and marginalized Roma communities;

Box 2.4 Roma Mediators Help Link Roma Communities with the Romanian Education System

Romania was the first country in the region to institutionalize the concept of the Roma school mediator, which was introduced by the NGO Romani CRISS. The mediator is a respected and trusted Roma community member that connected community members with schools or public officials. Between 2003 and 2013, a total of 1,001 school mediators were trained in Romania under various programs. Out of these, about 400 mediators are currently active. As an extension of the mediators' activity, the Council of Europe's ROMACT program (launched in November 2013) uses European funds to target a number of urban municipalities. It aims to use community mediators (health and school mediators) to strengthen the local policies related to Roma inclusion, and to mainstream Roma inclusion into general public policies. Since the 2011 education reform, the school mediator function has been mainstreamed into the education infrastructure.

box continues next page

Box 2.4 Roma Mediators Help Link Roma Communities with the Romanian Education System
(continued)

Recent research indicates that school mediators have had a positive impact on a number of issues, including considerably decreasing the number of school dropout and nonenrollment cases; achieving better school attainment and academic performance of Roma students; reducing absenteeism among students; combating Roma students' class segregation and the general desegregation of schools; and improving communication between the school and the Roma community. Teachers' attitudes toward the Roma have also improved, which has promoted the overall development of the Roma communities beyond their narrower education mandate.

Nevertheless, the school mediator program has important shortcomings that need to be addressed in future policy making. Teachers and school administrators from institutions that benefit from a school mediator's services tend to relegate all activities related to Roma to the mediator, which disengages teachers from the Roma communities they serve. Furthermore, the lack of sustainability and security regarding employment has placed some of the mediators in the position of being unable to raise concerns or take effective measures regarding the discrimination of Roma children in the school environment.

Box 2.5 Subsidized School Dining in the Slovak Republic and the "Bread Roll and Milk" Program in Romania

One measure introduced by the Slovak government to support children from socially disadvantaged environments—a category defined mainly on the basis of family income—are the so-called "one koruna lunches" in kindergartens and primary schools (ISCED 1 and 2). This program significantly subsidizes school lunch costs (a family without the subsidy covers 45 percent of the actual cost of the meal). In schools where more than 50 percent of children are entitled to the subsidy, the program automatically extends it to all children regardless of whether they meet the means test.

In Romania, a nutrition program called "Bread Roll and Milk" (*Cornul și laptele*) was launched in 2002, first in public primary schools and later in kindergartens (2004) and lower secondary education schools (2008). The program is not exclusively targeted at socially disadvantaged families but covers all children; it aims to support children's nutrition, and at the same time, reduce the dropout rate and improve attendance. Each child is eligible for a roll and a glass of milk a day. UNDP and UNICEF report that the program has improved attendance rates (Cace et al. 2006; UNICEF, n.d.), and an evaluation of the program (Arpinte et al. 2009) concluded that its strengths include the fact that it supports nutrition (for some children, this is their first meal of the day) and is universal (no one is excluded or feels stigmatized as the poorest in the class). On the other hand, the program's weaknesses include poor quality food and lack of variety, and the subsequent waste generated (especially in larger towns) when children throw away the food. Further problems relate to the distribution of school snacks, especially in rural areas, where distribution companies deliver food to schools usually twice per week, in an effort to cut costs.

- Afterschool programs to compensate for insufficient resources and lack of support in the family environment, including tutoring and mentoring to address individual needs as they arise; and
- Preparatory grades for children who have not attended preschool.

It is important to note that some integrated programs that go beyond education policies (such as urban or community development) may also have a positive impact on education outcomes. For example, the IRIS Subsidized Rental Housing Project in Spain—discussed in Initiative 4.5 of chapter 4 of this book—has demonstrated considerable positive effects on the education outcomes of the children rehoused by the program; educational outcomes—as measured by the probability that the child is in a grade that corresponds to his or her age—improve considerably among these pupils (Santiago 2012).

Further examples of good initiatives can be found in boxes 2.6 and 2.7.

Box 2.6 Select Examples of Measures That Support Marginalized Roma Children in Primary Schools

In all the examined countries, a Roma teaching assistant position has been established for more than a decade, with first pilots starting in 1993–94 in the Czech Republic and the Slovak Republic (Rus 2006). Interestingly, the idea (and piloting) originated in the nongovernmental sector, and education authorities later adopted it as part of their policies, legislation, and financing. Roma teaching assistants mainly facilitate communication between schools and families (similar to the Roma school mediators in Romania), or facilitate communication between the teacher and Roma students, and support Roma children outside of the classroom by helping them with homework, organizing leisure time activities, and so on (for example, in the Czech Republic, the Slovak Republic, and Bulgaria). Roma teaching assistants are most common at the ISCED 1 level, but they work also in ISCED 0 and ISCED 2, and sometimes in ISCED 3 programs.

The Teach for Bulgaria program, inspired by Teach for America (where graduates from competitive colleges are placed in low-performing schools nationwide) was rolled out in Bulgaria in July 2010. Several independent studies have shown that the Teach for America program tends to positively impact student test scores relative to students instructed by teachers not affiliated with Teach for America. Such effects are particularly strong in math and science.

In 2012, the Slovak Republic introduced another measure aimed at improving the outcomes of Roma pupils in primary schools—the so-called Full-Day Education System, part of an EU-funded national project. The system is based on pedagogic experiments carried out in the Slovak Republic in the late 1970s, which showed the benefits of keeping Roma children from marginalized backgrounds engaged in class for the full day rather than just part of it. The project introduced varied combinations of afternoon activities (tutoring, extracurricular activities, sports) at some 200 Slovak schools with higher shares of pupils from so-called disadvantaged backgrounds.

Box 2.7 Helping Disadvantaged Roma Children Complete Secondary Education

All CEE countries have support programs for students at upper secondary levels, including means-tested programs that target only the poorest students or explicitly Roma students, with differences in eligibility criteria such as attendance, academic merit, or talent. Public and private grant schemes are in place; the scholarship scheme of the Roma Education Fund (REF) is the most significant private initiative that supports Roma students across CEE.

For example, Hungary has extensive public support programs in place. Its For The Road—MACIKA program supported 14,481 students with a total of €7.2 million in the 2013–14 school year. The program targets disadvantaged or multiple-disadvantaged students and is required to award at least 50 percent of the grants to Roma students.[a]

In Bulgaria, state scholarships are provided to students to award their performance, ensure access to education, prevent drop out, and support children with disabilities or without parents. In addition, one-off support could be provided to students in order to surmount the issues that negatively affect school access and regular attendance. Children from poor families receive free textbooks in grades 1 through 8 (ISCED levels 1 and 2) and are entitled to subsidized school meals.

In Romania, the program Money for High School has been in place since 2004. It makes students from low-income families eligible for a monthly scholarship of about €42 if their attendance rate is acceptable (that is, if they have no more than 20 unexcused absences per year). Priority is given to students from rural areas who study in other localities.

In 2008, the Czech Republic's Ministry of Education launched a grant program to support Roma students from low-income families who study at general or vocational secondary schools. Schools are given funding to pay for dining, dormitory fees, travel costs, and school aids, or are reimbursed for these costs if students have covered them. In 2014, 487 students at 130 secondary schools were supported with a total of €78,000. Full-time students from low-income families who declare Roma ethnicity and have not received a formal reprimand by their school concerning discipline or attendance are eligible. Grant sum per student increases with the grade, from €140 in grade 1 to €250 in grade 4 per semester of secondary school. Private support is provided by the REF and in a separate program by the Verda Foundation.

A similar public program is in place in the Slovak Republic, with two major differences: ethnicity is not an eligibility criterion, and the grant sum is higher for students with higher academic achievement. The grant amount ranges from €45 per month for the best students, down to €22 for students with grade averages between 2.5 and 3.5 (on a scale of 1, the best, to 5, the worst).[b] Students with grade averages below 3.5 are not eligible for the grant. According to school principals (Kubánová 2011), such scholarships are effective if schools link them to stricter internal rules concerning attendance; if other decentralized subsidies are available for low-income students, such as subsidized fees for school dining and dormitories; and if the school cooperates with students/parents and pays for the associated costs directly rather than allowing the funds to be used by the students/parents for other purposes. The governmental unit Plenipotentiary for Roma Communities provides further resources to Roma students at secondary schools who are from families in need, except for special needs students in 2-year programs at secondary schools. There are also private donors. For example, the program "Divé maky"

box continues next page

Box 2.7 Helping Disadvantaged Roma Children Complete Secondary Education *(continued)*

provides funds, tutoring, and mentoring to Roma children with outstanding academic, artistic, or athletic talents. In addition, the REF in cooperation with the Slovak Republic's Open Society Foundation supports low-income Roma students in grades 2–4 who have outstanding academic achievements—in 2013, 110 applicants were funded with a total of €2,900.

a. See http://www.emet.gov.hu/_userfiles/felhivasok/ut_a_diplomahoz/2014/utr_ud_14_palyazati_kiiras.pdf (in Hungarian) for details of the program setup.
b. See http://www.uips.sk/sub/uips.sk/images/JE/stipendia/stipendia_v_skolskom_roku_2013-14.pdf (in Slovak) for details of the scholarship scheme.

Roma Children Face Challenges Completing Their Education—with Girls at a More Pronounced Disadvantage

The RRS highlights a considerable gender gap in Roma's educational attainment (see figures 2.1, 2.2, and 2.4), though the exact patterns and causes of this phenomenon remain difficult to determine. The RSS data shows that parental expectations for Roma girls either resemble or exceed those for Roma boys (Duminică and Ivasiuc 2013; UNDP, World Bank, and EC 2011). Furthermore, literacy indicators generally signal that girls perform slightly better in school than boys, except when it comes to computer literacy (Duminică and Ivasiuc 2013).

At the same time, social norms in Roma communities can strongly impact the educational attainment of Roma boys and girls. Qualitative research has found that in communities that adhere to traditional gender norms, boys skip classes or leave school altogether. This is particularly the case in poor communities. Under these circumstances, boys are expected to conform to the traditional gender norm of providing for the family; to be perceived as hardworking inside the family and community; and to supplement the family's income (World Bank 2014b).

The same research found that Roma girls are often constrained in pursuing their education once they hit puberty, due to the significant value that is attached to virginity in most traditional Roma communities. Concerns about virginity loss preclude girls from leaving the domestic space, as parents often deem the commute to and from school (and any interaction with boys) as too risky. Another important reason why Roma girls from traditional communities do not complete school seems to be the expectation that they will have children early and be in charge of the family, for which continued education does not seem to be relevant.

Teachers' expectations and stereotypes can negatively impact Roma students' school performance, particularly in the case of girls. One study found that, despite the fact that Roma children expressed high aspirations for their future, teachers viewed them as unmotivated and disinterested in studying (Fleck and Rughinis 2008). Stereotypes or expectations that Roma girls will drop out of school to get married seem to influence teachers' attitudes toward them, and even influence curricula—Roma girls are taught it is very common to marry early in Roma culture, even against evidence from their own communities (Duminică and Ivasiuc 2013).

However, it is important to note that Roma students who reach the university level do not conform to the same pattern; gender statistics collected by the Roma Education Fund (REF) within the Tertiary Scholarship Program in Albania; Macedonia, former Yugoslav Republic of; and Serbia show that the female beneficiaries ratios are higher than males (between 56 and 75 percent), in line with the relatively high share of female students in these countries in general (53 percent in Macedonia, former Yugoslav Republic of; 54 percent in Serbia; and 55 percent in Albania, in 2010).

Ethnic Segregation in the School and the Classroom

In CEE, segregation of Roma children in school takes three key forms. First, Roma children may attend Roma-majority schools that exist in predominantly Roma areas. Residential segregation is common in Bulgaria, for example, and ethnically Roma schools accommodate 70 percent of Roma pupils in the country (European Roma Rights Centre 2004). Second, even where schools are more heterogeneous, Roma students are often separated from the majority and placed into remedial classes (UNICEF 2011). Finally, Roma children might be placed in special education, even when they do not meet the specific requirements for it.

The analysis of PISA results points to a systemwide, ability-based, and social segregation of pupils in CEE, which has significant negative effects for the performance of pupils of lower socioeconomic status. In addition, the RRS (see figure 2.8) also reveals a high level of classroom-level ethnic segregation among Roma; in Bulgaria and the Slovak Republic, one-third of Roma children attend classes that have a Roma majority. Hungarian and Romanian rates were close—at 24 percent and 22 percent, respectively. In the Czech Republic, 10 percent of Roma children attend classes with a Roma majority. Recent evidence demonstrates that school segregation has been on the rise in both Hungary and the Slovak Republic. In Hungarian schools it grew substantially between 1980 and 2011. The size of the educational market, free school choice, and the share of

Figure 2.8 Roma and Non-Roma Children (Ages 7–15) with a Majority of Roma Schoolmates

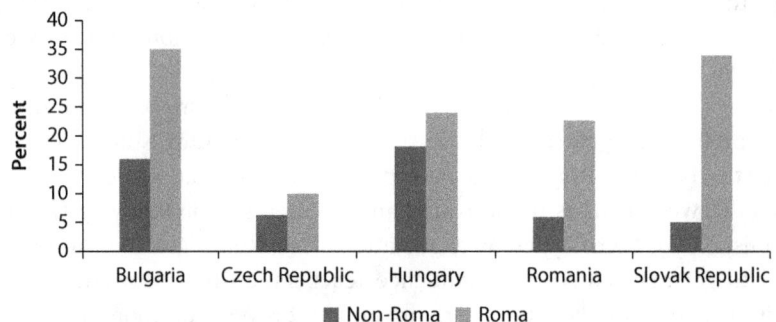

Source: UNDP, World Bank, and EC 2011.
Note: Respondents attend regular (that is, not special needs) schools.

Roma students are the main drivers of educational segregation. Given the higher mobility of most non-Roma students and the existing full free choice of school, non-Roma populations appear to increasingly commute to centers that have a lower density of Roma pupils (Kertesi and Kézdi 2012).

The issue of segregation seems to be particularly acute in the Slovak Republic, where special school attendance has been on the rise. The number of special education settings has grown due to a larger proportion of Roma children attending such schools in recent years. While only 6.4 percent of Roma currently older than the age of 30 attended special schools during their childhood, more than 11 percent of Roma children are enrolled in special education today. Although these schools should cater to the special needs of children with disabilities, only 13 percent of those enrolled report having special needs, as compared to 55 percent of non-Roma children who attend these centers (World Bank 2012a), which indicates that the special school system is being abused to perpetuate classroom segregation.

At the same time, the Slovak Republic example shows that issues such as preschool enrollment or parental education account for Roma children's disproportionate representation in special education: Roma parents' reasons for agreeing to send their children to special schools seem to reflect limited information about what it involves and its long-term effects on their children. The strongest predictor of whether a child goes to special school is whether the parents went to one themselves. In addition, the linkage between attendance, social assistance benefits eligibility, and funding mechanisms provides perverse incentives for both parents and educational institutions (World Bank 2012a).

International studies demonstrate the negative impact of segregation through, for example, the "peer effect," which seems to be most significant for low-achievement pupils, and increased feelings of inferiority and lower expectations (World Bank 2012b). In addition, school segregation in CEE also affects education quality and pupil achievement. For example, in Romania, research studies (Duminică and Ivasiuc 2010; Surdu 2008) indicate a high correlation between ethnic segregation and low quality of education. This arises from the segregated schools' poor infrastructure and learning resources, and teachers' lower qualifications and high turnover.

Findings from the evaluation of a Hungarian school integration program (Kézdi and Surányi 2009) have further demonstrated that ethnic integration in the classroom leads to improved results on standardized reading comprehension tests, has favorable effects on Roma students' noncognitive skills, and does not negatively affect performance for non-Roma students.

Directions for Policy

Improve Access to and Quality of Education throughout All Grades

At the policy level, as part of policy efforts aimed at improving education systems' competitiveness and inclusiveness, all CEE governments need to develop both systemic interventions to improve the educational system overall

Being Fair, Faring Better • http://dx.doi.org/10.1596/978-1-4648-0598-1

(see "The Path Ahead" in this chapter) and targeted measures to address Roma students' learning gap.

In terms of overall teaching quality, several European countries have implemented performance-based pay for teachers, and currently about half of all OECD countries reward teacher performance in various ways; CEE governments may wish to explore these. In addition, an analysis of Bulgaria's PISA results shows that a class that is orderly and has fewer disruptions is more conducive to learning. To this end, governments may wish to institute classroom observation methods and international best practices on classroom management, as well as teacher development programs that advise on more effective classroom management.

Improving the quality of educational resources (instructional materials, lab equipment, computer and software materials, library materials, and so on) can have a major impact, especially for low-achieving students. Doing so can also contribute to improved quality and equity throughout the education systems. As an example, Hungary has an H2O network of schools that follow the Hejőkeresztúr model. These are based on the Complex Instruction Program (CIP) method from the United States, and offer higher quality educational services to children from disadvantaged backgrounds (see box 2.8).

Another way to improve marginalized Roma's access to education is to scale up and improve the effectiveness of school mediator and Roma teacher assistant programs, particularly in countries where a significant share of the Roma population lives in rural, hard-to-reach locations (Romania, the Slovak Republic). This can involve training new and existing mediators in school mediation (in addition to health mediation) as well as making commitments regarding mediators' formal employment. These measures should be accompanied by awareness campaigns on mediators' roles and responsibilities, which could target teachers and school principals in institutions with high shares of Roma.

While spatial segregation[15] could often be a key source of segregation in service provision (including education), it is not always the cause of education segregation. Avoidable school segregation should not be justified or continued on the basis of spatial segregation. Authorities need to follow an integrated approach when designing and implementing desegregation interventions; desegregation should be supplemented with remedial education interventions so as to reduce the dropout rate of Roma children who lag behind in terms of education performance. At the same time, adequate accountability mechanisms should be introduced to ensure that antisegregation measures are adhered to in countries where classroom-level ethnic segregation persist (the Slovak Republic, Hungary, Bulgaria). In the case of the Slovak Republic, special schools for children who do not suffer from a severe mental or physical disability should be closed, or transformed into regular schools (World Bank 2012a).

At the program level, in countries where a large share of the disadvantaged population attends low-performing schools (for example, in Romania, Bulgaria, and Hungary), special incentives could be offered to attract the most talented teachers to work in hard-to-staff schools and preschools. Models based on the

Teach for America/Teach for Bulgaria programs could also be explored. In addition, teachers must be adequately motivated and trained to effectively offer inclusive education. For example, in Romania, the current teacher system should be revised to improve the selection process and the general curriculum, and to include specific modules on inclusive education and reducing school dropout.

Several countries promote integrated educational support for communities that can transform the school into an active institution that is open to the real needs of the community. Successful measures that increase Roma's education attainment require large-scale integrated interventions that also deal with such populations' socioeconomic environment, employment prospects, and health status. Cross-sectoral interventions at the community level are more efficient than singular interventions. For example, the concept of a community school (Blank et al. 2003) that was promoted by a coherent policy decision in the United Kingdom in 1996 was regarded as a significant attempt to overcome educational disadvantages among different communities. Under this approach the school becomes a center of the community, allowing school buildings to serve as the setting for other community services, in addition to formal education.

A description of a good example of integrated academic support can be found in box 2.8.

Box 2.8 The Complex Instruction Program in Hungary

The Complex Instruction Program (CIP) evolved from more than 20 years of research at the Stanford School of Education. Its objective is to ensure academic access and success for *all* students in heterogeneous classrooms. This methodology has three major components: (a) multiple ability curricula and independent/group work that involves open-ended tasks on a topic that requires a wide array of intellectual abilities; (b) special instructional strategies, as the teacher trains the students to use cooperative norms and specific roles to manage their own groups; and (c) teachers who learn to recognize and treat status problems, so that all students from diverse backgrounds can make meaningful contributions. Research has shown significant achievement gains in classrooms that have adopted such methods, which are widely used in schools in the United States and Europe.

In Hungary, the H_2O program started at the Hejőkeresztúr Primary and Middle School (where the rate of Roma pupils has been gradually rising). It has used the CIP methodology (among other innovative and educational inclusion tools) as a means to counteract potential achievement gaps and segregation, and to improve learning and performance for all students, regardless of their backgrounds.

By replicating the school's success, the H_2O program aims to reduce differences between students and make sure each one reaches the highest level attainable, given their abilities, motivation, and goals. The H_2O program transfers this educational method—in the form of a 90-hour accredited teacher training course—to the entire staff of primary schools that have disadvantaged indicators.

box continues next page

Box 2.8 The Complex Instruction Program in Hungary *(continued)*

The H_2O program's educational method is diverse. It strengthens student motivation; supports classroom differentiation; encourages teaching to learn and autonomy; strengthens communication, socialization, ICT, language, and other skills and abilities; develops problem-solving and cooperation skills; and encourages teamwork, tolerance, and practice-oriented education. Students who lag behind others are prioritized and prompted to work cooperatively, creatively, and multiculturally. Cognitive, meta-cognitive, and socioemotional skills are given special importance; parents' role in their children's overall development and learning process is also emphasized.

Prevent Roma Children from Dropping Out of Primary and Secondary Education

At the policy level, education systems should be able to identify at-risk children via monitoring systems. These children should receive counseling and mentorship services, and their families should receive information about the returns on education, the risks of limited school attendance (such as due to child labor) and its impact on the broadening performance gap, and the risks associated with eventual school dropout (see box 2.9). These counseling services should also be tailored to specifically address the challenges that adolescent Roma boys and girls face in negotiating traditional gender roles and the community's social norms with the expectations of mainstream society, such as the public education system. A successful example of addressing gender-specific challenges to prevent school dropout is the Adolescent Girls Initiative (AGI).[16] AGI aims to promote school completion and ease the transition of adolescent girls and young women from school to productive employment by providing tailored support that is adapted to the local context and addresses the specific constraints faced by girls.

To offset problems related to stereotyping and to proactively address the cultural and social factors that contribute to Roma's low school completion rate, the curricula should be adapted to take into account cultural and context-relevant factors (for example, it could incorporate components on Roma language, identity, and culture). Teacher training programs should be launched on culturally sensitive instruction. Working with experienced school mediators and counselors in this context would be useful, as they can bridge Roma communities with school facilities.

Based on recent pilots run in schools with a high share of children at risk for dropping out, teacher training programs may help promote individual learning strategies. These may involve establishing achievable learning objectives for each child, in line with their skills and competences; communicating learning objectives to students to increase awareness of their own progress; providing meaningful learning experiences that relate to students' real family and community lives; promoting positive approaches in learning and "learning-to-learn" strategies for children; and improving socio-emotional learning, including self-regulation and social skills.

At the program level, extracurricular activities can provide compensatory learning stimulation for marginalized children who are at a significant learning disadvantage relative to their more advantaged peers. For example, in Romania, localities with large Roma populations have implemented a large set of extracurricular activities, which are positively valued by the involved stakeholders. In addition, several countries have opted to equalize extracurricular opportunities by increasingly using their schools as community centers. For example, many Dutch schools have been expanded into community centers that offer a variety of afterschool enrichment activities. Similarly, the highest performing public school districts in the U.S. feature afterschool programs that offer a wide range of sports, arts, and other activities, often with the help of volunteers (such as parents or other family members). To address the problem of dropout among Roma girls, school environments should be made compatible with Roma communities' social norms and values (such as regarding adolescent girls' safety). In addition, child-care could be provided for families in which girls are at risk of dropping out because they need to help care for siblings or other young children

---

Box 2.9 Developing a School Dropout Early Warning System—Lessons from Romania

An early warning system for monitoring dropouts could be based on the following building blocks (Jigau and Fartusnic 2012):

- Clarify the definition of school dropout and draft guidelines for how the school can participate in completing statistical questionnaires that are administered by the national statistical authorities.
- Collect and report dropout data at the school and inspectorate levels. School staff that holds relevant responsibilities should be better trained, and more efficient monitoring and checking instruments should be instituted both at the school inspectorate level and at each school.
- Develop a school cohort evolution tracking system for deeper analysis of out-of-school children's characteristics (for example, family living conditions, engagement in circulatory or work migration, sibling influence, academic failure record, and so on). In addition, a long-term school cohort evolution tracking system needs to be developed and implemented. A national representative sample could be surveyed in various stages of the educational pathway, with research repeated every four-school cohorts (Voicu 2010). Alternatively, an electronic matriculation register could be created, which would allow for the real-time monitoring of each student's school pathway. In this case, basic information would be collected for every child that a school identifies to be most at risk of dropping out.
- Schools should strictly monitor truancy, dropout, and the situation of children who have never attended school. Public awareness campaigns on the importance of education must equally target parents, the public, and all school stakeholders (students, teachers, management, and

box continues next page

Box 2.9 Developing a School Dropout Early Warning System—Lessons from Romania *(continued)*

support staff). Moreover, schools and local authorities need to be made accountable for managing dropouts, while local cooperation organizations should be consolidated to also involve school and health mediators, informal community leaders, child protection structures, and NGO representatives that run relevant local projects.

• Monitor the situation of children caught in circulatory migration. National governments may wish to consider introducing a fly grade book/academic passport for those children who must accompany their parents to work outside of the community (either in other countries or elsewhere in their home country) in order to recognize the grades attended and completed. Students can more easily move between education systems if they have a certificate that documents their record (World Bank 2014a).

---

in the family. A good example of developing a school dropout early warning system can be found in box 2.9.

University Degree: A Pathway to Equal Access to Labor Markets

Very Few Roma Students Reach the University Level

The share of Roma students who complete tertiary education is extremely small. According to the RRS, the share of Roma among tertiary education graduates does not exceed 1 percent in any CEE country. While there are indications that the number of Roma university graduates in the region is on the rise (Brüggemann 2012), they remain a small fraction relative to national averages. Parents' commitment to supporting their children's education is the most prominent characteristic of students who pursue higher education. Family support for and investments in education seem to be the key factors that positively impact the life trajectory of Roma students, particularly girls. Nevertheless, in addition to early school leaving, the prohibitively high costs and expected low returns on tertiary education may be a contributing factor to nonattendance.

Roma with upper secondary education rarely continue their education at the tertiary level, which can be explained by financial barriers and perceived few gains, given the opportunity cost (such as missing out on income from employment or social benefits while in school) and expected labor market discrimination (O'Higgins 2009). As indicated by research in other countries, negative estimates of prospective success discourage students from more disadvantaged backgrounds from enrolling in university (Becker and Hecken 2009).

Poverty and unemployment are widespread among the region's Roma, making university unaffordable for the majority of Roma students. As figure 2.9 shows, in all five countries, the need-based support for full-time university students is not sufficient to cover even the cost of minimum tuition (where applicable) for first-cycle higher education programs and student dormitory fees (given that such housing is usually the cheapest), let alone the cost of food, utilities, transportation, textbooks, and clothing.

Figure 2.9 Minimum Cost of Tuition and Accommodation versus Average Need-Based Student Support (Per Academic Year)

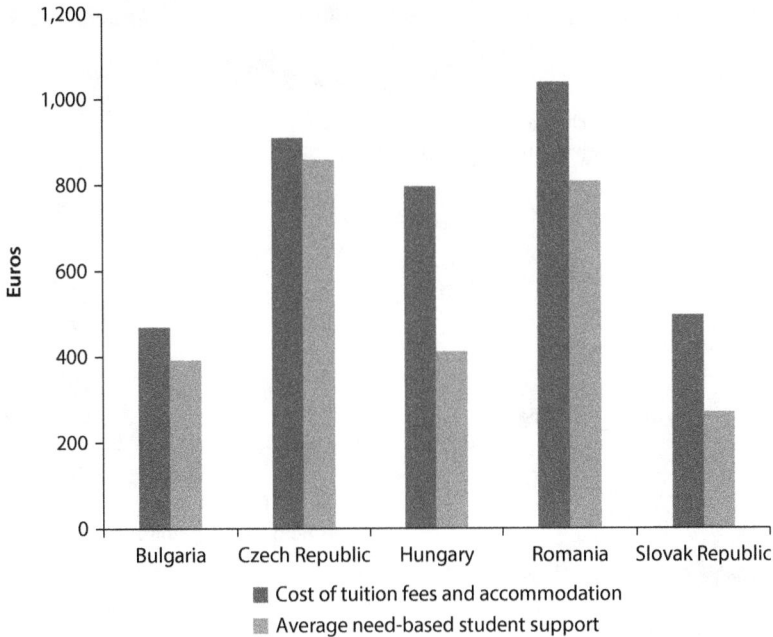

Sources: EACEA 2014 (for tuition fees and need-based student support); Eurostudent (n.d.) and Study in Bulgaria (n.d.) (for accommodation fees).
Note: Tuition fees are not charged in the Czech Republic and the Slovak Republic; there are admission fees (€20–21 per cycle) in the Czech Republic and registration fees in the Slovak Republic (€10–100 per academic year). In both countries, only tertiary students who exceed a regular length of study by one year pay tuition fees, except students in the Czech Republic who take leave because of parenthood. In the case of Hungary, student hall accommodation costs were not included because of unavailable data, and only the cost of the minimum tuition fee was included.

Tertiary Degree: A Passport to Equally Accessing the Labor Markets

Despite the evident gap in school completion between Roma and non-Roma, more young Roma have entered universities over the past few years. Based on data from the REF's tertiary education scholarships program (Roma Memorial University Scholarship Program [RMUSP] the largest higher education scholarship program for Roma in Europe), the number of Roma students who apply for scholarship support has been steadily increasing. In the 2012–13 academic year, RMUSP granted support to 1,076 young Roma students (out of 1,903 submitted applications). Among the scholarship recipients, 72 percent are pursuing bachelor degrees and 25 percent are pursuing master's degrees; 3 percent are enrolled in doctorate programs (Roma Education Fund 2013). On average, about 60 percent of scholars' parents have a minimum secondary education level.

A recent analysis in Romania highlights that among Roma, the probability of being employed increases significantly with one's level of education. As shown in figure 2.10, among Roma and non-Roma who are ages 15–64 and not in school,

Figure 2.10 Roma versus Non-Roma Education Levels for Employees (Ages 15–64), Romania

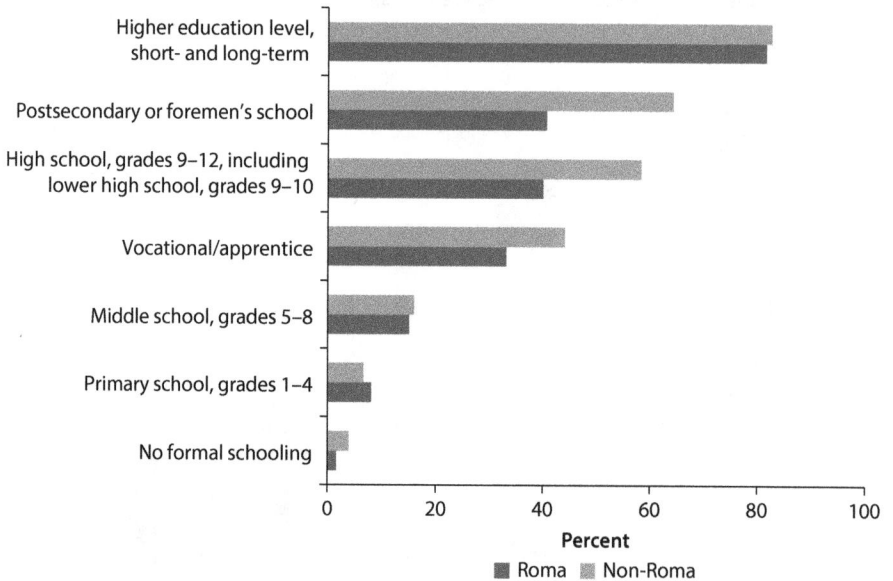

Source: National Institute of Statistics 2013.
Note: High school includes also lower high school, grades 9–10. Postsecondary or foremen's school not included for Roma because of the low number of cases.

the proportion of employees increases steadily from 2 to 4 percent among persons with no formal schooling, to 82–83 percent among graduates with tertiary education. The differences between Roma and non-Roma are notable in vocational and high school graduates, and virtually disappear at the tertiary level, effectively meaning that earning a college or university degree equalizes a Roma individual's chances of finding a job. Increasing the pool of Roma higher education graduates not only contributes to individual advancement, but also uplifts Roma communities. Roma with higher education can serve as role models and make a positive difference in their community.

According to a study by the REF and Gallup–Romania (Bojinca et al. 2009), the majority of beneficiaries of state-funded affirmative action tertiary education in Romania are proud of being Roma; at the same time, another in-depth study of the same policy reveals a more nuanced picture, suggesting that a poorly articulated policy of "special places" can be inclusive while simultaneously generating tensions, dilemmas, and social costs for beneficiaries (Pantea 2014). Among the beneficiaries of the privately funded Romaversitas program in Hungary, 72 percent of students and 57 percent of graduates report that the program helped them strengthen their Roma identity (Arnold et al. 2011). These figures suggest that affirmative action contributes to expanding the pool of Roma intellectuals and professionals.

Good initiatives of programs supporting Roma students in tertiary education can be found in box 2.10.

Box 2.10 Programs Supporting Roma Students in Tertiary Education

Existing merit-based support initiatives aim to facilitate tertiary access. The Roma Education Fund (REF) provides support to Roma students to attend university inside and outside their countries of residence, so as to expand the number of Roma graduates who can become agents for change in their respective communities and countries. In Bulgaria, the Czech Republic, Hungary, Romania, and the Slovak Republic, REF offers academic merit-based scholarships under its Roma Memorial University Scholarship Program and Roma International Scholar Program. In Bulgaria and Romania, scholarships are also provided under REF's Roma Health Scholarship Program (RHSP). These scholarship schemes support Roma students who are pursuing bachelors, master's, and doctorate degree programs; RHSP scholarships are also offered to students pursuing vocational level education. Scholarships are provided for one academic year, and students can renew their application provided they have successfully completed the prior academic year (Roma Education Fund 2013). The scholarship amounts vary from €910 to €2,010 per year, out of which €800–1,000 are intended for living costs and the rest for tuition (Arnold et al. 2011). Besides the REF scholarships, Romania has state-funded, tuition-free spots in the public universities that are reserved for Roma applicants who score at least five out of ten points on an entrance examination. In Hungary, the privately funded Romaversitas program provides applicants who successfully complete written and oral examinations with a monthly stipend of about €110 during the academic year and an approximately €73 annual textbook allowance, as well as free language courses, mentoring, and tutoring. Despite promising signs from these interventions, their impact on improving Roma's access to and completion of tertiary education—like programs that target students in secondary education—has yet to be rigorously evaluated.

Directions for Policy

Across the whole region, it is critical to improve marginalized Roma's access to tertiary education. In addition to the existing merit-based scholarships, governments may want to consider rolling out well-targeted affirmative action policies and programs for tertiary education, focusing on students from marginalized Roma communities. It is just as important to provide role models by encouraging strong linkages between Roma graduates and their communities. Roma children and parents should be made more aware of such measures, which should be accompanied by systematic monitoring and evaluation to accurately measure their real impact. Transportation subsidies may be provided for Roma from rural areas who continue their education in a different locality.

The Path Ahead

New member states face the challenge of delivering universal quality education (World Bank 2012d). Anywhere between 21 percent (the Czech Republic) and 43 percent (Bulgaria) of 15-year-olds are functionally illiterate, and the differential between student performance—as measured by PISA scores—in the highest and lowest socioeconomic quintiles is wide (Gortazar et al. 2014). For example, in

Bulgaria, students' circumstances play a dispropotionate role in explaining PISA scores. Furthermore, if the primary language spoken at home is different from Bulgarian, it accounts for a gap equivalent to three years of schooling in math and science, suggesting a considerable performance gap between students from ethnic minorities and their Bulgarian peers. It is important to note that in countries such as Bulgaria and Romania, many marginalized students (including Roma) have already dropped out of school before age 15, when PISA is administered.

The inability of the majority of students in these countries to get a quality education often results from the systems' very design, be it streaming into special education, early tracking, school assignment mechanisms that result in segregation, or curriculum design. The countries that have been most successful in improving the quality of learning—for example, Finland and Poland—have done so by over-hauling their education systems to be more inclusive. In other words, in education, improving quality and delivering equity amount to the same challenge.

Looking forward, ensuring that education systems can be society's "great equalizer" will require a changed approach, both at the systemic level and regarding interventions that can address the multiple barriers faced by the most marginalized. Reorienting education systems' architecture toward more inclusion will require changing designs and incentives, as well as establishing better measurement mechanisms for evidence-based policy making. This will include strengthening the selection of motivated and competent teachers; designing monetary and nonmonetary (career progress) incentives to entice high-performing teachers to segregated or remote schools; delaying early tracking of students (including via high-stakes exams at an early age, as is the current case in Bulgaria) to reduce segregation in schools; and transitioning away from special schools, where Roma children continue to be overrepresented.

More actively and accurately measuring learning outcomes (and using the results to make policy decisions) will also help improve teaching and learning (World Bank 2012d). The case for more and better measurement is particularly relevant for understanding the impact that government and NGO-led initiatives have on disadvantaged students' learning, including Roma. In particular, the RRS and all initiatives discussed in this chapter point to a growing need for data, evidence, and lessons from implementation experiences. A common weakness of government support schemes and some NGO-led initiatives is that they rarely incorporate rigorous monitoring and evaluation frameworks, and—in some cases—lack even basic data and information about grantees. For example, some programs explicitly target Roma based on self-declaration of ethnicity, but do not take into account social needs. These issues highlight the need to collect ethnically disaggregated data on education outcomes through regularly conducted surveys or student assessments, and to collect data during program implementation so as to rigorously evaluate the effect of various interventions.

At the same time, specific interventions—ranging from parenting skills and early nutrition interventions, afterschool support and mentoring, to mediation and better training for teachers and other stakeholders—are needed. These combined efforts can help education systems' ability to respond effectively to individual students' needs (World Bank 2005).

There are many areas in which research could add important elements to the successful design and implementation of these reforms. These include understanding how the capacity of local level service providers affects the delivery of education services to Roma, and how bottlenecks could be lessened; knowing the key drivers of the early school leaving/dropout phenomenon, which disproportionately affects Roma children; examining the role social norms and discrimination play regarding education outcomes; and recognizing the potential impact the "social network effect" and discrimination have on learning outcomes for marginalized Roma children.

Notes

1. Controlling for socioeconomic background and parenting characteristics.

2. Disadvantaged children are those who are eligible for the regular child protection allowance (rendszeres gyermekvédelmi támogatás); that is, those who come from families with income below 130 percent of the lowest pension benefit; single-parent families; and families with disabled children. Moreover, multiple-disadvantaged children are those whose parents reached only eight grades of primary education (Kontseková in Kriglerová 2010).

3. At least six hours per day spent in kindergarten and share of absences below 25 percent.

4. It is, however, important to take note of evidence from Hungary suggesting that it is in fact socioeconomic status, rather than bilingualism, that determines a child's performance in school. The vocabulary and concepts used in the "school language" are so distant from those used within the community that ultimately it does not matter whether the child and the teacher have a common mother tongue; a significant gap in understanding will persist (Derdak and Varga 1996).

5. The assessment varies between schools and individual teachers. Children are expected to talk about pictures, recognize colors, compare the size of objects and count them, and tell a simple story or similar tasks. If any problems occur, the teacher may recommend that the child see a specialist at a center for pedagogical and psychological counseling, where standardized assessment tools will be used to examine the child and make a recommendation.

6. In the Czech Republic, 15 percent of 6-year-olds (boys more often than girls) postpone their entry to compulsory education by a year. At primary schools for special needs students, the share of postponed entries is as high as 42 percent of 6-year-olds. See additional data from the Ministry of Education, Youth and Sport of the Czech Republic at http://www.msmt.cz/vzdelavani/skolstvi-v-cr/statistika -skolstvi/zapisy-do-1-rocniku-zakladnich-skol. In the Slovak Republic, 9 percent of children who came to enroll in primary education in 2012 had their entry postponed by one year (Ministry of Education, Science, Research and Sport of the Slovak Republic 2013).

7. Data from the Regional Roma Survey (UNDP, World Bank, and EC 2011).

8. Data from Brüggemann (2012).

9. Many other aspects of testing at the entry to primary school are considered controversial. See White (2012) for a comparative analysis of several CEE and Balkans countries; Tomatová (2004) for a detailed overview of the Slovak case; and Valenta et al. (2009) for an analysis of the Czech Republic.

10. In Hungary, compulsory education starts in kindergarten at age five, and most children enter primary school at age six or seven. In Romania, compulsory education starts at age six (before 2003 the entry age was seven, and parents still widely exercise their right to postpone enrollment by one year). However, as of 2012, children who are not in kindergarten are required to enter the preparatory class of the primary school. In Bulgaria, primary education starts at age seven and follows two years of compulsory preschool preparation of children ages five and six; this was introduced in the 2010–11 school year for some municipalities, and mainstreamed in the subsequent year. Eurydice (2012) finds that Bulgaria had the highest share of children in Europe who were not enrolled at time of their first year of compulsory primary education (10 percent of 7-year-olds in Bulgaria in 2009).

11. Data from the Hungary Life Course survey provide a considerably better picture: the upper secondary school completion rate in Hungary by age 20–21 is 46 percent of those who started the first grade of primary school and 52 percent of those who started upper secondary school (Hajdu, Kertesi, and Kézdi 2014). These differences may be attributed to the different characteristics of survey samples.

12. Online source accessed June 20, 2014: http://www.minv.sk/?atlas_2013.

13. Eight percent of 7-year-olds are still enrolled in preschool in the Czech Republic, 6 percent in Romania, 4 percent in Hungary, and 2 percent in the Slovak Republic (Eurydice Network 2012).

14. According to the National Statistical Office in Bulgaria, a decade ago there were two main reasons for dropping out from primary and lower secondary education: family reasons and unwillingness to continue in studies. Currently, the main reasons students drop out are unwillingness, family reasons, and migration of the family abroad. See http://www.nsi.bg/en/content/4830/students-and-drop-outs-reasons-and-level-education.

15. Spatial segregation is discussed in more detail in chapter 4 of this study.

16. For more information, see http://www.worldbank.org/en/programs/adolescent-girls-initiative.

References

Arnold, P., R. Ágyas, G. Héra, I. Katona, J. Kiss, Z. Mészáros, J. Péter, A. Pletser, A. Rácz, G. Rostás, and A. Szépe. 2011. *Evaluation Research of Romaversitas Hungary: Final Study.* Budapest: Kurt Lewin Foundation. Cited in E. Friedman and S. Garaz. 2013. "Support for Roma in Tertiary Education and Social Cohesion." In *Roma Education in Europe: Practices, Policies and Politics*, edited by Maja Miskovic, 149–66. London: Routledge.

Arpinte, D., S. Cace, M. Preotesi, and C. Tomescu. 2009. *Cornul și laptele—percepții, atitudini și eficiență.* Bucharest: ECOSOC. http://www.publicinfo.gov.ro/library/lapte_si _corn_expert.pdf.

Baslová, M., and M. Homrová. 2012. *Analýza role ZŠ praktických v procesu vzdělávání.* Report, University of West Bohemia, Plzeň. http://www.clovekvtisni.cz/uploads /file/1360764203-an_KA2_prakticke_skoly.pdf.

Becker, R., and A. E. Hecken. 2009. "Why Are Working-Class Children Diverted from Universities—An Empirical Assessment of the Diversion Thesis." *European Sociological Review* 25 (2): 233–50.

Bennett, J. 2012. *Roma Early Childhood Inclusion*. RECI Overview Report, Open Society Foundations, Roma Education Fund, and UNICEF, Budapest. http://www.romachildren.com/wp-content/uploads/2010/12/RECI-Overview-final-WEB.pdf.

Blank, Martin J., Atelia Melaville, and Bela P. Shah. 2003. *Making the Difference. Research and Practice of Community Schools*. Report, Coalition for Community Schools, Institute for Educational Leadership, Washington, DC. http://www.communityschools.org/assets/1/Page/CCSFullReport.pdf.

Bojinca, M., D. Munteanu, A. Toth, M. Surdu, and J. Szira. 2009. "Analysis of the Impact of Affirmative Action for Roma in High Schools, Vocational Schools and Universities." Working Paper 3, Roma Education Fund and the Gallup Organisation Romania, Budapest. http://www.romaeducationfund.hu/sites/default/files/publications/gallup_romania_english.pdf.

Brüggemann, C. 2012. "Roma Education in Comparative Perspective. Analysis of the UNDP/World Bank/EC Regional Roma Survey 2011." Roma Inclusion Working Papers, United Nations Development Programme, Bratislava. http://www.unesco.org/new/fileadmin/MULTIMEDIA/HQ/ED/pdf/Roma-Education-Comparative-Perspective-UNDP.pdf.

Cace, S., M. Preda, and G. Duminica. 2006. *Evaluation of Programmes Targeting Roma Communities in Romania*. Report, "Impreună" Agency for Community Development and UNDP Romania, Cluj-Napoca. http://www.undp.ro/pdf/Evaluation%20of%20Programmes%20Targeting%20Roma%20Communities%20in%20Romania.pdf.

CARE. 2011. *Situational Analyses of Education and Social Inclusion of Roma Girls in Serbia*. Report, CARE Serbia, Belgrade. http://www.care.rs/wp-content/uploads/2011/08/Situational-Analysis-of-Education-and-Social-Inclusion-of-Roma-Girls-in-Serbia.pdf.

Csapó, B., V. Csépe, K. Fazekas, G. Havas, M. Herczog, A. Kárpáti, G. Kertesi, J. Köllő, J. Lannert, I. Liskó, J. Nagy, A. Schleicher, and J. Varga. 2009. *Green Book for the Renewal of Public Education in Hungary*. Budapest: Prime Minister's Office.

Derdák, T., and A. Varga. 1996. "Az iskola nyelvezete—idegen nyelv." *Regio—Kisebbség, politika, társadalom*. http://epa.oszk.hu/00000/00036/00025/pdf/07.pdf.

Duminică, G., and A. Ivasiuc. 2010. *One School for All? Access to Quality Education for Roma Children*. Research Report, UNICEF, Bucharest. http://www.unicef.org/romania/One_school_for_all_pt_WEB.pdf.

———. 2013. *The Roma in Romania: From Scapegoat to Development Engine*. Report, "Impreună" Agency for Community Development, Cluj-Napoca. https://www.academia.edu/6037269/IN_ROMANIA_ROMA_From_Scapegoat_to_Development_Engine.

EACEA (Education, Audiovisual and Culture Executive Agency). 2014. *National Student Fee and Support Systems in Higher Education, 2013/14*. Report, Eurydice—Facts and Figures, European Commission, Brussels.

Engle, P. L., L. C., Fernald, H., Alderman, J., Behrman, C. O'Gara, A. Yousafzai, M. C. De Mello, M. Hidrobo, N. Ulkuer, I., Ertem, S., Iltus, and the Global Child Development Group. (2011). "Strategies for Reducing Inequalities and Improving Developmental

Outcomes for Young Children in Low-Income and Middle-Income Countries." *The Lancet, 378,* 1339–53.

European Roma Rights Centre. 2004. *Stigmata: Segregated Schooling of Roma in Central and Eastern Europe.* Report, European Roma Rights Centre, Budapest.

Eurostudent. n.d. "Average Student Hall Monthly Rent, Czech Republic, Romania and Slovakia." http://www.eurostudent.eu.

Eurydice Network. 2012. *Key Data on Education in Europe, 2012.* Brussels: Education, Audiovisual and Culture Executive Agency (EACEA P9 Eurydice). http://eacea.ec .europa.eu/education/eurydice.

Ferreira, F. H. G., and J. Gignoux. 2011. "The Measurement of Educational Inequality— Achievement and Opportunity." Working Paper 019, Rede de Economia Aplicada, Paris. http://reap.org.br/wp-content/uploads/2011/12/019-The-Measurement-of-Educational -Inequality.pdf.

Fleck, G., and C. Rughinis. 2008. *Come Closer: Inclusion and Exclusion of Roma in Present-Day Romanian Society.* Report, European Commission, Bucharest.

GAC (Governmental Advisory Committee). 2009. *Vzdělanostní dráhy a vzdělanostní šance romských žákyň a žáků základních škol v okolí vyloučených romských lokalit.* Prague: GAC.

Gortazar, L., K. Herrera-Sosa, D. Kutner, M. Moreno, and A. Gautam. 2014. "How Can Bulgaria Improve Its Education System? An Analysis of PISA 2012 and Past Results." Working Paper 91321. Washington, DC: World Bank Group. http://documents .worldbank.org/curated/en/2014/09/20289139/can-bulgaria-improve-education -system-analysis-pisa-2012-past-results.

Hajdu, T., G. Kertesi, and G. Kézdi. 2014. "Roma fiatalok a középiskolában: Beszámoló a Tárki Életpálya-felvételének, 2006 és 2012 közötti hullámaiból." Budapest Working Papers on the Labour Market, BWP 2014/7, Budapest. http://www.econ.core.hu/file /download/bwp/bwp1407.pdf.

Heckman, J. J. 2006. "Investing in Disadvantaged Young Children Is an Economically Efficient Policy." Paper presented at the Committee for Economic Development/Pew Charitable Trusts/PNC Financial Services Group Forum, "Building the Economic Case for Investments in Preschool," New York, January 10. http://jenni.uchicago.edu /Australia/invest-disadv_2005-12-22_247pm_awb.pdf.

Ivan, C., and I. Rostas. 2013. *Equal Opportunities in Education.* Bucharest: REF Romania.

Jigau, M., and C. Fartusnic. 2012. *Estimarea dimensiunii fenomenului de abandon şcolar folosind metodologia analizei pe cohortă.* Report, UNICEF, Bucharest. http://www .unicef.ro/wp-content/uploads/Studiu-cohorte-RO-22-nov-2012-pt-web-1.pdf.

Kertesi, G., and G. Kézdi. 2006. "Expected Long-Term Budgetary Benefits to Roma Education in Hungary." Budapest Working Papers on the Labour Market BWP— 2006/5, Institute of Economics, Hungarian Academy of Sciences, Corvinus University of Budapest. http://www.econ.core.hu/doc/bwp/bwp/bwp0605.pdf.

———. 2011. "The Roma/Non-Roma Test Score Gap in Hungary." *American Economic Review* 101 (3): 519–25.

———. 2012. "Ethnic Segregation between Hungarian Schools: Long-Run Trends and Geographic Distribution." Budapest Working Papers on the Labour Market, BWP 2012/8, Budapest. http://www.econ.core.hu/file/download/bwp/bwp1208.pdf.

———. 2014. "The Kindergarten Allowance in Hungary: Evaluation of a Conditional Cash Transfer Program." *Acta Oeconomica* 64 (1): 27–49.

Kézdi, G., and E. Surányi. 2009. *A Successful School Integration Program*. Report, Roma Education Fund, Budapest. http://www.romaeducationfund.hu/sites/default/files /publications/a_succesful_school_integration_kezdi_suranyi.pdf.

Kontseková, J. 2010. In *Žiaci zo znevýhodneného prostredia na Slovensku a v zahraničí: Komparatívna analýza slovenskej legislatívy a štatistických údajov s prístupmi v piatich európskych krajinách*, edited by Gallová Kriglerová. Slovak Governance Institute. http://www.governance.sk/index.php?id=1834.

Kubánová, M. 2011. "Sú stredoškolské štipendiá efektívny nástroj, aby viac študentov z chudobných rodín zvládlo strednú školu?" Slovak Governance Institute. http://www .scribd.com/doc/56056032/Reportaz-Stredoskolske-Stipendia-Final-2305.

Martinez, L. M., M. F. Enguita, and J. R. Gómez. 2010. "Disengaged from Education: Processes, Experiences, Motivations and Strategies of Early School Dropout and School Failure." *Revista de Educación Número Extraordinario 2010*, pp. 119–45. http:// www.mecd.gob.es/dctm/revista-de-educacion/articulosre2010/re201005.pdf?docum entId=0901e72b81203eb3.

Ministry of Education, Science, Research and Sport of the Slovak Republic. 2013. *Report on the Slovak Education and Systemic Measures to Support Its Further Advancement, Annex 1*. Report, Ministry of Education, Science, Research and Sport of the Slovak Republic, Bratislava.

National Institute of Statistics. 2013. Household Budget Survey Romania.

OECD (Organisation for Economic Co-operation and Development). 2010. *PISA 2009 Results: Equity in Learning Opportunities and Outcomes*. Vol. 2. Paris: PISA, OECD.

———. 2013. *PISA 2012 Results in Focus: What 15-Year-Olds Know and What They Can Do with What They Know: Key Results from PISA 2012*. Paris: PISA, OECD.

O'Higgins, N. 2009. "'It's Not That I'm a Racist, It's That They Are Roma': Roma Discrimination and Returns to Education in South Eastern Europe." IZA Discussion Paper 4208, Institute for the Study of Labor, Bonn. http://ftp.iza.org/dp4208.pdf.

Pantea, M.-C. 2008. "Challenges Regarding the Combating of Roma Child Labor via Education in Romania and the Need for Child-Centered Roma Policies." International Policy Fellowship Program, Open Society Institute, Budapest. http://www.policy.hu /document/200808/maria_carmen.pantea.pdf&letoltes=1.

———. 2014. "Affirmative Action in Romania's Higher Education: Roma Students' Perceived Meanings and Dilemmas." *British Journal of Sociology of Education* 1–19. doi: 10.1080/01425692.2013.869172. http://www.tandfonline.com/doi/abs/10.1080/01 425692.2013.869172.

ROCEPO (Rómske vzdelávacie centrum Prešov). 2011. *Správa o výsledkoch prieskumu o postavení žiaka zo sociálne znevýhodneného prostredia v školskom systéme v Slovenskej republike*. Metodicko-pedagogické centrum Bratislava, RegionálnepracoviskoPrešov.

Roma Education Fund. 2013. *Annual Report, 2012*. Budapest: Roma Education Fund.

Rus, C. 2006. *The Situation of Roma School Mediators and Assistants in Europe*. Report, DGIV/EDU/ROM(2006)3, Council of Europe, Strasbourg. http://www.coe.int/t /dg4/education/roma/Source/Mediators_Analyse_EN.PDF.

Santiago, L. 2012. *Leaving the Slums Behind: Measuring the Impact of IRIS Pro-integration Housing Program*. Policy Report, IRIS, Madrid. http://www.romadecade.org/cms /upload/file/9713_file1_iris-policy-report.pdf.

Singhal, A., and J. Lanigan. 2007. "Breastfeeding, Early Growth and Later Obesity." *Obesity Review* 8 (Suppl 1): 51–4. http://www.ncbi.nlm.nih.gov/pubmed/17316302.

Study in Bulgaria. n.d. "Living Expenses in Bulgaria—Student Accommodation." http://
www.studyinbulgaria.com.

Surdu L. 2008. *Monitorizarea aplicării măsurilor împotriva segregării şcolare în România.*
Report, UNICEF, Bucharest. http://www.unicef.ro/wp-content/uploads/monitorizarea
-aplicarii-masurilor-impotriva-segregarii-scolare-in-romania.pdf.

Tomatová, J. 2004. *Na vedľajšej koľaji, Je process zaraďovania rómskych detí do špeciálnych
základných škôl znevýhodňujúcim činiteľom?* Report, Slovak Governance Institute,
Bratislava.

UNDP (United Nations Development Programme), World Bank, and EC (European
Commission). 2011. *Regional Roma Survey.* Report, UNDP, World Bank, and EC,
New York.

UNECSO Institute for Statistics. 2012.

UNICEF (United Nations Children's Fund). n.d. *Early Childhood Development.* http://
www.unicef.org/romania/education_1616.html.

———. 2011. "The Right of Roma Children to Education." Position Paper. http://www
.unicef.org/ceecis/UNICEF_ROE_Roma_Position_Paper_Web.pdf.

———. TransMONEE Database. http://www.transmonee.org.

Valenta, M., J. Michalík, J. Petrášová, H. Balabánová, V. Hloušek, M. Lečbych, and
M. Procházka. 2009. *Analýza diagnostických nástrojů užívaných vůči žákům ze
sociokulturně znevýhodněného prostředí s přihlédnutím k romským dětem.* žákyním a
žákům Výzkumné centrum integrace zdravotně postižených.

Voicu, B. 2010. *Renunţarea timpurie la educaţie: Posibile căi de prevenire.* Report, UNICEF,
Bucharest. http://www.unicef.ro/wp-content/uploads/renuntarea_1.pdf.

White, J. 2012. *Pitfalls and Bias: Entry Testing and the Overrepresentation of Romani
Children in Special Education.* Report, Roma Education Fund, Budapest.

World Bank. 2005. *Expanding Opportunities and Building Competencies for Young People:
A New Agenda for Secondary Education.* Report, World Bank, Washington, DC.

———. 2012a. *Diagnostics and Policy Advice on the Integration of Roma in the Slovak
Republic.* Report, World Bank, Washington, DC.

———. 2012b. *Protecting the Poor and Promoting Employability: An Assessment of the Social
Assistance System in the Slovak Republic.* Report, World Bank, Washington, DC.

———. 2012c. *Reducing Vulnerability and Promoting the Self-Employment of Roma in
Eastern Europe through Financial Inclusion.* Report, World Bank, Washington, DC.

———. 2012d. *Skills, Not Just Diplomas: Managing Education for Results in Eastern Europe
and Central Asia.* Report, World Bank, Washington, DC.

———. 2012e. *Toward an Equal Start: Closing the Early Learning Gap for Roma in Eastern
Europe.* Report, World Bank, Washington, DC. http://www-wds.worldbank
.org/external/default/WDSContentServer/WDSP/ECA/2013/01/23/090224b0818b
963c/1_0/Rendered/PDF/Overview0of0Ma0ation00EU0Financing0.pdf.

———. 2013. *Economic Cost of Roma Exclusion.* Policy Note, World Bank, Washington,
DC. http://go.worldbank.org/G1EL5HZ8S0.

———. 2014a. *Diagnostics and Policy Advice Supporting Roma Inclusion in Romania.*
Report, World Bank, Washington, DC.

———. 2014b. *Gender Dimensions of Roma Inclusion: Perspectives from Four Roma
Communities in Bulgaria.* Report, World Bank, Washington, DC.

CHAPTER 3

Accessing Productive Employment

Celine Ferré

Summary

Roma in marginalized communities face poor labor market integration. Employment rates among the Roma are low, and markedly worse than their non-Roma neighbors. Women and youth have especially low market participation rates. These rates do not reflect Roma preferences for work, however; Roma men and women look for work as much as non-Roma but cannot find reliable employment. Furthermore, those who do work often have precarious, unstable, and informal jobs (figure 3.1 presents some of the most salient facts about employment for Roma in marginalized communities).

Constraints to employability constitute the first and most important set of barriers faced by Roma. Unemployment and low wages are often the result of a mismatch between the specific skills that employers require—both technical and nontechnical—and those usually possessed by the work-able Roma population, which is characterized by low levels of education, limited work experience, and long stretches of unemployment.

Constraints to participation constitute the Roma's second set of barriers, and include discrimination, discouragement, residential segregation, and lack of financial resources. Lack of access to social services, health care, and housing result in mutually reinforcing barriers, all of which create obstacles to access the labor market. Moreover, many marginalized communities are located in areas where unemployment is structurally high. In addition, many Roma job seekers lack social capital and the network of information about job and training offers. Recent qualitative research findings suggest that Roma are often discouraged from looking for jobs when their job-searching peers are continuously unsuccessful. Last but not least, capital constraints can also be a major impediment for those trying to start a business or become self-employed.

Public employment services (PES) can potentially play an important role in promoting access to productive employment for Roma. However, to do so effectively, they need to strengthen their focus on hard-to-reach populations, and refine some marginal elements to address Roma job seekers' specific needs, including how programs are delivered.

First, given the widespread functional illiteracy among Roma in marginalized localities, second-chance education and literacy programs should become core pieces of any labor market initiative focused on improving employability for marginalized Roma, including systems to detect at-risk groups early on and give them prioritized and individualized attention. In particular, youth could benefit from career counseling and professional orientation programs offered at school, both of which should be connected to the market employability capacity.

Second, and consistent with international good practices, there is room for Active Labor Market Programs (ALMPs) to concentrate financial and human resources away from skilled secondary school and university graduates and toward low-skilled and disadvantaged job seekers. Moreover, training and retraining programs should be better linked to actual employment and build on client choice. Public works programs should remain an important intervention, especially for unskilled Roma and those in low labor demand regions.

Figure 3.1 Notable Facts about Employment among Roma

Roma have similar labor participation rates as non-Roma but are 2 times less likely to be employed.

Irregular work is 2 to 6 times more common for Roma than their non-Roma neighbors.

72% of unemployed Romanian Roma are not registered with an employment service agency.

In Bulgaria, Hungary, and Romania, less than 4% of Roma have savings.

One additional year of experience decreases the probability of being out of the labor market by 11 to 19 percent.

In the Czech Republic, Roma workers earn 1/3 of their non-Roma neighbors' wages.

2/3 of Roma are unskilled workers.

Source: UNDP, World Bank and EC 2011.

Being Fair, Faring Better • http://dx.doi.org/10.1596/978-1-4648-0598-1

Jobs Are More Than Just Earnings

Jobs are more than just the earnings they provide—jobs are part of who we are, how we define ourselves, and how we interact with others in society. Jobs are the cornerstone of economic and social development; they can boost living standards, raise productivity, and foster social cohesion (World Bank 2013). People work their way out of poverty and hardship through better livelihoods. Economies grow as people get better at what they do, and as more productive jobs are created and less productive ones disappear. Through these processes, jobs are transformational for development, and as a key pathway out of poverty, they are a critical element for improving the circumstances in which the next generation can grow and flourish. Conversely, unequal opportunities in labor markets can perpetuate the cycle of exclusion for Roma in relation to non-Roma populations. As seen in chapter 2, socioeconomic background plays an important role in children's success in schooling. Similarly, family background can play a relevant role in Roma youths' transition from school into the labor market—indirectly through education but also directly through access to social networks, for example.

Without jobs, competitive skills, and a fair access to the labor market, many Roma lack the tools to succeed and advance economically. While there is no substitute for creating jobs through a healthy and dynamic labor market, several complementary interventions are needed to better integrate marginalized Roma communities into their countries' economic development. These include investing in more and better jobs for the most marginalized, including the Roma; tearing down the labor market barriers they face; and developing effective labor market programs that connect the most vulnerable to jobs.

Because of the widespread influence on the economy, improving labor market opportunities and outcomes for marginalized Roma will have an even greater value to broader society than it will to the Roma alone. A substantial and growing proportion of new labor market entrants in Eastern Europe are Roma. Meanwhile, majority populations throughout much of Central and Eastern Europe (CEE) and the Balkans are declining—for example, Romania's working-age population is expected to shrink by 30 percent by 2050. At the same time, the Roma population is young and continues to grow. While unofficial estimates of the share of Roma ranges from 2 to 10 percent across countries, the share of young Roma in the ages 0–14 group—future labor market entrants—is estimated at between 7 and 20 percent. Thus, investing in young Roma's employability is an important strategy for CEE countries to sustain productivity gains.

Labor Market Participation Is Similar to Non-Roma, but There Is a Large Employment Gap...

Roma in marginalized communities face poor employment outcomes—employment rates among the Roma are low, and markedly poorer than their non-Roma neighbors. Figure 3.2 shows that between 15–34 percent of working-age Roma are unemployed, and 43–55 percent are out of the labor force (inactive). The situation is, however, far from uniform when looking at different demographic groups.

Figure 3.2 Roma versus Non-Roma Employment for Men, Women, and Youth

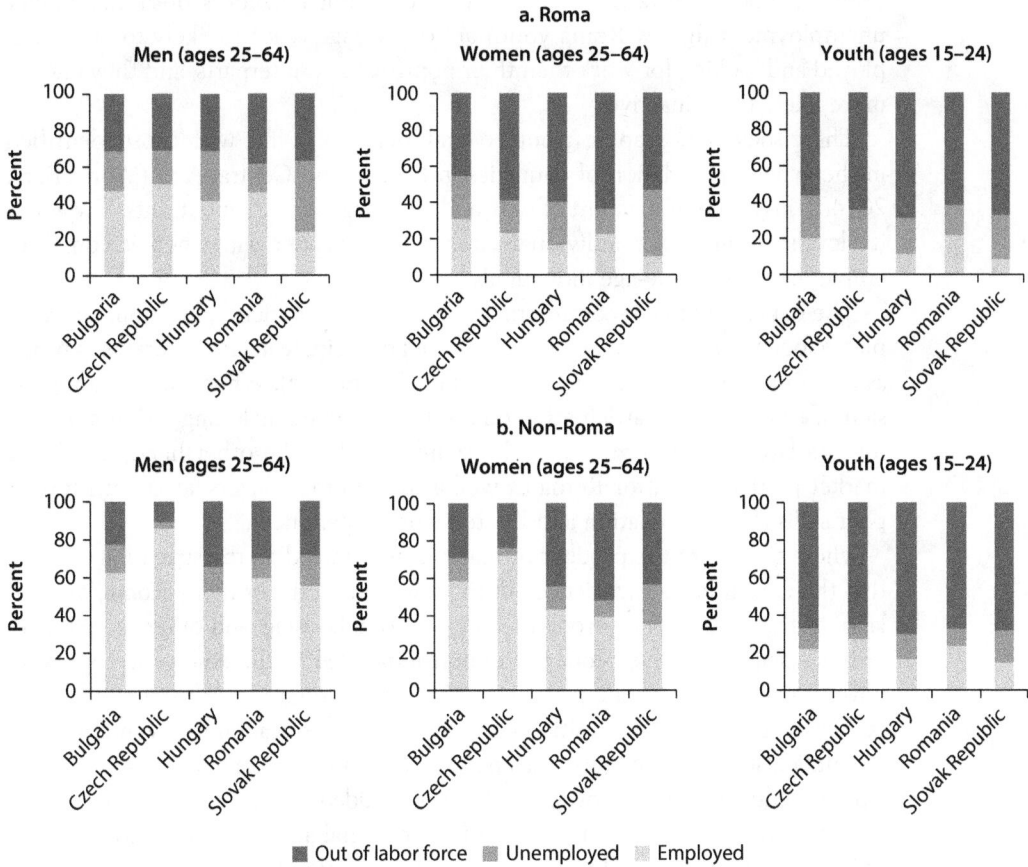

a. Roma

Men (ages 25–64) — Women (ages 25–64) — Youth (ages 15–24)

b. Non-Roma

Men (ages 25–64) — Women (ages 25–64) — Youth (ages 15–24)

■ Out of labor force ■ Unemployed ▨ Employed

Source: UNDP, World Bank, and EC 2011.
Note: Sample restricted to working-age individuals (ages 15–64). An unweighted average across the five countries of interest shows that only one in four working-age marginalized Roma is employed, which represents half of non-Roma neighbors' employment rates.

The group of men ages 25–64 is the most integrated into the labor market. This cohort displays relatively high employment rates. Employment and inactivity gaps are limited compared to non-Roma neighbors, but the unemployment gap is larger, ranging from 5 percentage points in Romania to 23 percentage points in the Slovak Republic.

Roma women (ages 25–64) appear to face a double disadvantage in securing employment. Their employment rates are low: only 10 (the Slovak Republic) to 31 (Bulgaria) percent of Roma women are engaged in some form of labor activity. The employment gap with non-Roma neighbors is considerable, with estimates above 25 percentage points in all countries but Romania. In the Czech Republic, non-Roma women are more than three times as likely to work than marginalized Roma women. In addition to low levels of participation and large employment gaps, inactivity is of great concern among Roma women—between 45 and 64 percent of working-age women are neither working nor looking for a job.

In sharp contrast to working-age men and women ages 25–64, Roma youth display employment rates similar to their non-Roma neighbors, but much higher unemployment figures. Roma youth are on average twice as likely to be unemployed and looking for work than their non-Roma counterparts, and they are not more likely to be inactive.

These sociodemographic groups overall perform in line with those identified in the general population of countries in Europe and Central Asia (World Bank 2014d): high unemployment of new and young labor market entrants, low activity levels among older individuals, and a large gender gap when it comes to employment of prime-age individuals.[1]

The data show that—controlling for education, experience, location, and simple sociodemographic characteristics—Roma participate in labor markets as much as non-Roma (see table 3B.2 at the end of the chapter). When running a regression of labor market participation on a set of variables, including a Roma indicator, the latter never turns out to be significant. On the other hand, low labor market participation (for Roma as well as non-Roma) is associated with few or poor skills (lower education and limited work experience).

These trends are the product of many factors, including the structural changes that these economies experienced during the transition. For many Roma, the collapse of the socialist state eroded security in jobs, housing, and other sectors, and, in the absence of viable economic opportunities, led to the emergence of severe poverty (Revenga, Ringold, and Tracy 2002). The Roma's labor market disadvantage at the outset of the transition period—with low education levels and overrepresentation in low-skilled jobs—deepened over time, especially in those countries where production moved toward higher value-added sectors and services.

Even when Roma have a job it is often informal and unstable. Less than half of Roma employment falls under a permanent contract. The average job tenure of Roma workers is short, indicating high turnover and job instability (see figure 3.5). Roma workers are more likely to do temporary and seasonal work, and irregular work (that takes place "from time to time") is two to six times more common for Roma than for their non-Roma neighbors. In fact, Roma workers are quite active in the construction and agriculture sectors, both of which are characterized by informality and seasonality. Between 15 and 32 percent of Roma workers are employed in the construction sector, and the shares are similar in agriculture.[2] In contrast, fewer than 15 percent of non-Roma work in either of these two sectors (author's calculations using UNDP, World Bank, and EC 2011). Job instability often translates into high turnover for Roma workers; in the Czech Republic, nearly 50 percent of Roma workers have held their jobs for less than a year (World Bank 2008, using the 2008 Excluded Roma Labor Force Survey). This is in sharp contrast with non-Roma workers, the majority of whom work under a permanent contract.

In addition to job instability, the Roma experience high levels of job informality (see figure 3.6). When it comes to signing a written contract for hiring and paying social contributions, the gap between Roma and non-Roma workers is large—about 25 percentage points. Roma workers are therefore in a more precarious situation; they are less likely to receive health benefits when they are sick, unemployment benefits when they are out of work, or pensions when they retire, all of which places them at a higher risk of falling into poverty when faced with a health or labor shock.

Around 72 percent of the Roma looking for a job in Romania indicate that they are prepared to work under harsh conditions and regardless of contract availability, meaning that they will most likely not contribute to a pension fund and will miss out on benefits in the future (Social Observatory, University of Bucharest 2010). Asenov et al. (2014) report precarious working conditions among Roma workers that include full-time work requirements for part-time positions; the inability to take leave; and health insurance deductions from their wages despite the employer's lack of contribution to health insurance.

Even when the Roma hold a job, they do not always receive a sufficient or regular salary (see figure 3.7). Low participation rates coupled with limited access to stable, gainful employment reinforces precarious incomes and heightens the risk of poverty and social exclusion. Roma workers earn from less than half (Bulgaria, Hungary, Romania) to less than one-fourth (the Czech Republic) of their non-Roma neighbors' income.

... Despite a Strong Preference for Work

The lower labor market outcomes observed among Roma populations across these five countries do not match the work preferences that Roma populations report. Many Roma men and women declare they are looking for work but are unable to find secure employment (see figure 3.3). The majority of Roma say they value lower paid but secure employment and prefer to work full-time rather than irregular jobs that would let them be free to manage their time. Between 59 percent (the Czech Republic) and 89 percent (Hungary) of Roma men in the region, and between 63 percent (the Czech

Figure 3.3 Self-Reported Inability to Find Lower Paid But Secure Work

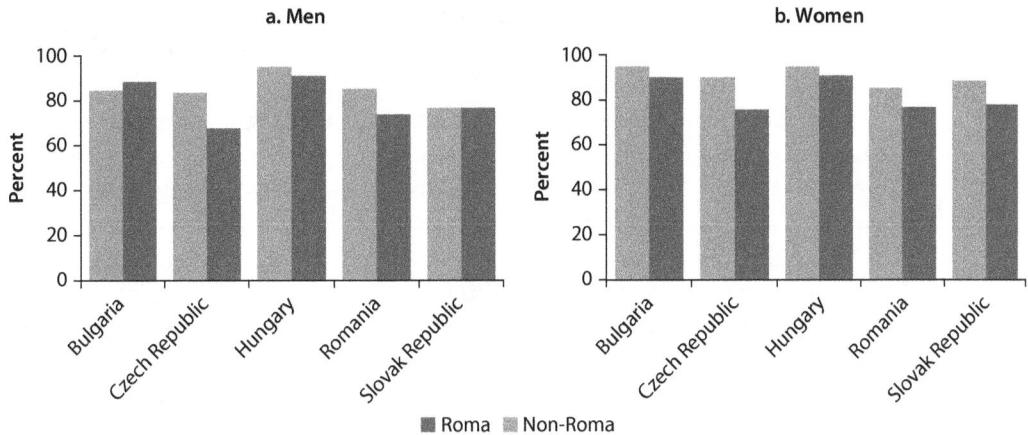

Source: UNDP, World Bank, and EC 2011.

Figure 3.4 Roma versus Non-Roma Preference for Earning a Living versus Depending on Social Assistance

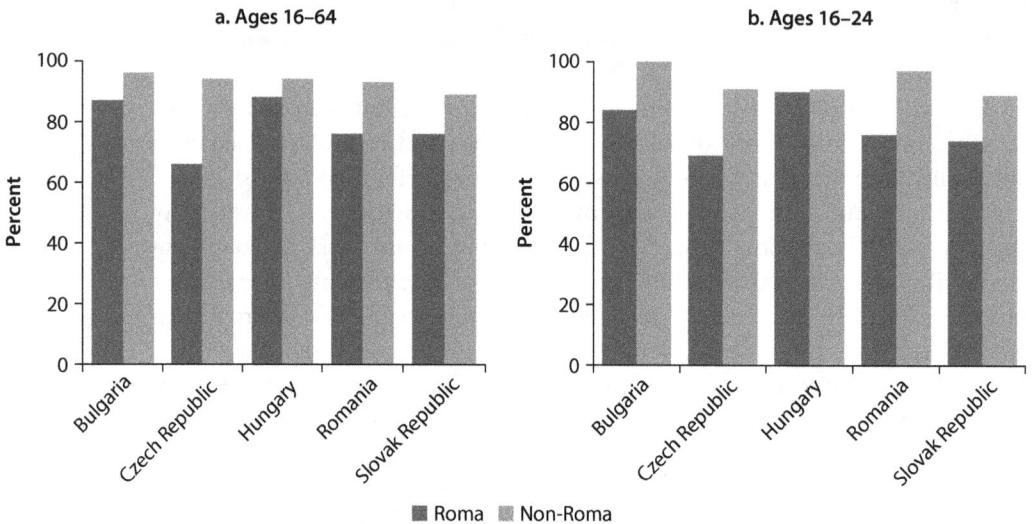

a. Ages 16–64

b. Ages 16–24

■ Roma ■ Non-Roma

Source: UNDP, World Bank, EC 2011.
Note: Share of adult persons who prefer to have higher standards of living but work hard to earn their living, rather than live on social assistance with problems making both ends meet but with no particular effort.

Republic) and 91 percent (Hungary) of women indicate they would rather have "secure employment but [be] low paid" than have "higher income but insecure and irregular" employment. These responses are similar to those provided by non-Roma neighbors. Comparable majorities of Roma and non-Roma neighbors similarly prefer to "have higher standards of living but working hard to earn your living" rather than "live on social assistance with problems making both ends meet but with no particular effort" (see figure 3.4).

Barriers to Employment: Participation and Employability

Roma face many barriers when accessing employment. Using a classification similar to that of Almeida et al. (2012), we identify six major barriers to Roma's integration in the labor market, which fall into two broad categories: constraints to employability and to participation.

Inadequate skills constitute the first and most important set of barriers that Roma face. Unemployment and low wages are often the result of a mismatch between the specific skills that employers require and those usually possessed by the work-able Roma population. As discussed in chapter 2, marginalized Roma arrive to the labor market with low levels of education, limited hard and soft skills, little or no work experience, and often, long stretches of unemployment.

Constraints to participation constitute the Roma's second set of barriers, and include discrimination, discouragement, residential segregation, lack of financial resources, and, in the case of women, lack of access to child care and safe transportation options. Roma are socially excluded and discriminated against in many dimensions, including access to social services, health care, and housing, all of

Figure 3.5 Roma versus Non-Roma Attainment of Permanent versus Other Employment

a. Roma   b. Non-Roma

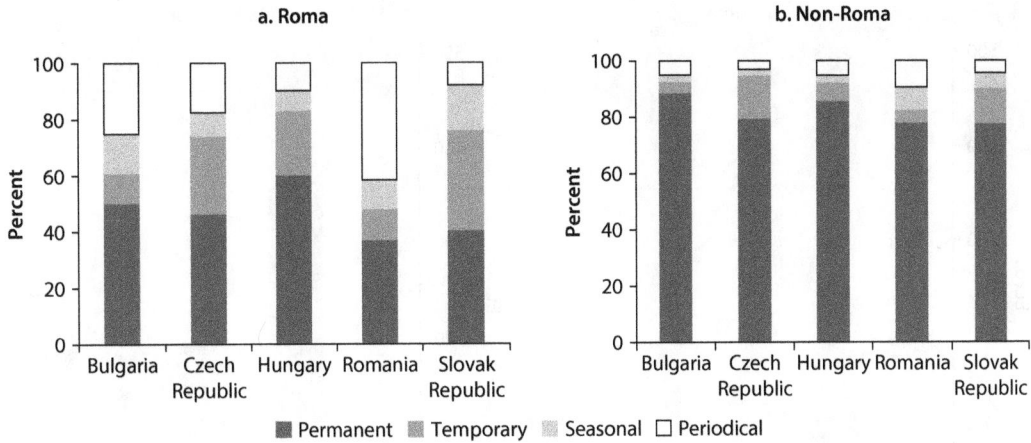

■ Permanent ▨ Temporary ▨ Seasonal ☐ Periodical

Source: UNDP, World Bank, EC 2011.
Note: Sample restricted to employed individuals (ages 15–64).

Figure 3.6 Roma versus Non-Roma Rates of Informal Employment

a. Signed a written contract   b. Pay social contributions

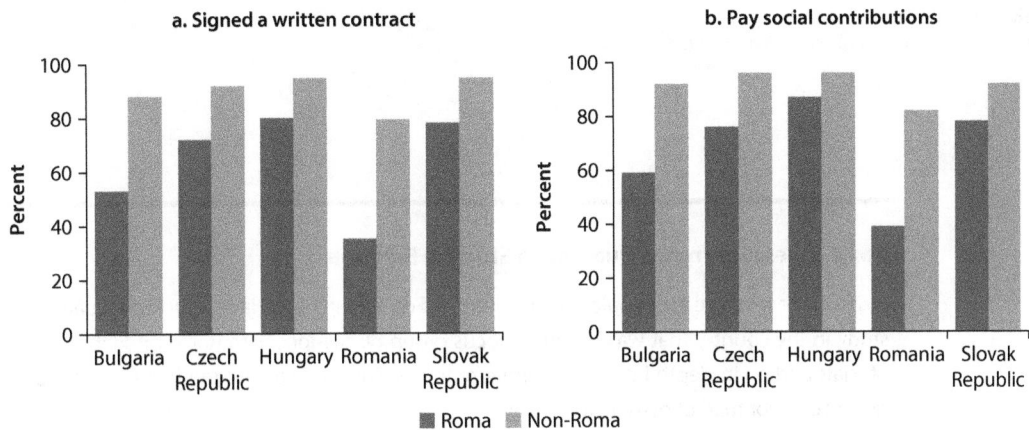

■ Roma ▨ Non-Roma

Source: UNDP, World Bank, EC 2011.
Note: Sample restricted to working-age individuals (ages 15–64). Social contributions include pension and health care, and can be paid for by the employer or employees.

which reinforce each other and create even more obstacles to access the labor market. Second, recent qualitative research findings suggest that Roma are often discouraged from looking for jobs when their job-searching peers are continuously unsuccessful (for more on disincentives, see box 3.1). Third, many marginalized communities are located in areas where unemployment is structurally high. Fourth, many Roma job seekers lack social capital and the network of information about job and training offers. Last but not least, capital constraints can also be a major impediment for those trying to start a business or become self-employed, as evidenced by a 2012 report on the Slovak Republic. For example, only 29 percent of Roma households in the Slovak Republic have a current

Figure 3.7 Roma versus Non-Roma Mean Monthly Income

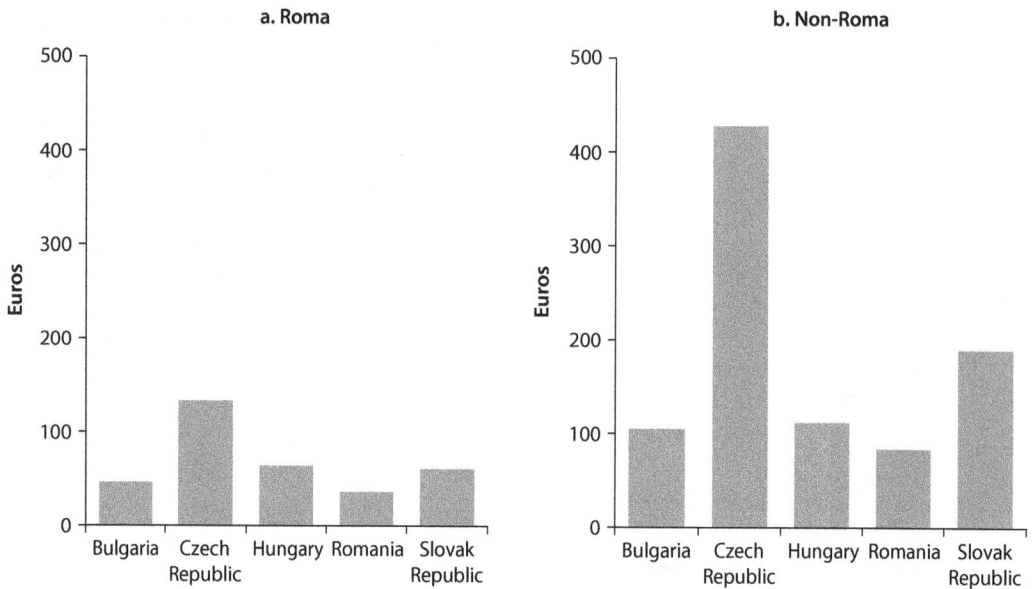

Source: UNDP, World Bank, EC 2011.
Note: Sample restricted to employed individuals (ages 15–64).

Box 3.1 Lessons from a Qualitative Study in Bulgaria

In 2014, the Institute for Population and Human Sciences in Bulgaria conducted a qualitative study in the country that was based on focus group discussions with Roma and labor office officials and on in-depth interviews with employers. The study aimed to identify causes and drivers of labor market barriers for Roma.

For low-skilled Roma with children, low salaries were cited as a disincentive to look for a job, both in the formal and informal sectors. Low educational attainment is generally considered a key reason for Roma's high levels of unemployment. For those looking for employment, specific challenges included having diplomas in areas that do not match in-demand skills; being unable to access training because of limited literacy and numeracy; and encountering negative attitudes and stereotyping from labor office staff and employers. It was generally those with the fewest or poorest skills that regard ethnic discrimination as their major barrier to employment. Although employers do not identify discrimination as a problem, many of them say that the Roma's negative attitudes toward work were central constraints. Language difficulties in particular appear to play a central role in explaining why employers often avoid hiring Roma individuals. Language-related barriers also prevent Roma from enrolling in training.

Source: Asenov et al. 2014.

---

account compared to more than three-quarters of the general population, and they have very limited access to credit as a result of indebtedness, low employment, lack of professional experience, and very low levels of education (World Bank 2012c).

Lack of Skills and Experience

Lack of skills and limited experience are the two most important barriers to employment (see box 3.2 for a definition of skills). Statistical models (see table 3B.1 at the end of the chapter) show that education is one of the most significant predictors of labor market participation among both Roma and non-Roma. Individuals who completed secondary school are much more likely to find employment than those who did not, after controlling for background characteristics. Similarly, one additional year of work experience decreases the probability of being out of the labor market by 11–19 percent.

The skills gap starts early in life for Roma, who have limited access to preschool (see figure 3.8). Few Roma children attend kindergarten, and thus have limited opportunities to engage in productive early childhood development. The preschool gap is particularly large in the Czech Republic, where Roma kindergarten enrollment rates are half those of their non-Roma neighbors. Low preschool attendance rates among Roma children, and poorer results for initial skills assessment often leads Roma children to be streamed early to the so-called 0th grades (preparatory grades within primary school) and to special education (see the discussion in chapter 2).

This low preschool enrollment undermines Roma children's school readiness, their chances of achieving higher educational levels, and obtaining the necessary skills for employment later in life. Evidence in and outside the European Union (EU) (including from the RRS data) demonstrates that early intellectual stimulation at home and in preschools develops the foundations of cognitive and socio-emotional skills, which improves adults' chances of socioeconomic success, especially for vulnerable groups and marginalized Roma communities.

Box 3.2 Skills Developed over the Life Cycle

Skills can be classified into three broad categories: (a) cognitive skills, involving the use of logic, intuition, and creative thinking, and including verbal ability, problem solving, memory, and mental speed; (b) socio-emotional or soft skills, which can be more associated with personality traits and include grit, self-regulation, perseverance, decision making, and interpersonal skills; and (c) job-specific or technical skills that involve manual dexterity and the use of methods, materials, tools, and instruments—such as skills related to a specific occupation like an engineer, economist, or IT specialist. These types of skills are available to individuals throughout all of life's developmental and educational stages. While socio-emotional and cognitive skills start developing from ages 0 to 3, and up to secondary education especially, job-specific skills take more relevance from the teenage years onwards.

Figure 3.8 Roma versus Non-Roma Children's Access to Preschool Education (Ages 0–6) and Impact on School Readiness and Later Life Success (Ages 6+)

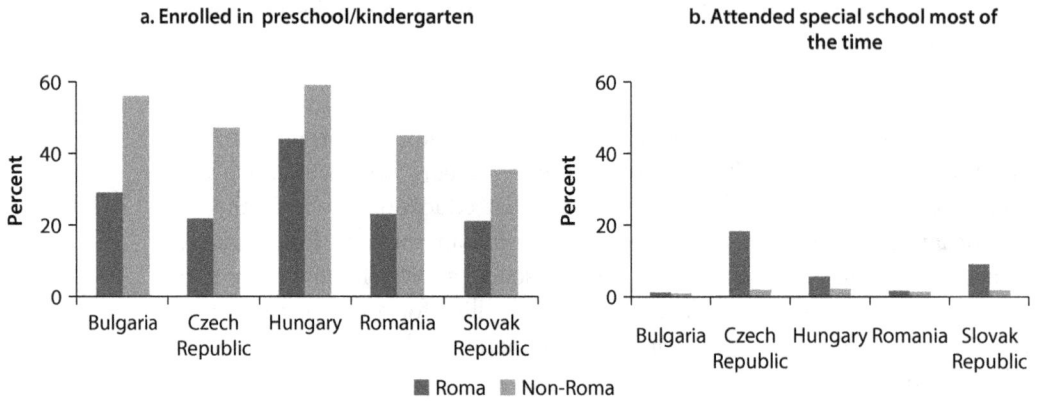

a. Enrolled in preschool/kindergarten

b. Attended special school most of the time

Roma   Non-Roma

Source: UNDP, World Bank, EC 2011.

As a result of these many factors, Roma have low education attainment, literacy, and numeracy skills. Illiteracy levels among the Roma population are extremely high. In Romania, about 25 percent of Roma cannot read or write (Research Institute for Quality of Life 2010). In the Czech Republic, as many as 44 percent of working-age Roma in excluded communities can be considered functionally illiterate. Another 44 percent have only some basic literacy and numeracy skills. Only 12 percent can be considered functionally literate—that is, able to answer most of the relatively simple questions that require knowledge on the primary school level (World Bank 2008).

Finally, the acquisition of vocational skills also depends on employment and on-the-job training, to which Roma have limited access (see figure 3.9). In CEE, lifelong learning is still rare, and Roma's participation in these kinds of programs is even rarer. In Romania, almost half of the working-age Roma population is ineligible for professional qualification courses that would give them an official certification, because they have not completed compulsory education. Indicators of professional qualifications point in the same direction as literacy and numeracy skills—computer literacy and participation in vocational training are twice as low as among non-Roma neighbors. However, vocational training greatly increases Roma employment opportunities; in the Czech Republic, among the Roma who received vocational training, 50 percent are employed, more than double the rate of those who received primary education and more than three times the rate of those who received special education or less (World Bank 2008). Similarly, employers interviewed in the Czech Republic (World Bank 2008) and in Bulgaria (Asenov et al. 2014) confirm that lack of skills is a key explanation for why Roma job seekers are not hired, including low literacy, numerical skills and poor soft skills.

As a result, unemployment is pervasive among Roma, and the majority of Roma workers hold unskilled jobs (see figure 3.10). More than two-thirds of Roma

Figure 3.9 Roma versus Non-Roma Access to Vocational Training

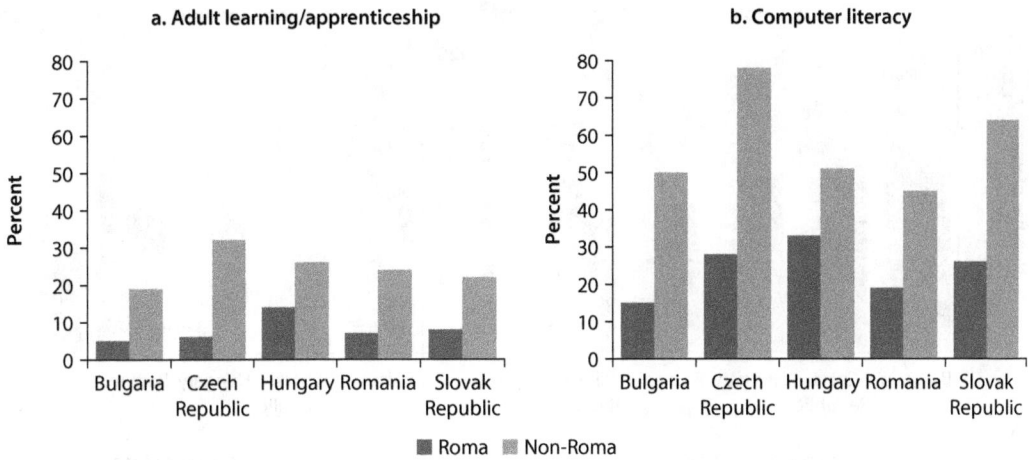

a. Adult learning/apprenticeship

b. Computer literacy

■ Roma ■ Non-Roma

Source: UNDP, World Bank, EC 2011.
Note: Sample restricted to working-age individuals (ages 15–64).

Figure 3.10 Roma versus Non-Roma Job Skill Level and Employment Sector

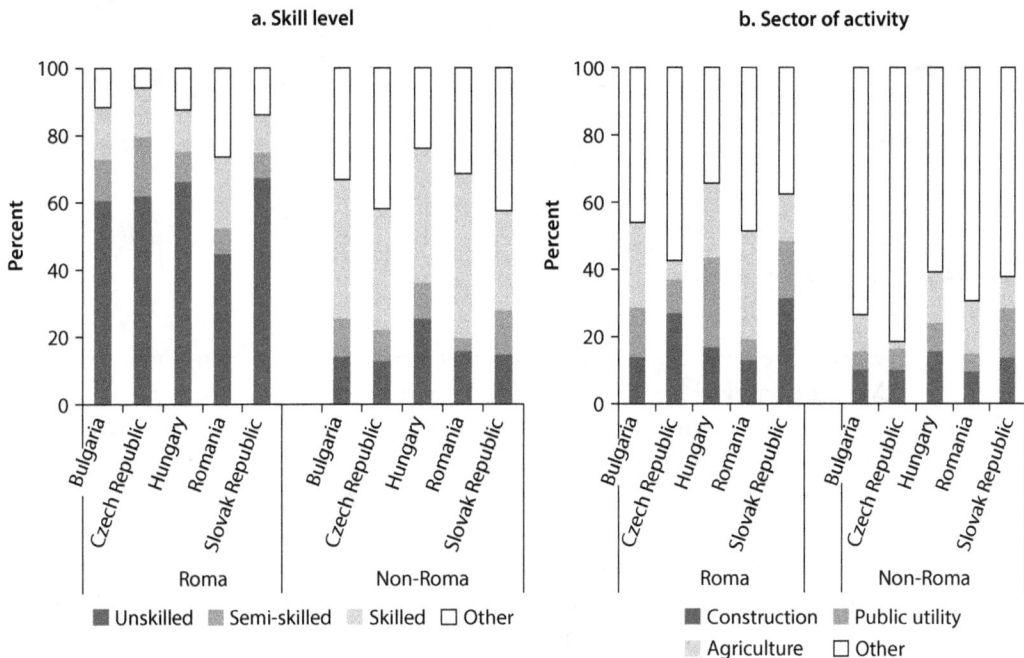

a. Skill level

b. Sector of activity

■ Unskilled ■ Semi-skilled ▨ Skilled □ Other

■ Construction ▨ Public utility
▨ Agriculture □ Other

Source: UNDP, World Bank, EC 2011.
Note: Sample restricted to working-age individuals (ages 15–64).

Figure 3.11 Roma versus Non-Roma Work Experience and Unemployment as Constraint to Labor Market Entry

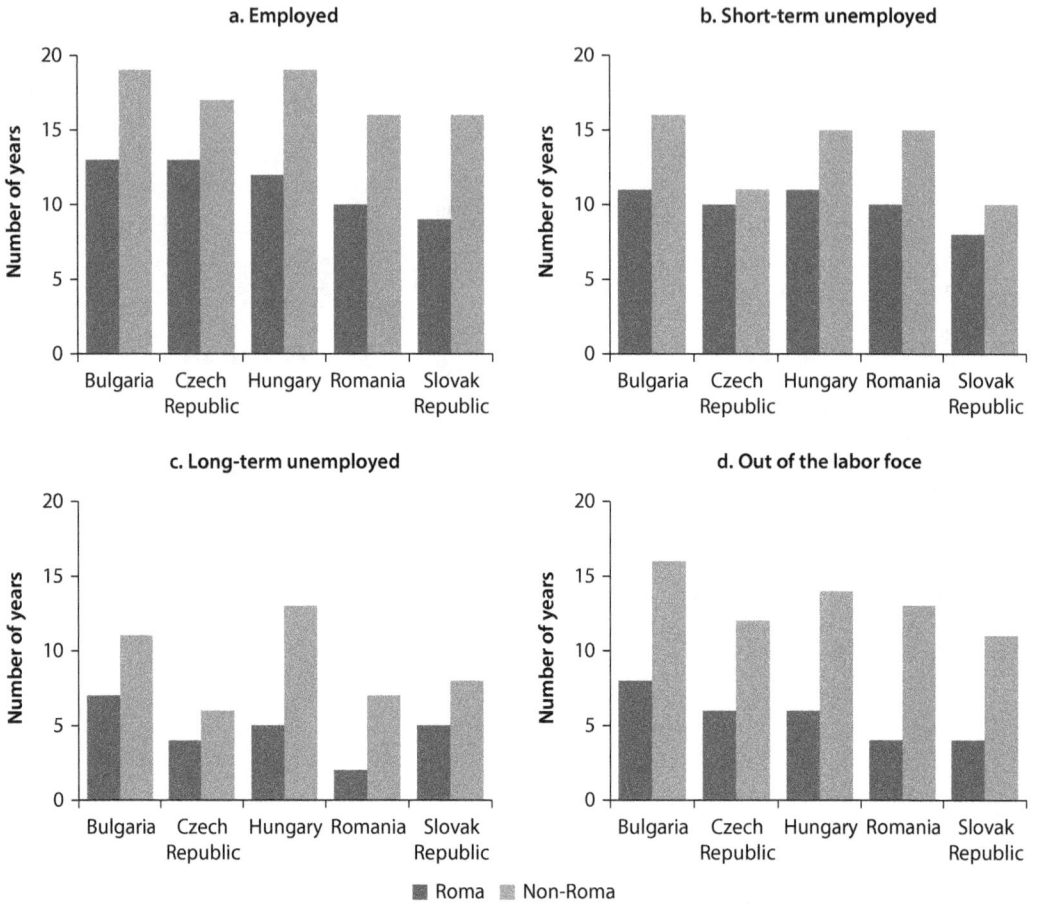

a. Employed

b. Short-term unemployed

c. Long-term unemployed

d. Out of the labor foce

■ Roma ▨ Non-Roma

Source: UNDP, World Bank, EC 2011.
Note: Sample restricted to working-age Individuals (ages 15–64).

workers are unskilled, compared to fewer than one-third of non-Roma neighbors. Most are engaged in construction (6–34 percent of all employed Roma), agriculture (13–32 percent), and public utilities (6–27 percent), which contrasts sharply with the situation of non-Roma workers, more than two-thirds of whom are not engaged in these three sectors where low-skilled positions are concentrated.

As for Roma job seekers, their access to the labor market is further hampered by their usually limited work experience, especially among the long-term unemployed (see figure 3.11). Roma workers have between 9 and 13 years of experience, compared to between 15 and 19 years among non-Roma in all five countries. This situation is much worse for the long-term unemployed, who report as little as two years of experience on average in Romania. This is compounded by the fact that the average age of this group is around 32, and these job seekers have been out of work for more than 10 years of their working life. It is precisely this latter group that has the worst chances of becoming employed.

Figure 3.12 Roma Job Seekers and Employees Report Systematic Ethnicity-Based Discrimination

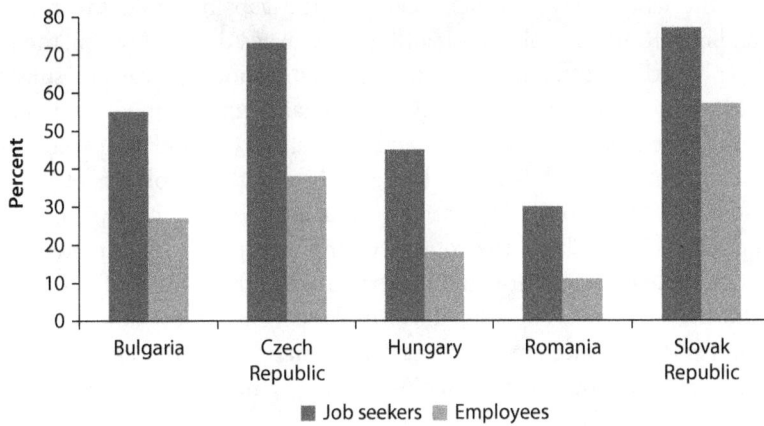

Source: UNDP, World Bank, EC 2011.
Note: Sample restricted to working-age Roma (ages 15–64). Discrimination is self-reported by Roma.

Preventing joblessness among the Roma would therefore primarily entail upgrading their skills. However, closing the human capital gap between Roma and non-Roma may not be sufficient to provide equal footing in the labor market, as differentials in returns to human capital, which signal unequal treatment, appear to be the norm. Kahanec (2014) further finds that a large part of the employment gap cannot be explained by differences in Roma and non-Roma characteristics (such as varying educational attainment) and is rather due to differences in returns to characteristics (such as paying different amounts for a university degree), or unobserved factors, which may include gaps in social capital as well as discrimination. In this regard, and according to recent qualitative research in Bulgaria, language-related barriers are of particular relevance for Roma individuals to both being able to find jobs and join ALMPs for general skills upgrading (Asenov et al. 2014).

Discrimination
A majority of Roma report labor market discrimination, both when they look for work and in the workplace (see figure 3.12). In the Czech Republic and the Slovak Republic, three in four Roma report that they experienced ethnicity-based discrimination when looking for work from 2006 to 2011. The numbers were slightly lower in Bulgaria, Hungary, and Romania—55, 45, and 30 percent, respectively. Discrimination in the workplace is lower across all five countries, with much higher figures in the Czech Republic and the Slovak Republic (38 and 57 percent, respectively). The most recent Social Inclusion Barometer (Social Observatory, University of Bucharest 2010) suggests that Roma in Romania are 10 times more likely to be laid off than workers in the general population, and 41 percent of Roma in search of a job said they were not hired because of their ethnicity (Social Observatory, University of Bucharest 2010).

Controlling for background characteristics, the large employment gap between Roma and non-Roma can be explained by a number of factors, including discrimination in the labor market. When analyzing the gap in employment between Roma and non-Roma neighbors using Blinder–Oaxaca decomposition, the largest part is explained by different endowments in education. However, a substantial part of the gap between the two groups remains unexplained: Romania and Bulgaria have relatively low unexplained differences (14 and 21 percent of the total gap, respectively), while more than one-third of the employment gap in the Czech Republic, the Slovak Republic, and Hungary remains unexplained. While it is impossible to attribute the totality of the unexplained component to discrimination, at least part of it could be attributed to these kinds of practices.[3]

Qualitative evidence suggests that employers' attitudes and behavior can compound and aggravate employment discrimination against Roma. The ERRC (2005) reports that some job vacancies are simply not open to Roma, as many companies practice a total exclusion policy (see box 3.3). In Romania, Messing et al. (2013) found a factory that displayed a sign on its gates stating, "We do not hire ethnic Roma." Furthermore, employers often resort to requesting educational qualifications for work that has no relation to such academic competencies, or demanding a level of literacy or numeracy that is not directly related to the job, in order to exclude Roma from basic employment.

Among 402 Roma surveyed by ERRC in Romania, Bulgaria, the Slovak Republic, the Czech Republic, and Hungary, 64 percent of those of working age indicated they had experienced discrimination, and an alarming 49 percent indicated that employers openly said they treated them differently because they were Roma; an additional 5 percent heard the same from labor offices (ERRC 2005). In the workplace, discrimination by employers proves to be quite

---

Box 3.3 "If You Are a Roma, You Can't Find Work Anywhere!"

In Romania, workplace Roma-related discrimination is very present, and takes several forms: (a) discrimination by employers and/or co-workers; (b) discrimination in Roma's working conditions; (c) discrimination regarding Roma's wages, compared to non-Roma; and (d) discrimination during firing procedures. The interviews and focus group discussions mainly reported cases of discrimination by employers against unemployed Roma who try to find a job. In the workplace, discrimination is primarily evident in the form of unpaid wages. Other types of discrimination seem to occur less often. As one focus group respondent put it, "There is discrimination because you are Roma. ... Yes, yes. If you are Roma, you cannot find work anywhere. ... It happens. They do not employ you if you are Roma. ... He [the employer] says he does not need you (the position was filled). Or he says: we'll call you. And they don't call."

While NGOs come across cases of discrimination against Roma by employers, especially in sectors like food industry and apparel, they report it is often difficult to find evidence of discriminatory hiring procedures.

Source: World Bank 2014b.

---

widespread and least concealed in the Romanian and Bulgarian cases (Messing et al. 2013). In Romania, labor market stakeholders—such as the PES staff—regarded discrimination as normal and explained its existence as the logical behavior of employers, who take stereotypes about Roma literally and believe they tend to steal, have a poor work ethic, cause problems for the employer, and have health problems (World Bank 2014b).

Discouragement

According to the *World Development Report 2013* (World Bank 2013), jobs empower, build agency, and are associated with greater trust and willingness to participate in society. Jobs influence how people view themselves, how they interact with others, and how they perceive their stake in society. Jobs also can have social consequences, shaping how societies handle collective decision-making, manage tensions, and resolve conflicts between different groups, such as Roma and non-Roma. Evidence from Bosnia and Herzegovina and Macedonia, former Yugoslav Republic of, shows that the number of people willing to work together or do business with someone of a different ethnicity is greater than the number in favor of interethnic cooperation in schools or neighborhoods. The prospect of doing business and working together has the potential to attenuate ethnic discrimination against Roma.

Roma, however, are often discouraged by the difficulty of the job search. As discussed previously, Roma workers are more likely to hold precarious, seasonal, and informal jobs due to their combination of low educational attainment, limited experience, and distance from work opportunities. Marginalized Roma job seekers, on the other hand, have little prospects of finding a job at all, given the general technical and nontechnical skills mismatch: few jobs are available for low-skilled and poorly educated workers (see World Bank 2008). Roma job seekers often have poor job prospects even when they are helped by local PES centers. Asenov et al. (2014) report that public employment officials sometimes send low or uneducated Roma job seekers home, as they do not think they can help them. The lack of perspective and motivation during the job search, and even after employment, further exacerbates the challenges and negative experiences that Roma adults face in education, likely leading to the intergenerational transmission of discouragement, with children of discouraged Roma adults scaling down their aspirations for school and work.

Roma are often oriented to large-scale public employment measures that promote and maintain a work habit, but have little effect on the employability of the unemployed workforce, thus fostering a vicious cycle of dependency on availability of public works. Messing et al. (2013) highlight the fact that Roma are often offered swiping jobs in workfare programs. The From Social Benefits to Employment program in Bulgaria, which includes large-scale public and community works, offers an example: About two-thirds of activities carried out under this program over the past few years were emergency activities, such as maintaining roads during the winter, without a clear investment in further skills. Roma job seekers also report being discouraged by the precarious and often humiliating

Box 3.4 Low Wages Combined with Travel Costs Discourage Roma

Low wages present a disincentive for working in the formal sector, especially for women who face a long commute to the workplace. "It's very difficult with jobs," said one NGO representative. "I met two situations: people who want to work but cannot find any and people who find work but outside their community. Let me take an example, in Pușcași commune [Romania] we found women seeking for work. The nearest jobs were available in a garment factory from Vaslui city and so they needed to commute. The money that they would get from that job was about 5 million, while the transportation related costs were almost 2 million, per month. With the remaining 3 million they would have covered the lunch for them and to provide for the family. And some have a small child at home who would have remained unsupervised. They have also a small plot … a household. So, it's a simple cost-benefit analysis to stay at home instead of commuting for a low-paid job: better stay and take care of the baby than earning so little money with so much time and effort."

Source: World Bank 2014b.

nature of the jobs they are offered, which can impact their dignity and self-respect. For example, Asenov et al. (2014) narrate the story of one unemployed Roma female, who used to be self-employed, and was invited to compete with other candidates for a job as a cleaner to assess her "skills with the broom."

With the combination of low-paying jobs, transport costs, and in some countries, the prospects of losing social benefits when employed, it is difficult to make work pay for many marginalized Roma (see box 3.4).

Residential Segregation
A large share of marginalized communities are located in areas where unemployment is structurally high, limiting the supply side of the labor market. In most countries, the majority of working-age Roma (ages 15–64) reside in small, secluded villages with insufficient public transportation and scarce job opportunities. In all but the Czech Republic, the majority of working-age Roma live in segregated rural settlements, and while more than three quarters of them live within 1 kilometer of a bus station, half live more than 10 kilometers from an urban location (see figure 3.13). Job opportunities may thus be located far from marginalized settlements, and the combination of distance, travel time, lack of access to child care services, and costs may deter Roma from participating in the labor market, as highlighted in box 3.4. Qualitative research by the World Bank (2014a) found that the lack of safe, accessible, and affordable transport options, especially after dark, was found to be particularly discouraging for Roma women in pursuing employment opportunities. In Hungary, for example, a large share of Roma live in the disadvantaged eastern, northeastern, and southern Transdanubian regions, where unemployment is high and connectivity is low. In the Czech Republic, the World Bank (2008) finds that job opportunities for the low skilled

Figure 3.13 Roma Connectivity Measured by Proximity to Bus Station or City Center

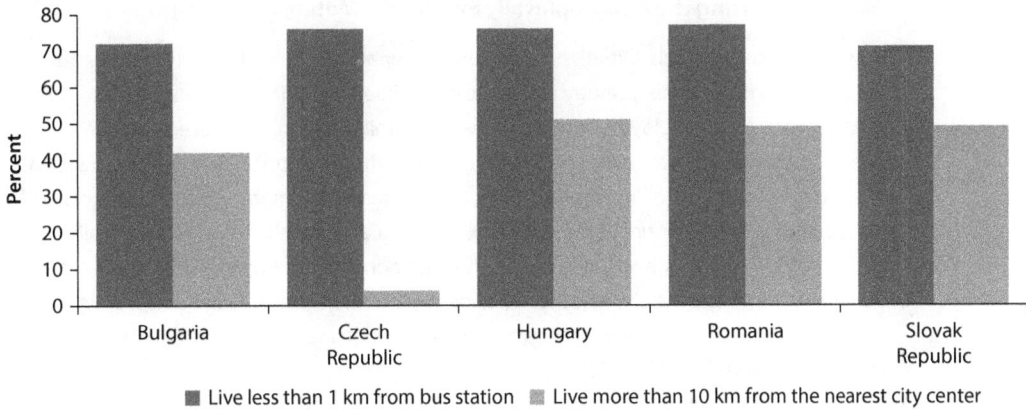

Live less than 1 km from bus station   Live more than 10 km from the nearest city center

Source: UNDP, World Bank, EC 2011.
Note: Sample restricted to working-age Roma (ages 15–64).

Figure 3.14 Rural Roma's Limited Access to Public Employment Service Centers

a. Nonworking Roma more than 10 km from employment centers

b. Unemployed adults not registered in employment centers

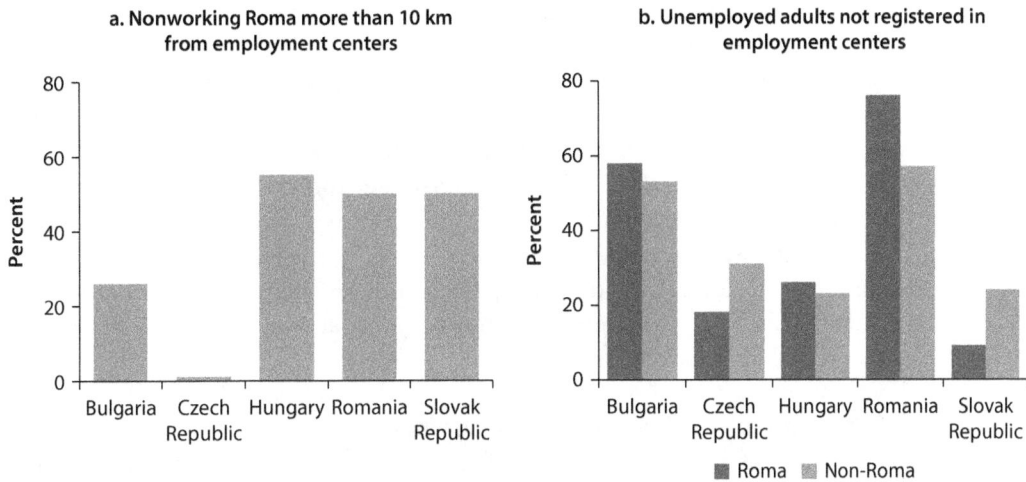

Roma   Non-Roma

Source: UNDP, World Bank, EC 2011.
Note: Panel a. is restricted to unemployed and out-of-labor force rural Roma (ages 15–64 year); panel b. is restricted to unemployed working-age individuals (ages 15–64).

are particularly constrained in traditional high unemployment regions where many socially excluded Roma reside.

PESs do not efficiently serve the marginalized rural Roma who live far from PES offices. In all countries, the majority of rural residents live more than 10 kilometers away from the closest PES centers. This is particularly problematic in the Slovak Republic, Hungary, and Romania. In these countries, the share of working-age Roma living in rural locations is 73, 65, and 61 percent, respectively (UNDP, World Bank, and EC 2011). In comparison, about half of the working-age Roma who live in urban areas are within 3 kilometers of a PES center. As a

Box 3.5 Servicing the Geographically Excluded—Mobile Offices, Hungary

Within the scope of this initiative, labor offices temporarily relocate their services to rural areas. An example of this strategy is the use of "mobile offices" in southwest Hungary, where the head of a local employment office in the Siklós microregion recognized that the region's lack of public transportation posed a barrier to labor market access. The manager proactively created a new position of "mobile officer" within the team. The mobile officer took a car and a laptop with a direct connection to the PES IT system and traveled around the small region, dedicating office hours every week in each settlement covered by the office's service area. Sending the office to the client, rather than having the clients travel to the office, proved to be very efficient; registration, as well as participation in various services and programs, has significantly increased within this microregion.

Source: Messing et al. 2013; World Bank 2014b.

consequence, many unemployed Roma (80 percent in rural Bulgaria and Romania) are not registered with PES (see figure 3.14). Distance to the closest PES becomes even more of a barrier for rural Roma job seekers if they are offered training, as both travel time and expenses pose serious obstacles to their participation. The timing of the trainings, in addition to distance and costs, has been identified as an additional challenge for female Roma job seekers in the event it is not compatible with their child-care and household duties (World Bank 2014c). Messing et al. (2013) report that the Romanian and Bulgarian labor offices do not cover travel expenses, while clients in Hungary and the Slovak Republic experience delays in travel cost reimbursements, which limits access to employment services and training opportunities. Hungary's "mobile offices" organized regularly in rural areas offer an example of an attempt to overcome these access problems (see box 3.5).

Social Capital and Information Constraints

Roma are further affected by significant information constraints regarding the labor market. Even where many positions exist and are vacant, low-income workers and low-skilled young people find it difficult to access them. Many Roma are not registered with PES centers (Asenov et al. 2014, in Bulgaria; World Bank 2008, in the Czech Republic). In fact, jobs are often obtained through informal contracts, door-to-door inquiries, and word-of-mouth. The marginalized Roma are at a particular disadvantage in finding work because of their lack of social capital and employment networks beyond the Roma community. The physical distance from the labor market and insufficient information about services available—trainings, counseling, job searches, and so on—may also restrict the available options. A recent qualitative study conducted in Bulgaria (World Bank 2014a) found that participating employers (small and medium-sized enterprises) usually recruit their employees through personal networks, to which Roma have limited access. This was also the general perception among the Roma,

---

Box 3.6 Bridging the Information Gap—US Steel, Slovak Republic

While discrimination is a barrier to employment, there are also employers interested in hiring Roma men and women, not only for corporate social responsibility reasons, but simply because they need productive workers to positively contribute to their firms. Information about employment—and employee—opportunities can be hard to come by, however. The government can play a key role in helping employers identify prospective Roma employees who are eager and able to work by reaching out to nonstate actors and government entities familiar with the local Roma community. A successful example comes from the US Steel factory in Košice, the Slovak Republic. It enlisted the help of a local church in Košice that had a strong presence in a large Roma neighborhood to identify prospective employees. In this case, church officials served as a bridge between the private company and skilled Roma who were eager to learn new skills on the job, or had informal skills from previous work experience that were relevant for the US Steel work. Similarly, nonstate actors, government social workers, and community mediators can help connect employers and prospective Roma employees.

Source: Salner 2013.

---

who largely reported that access to jobs was only possible with membership to certain social and/or political networks (Asenov et al. 2014).

Even when Roma have the skills and training to be good employees, they have trouble signaling that to employers. Signaling can be especially challenging for Roma job seekers, as research has shown that those who have already held a job are less likely to be unemployed than those who have never worked. Young, long-term unemployed, and discouraged inactive Roma—all of whom are more likely to have low skills and limited work experience—lack the ability to signal their skills to prospective employers, either because they lack the necessary knowledge and experience and/or because their skills cannot be objectively assessed (see box 3.6).

Working Capital Constraints

A large share of Roma say they are interested in becoming self-employed but face too many financial barriers (World Bank 2012d). Across the five countries of study, 24–40 percent of all working-age Roma men and between 14 and 35 percent of working-age Roma women report being interested or somewhat interested in becoming self-employed. Roma who report this interest are employed, unemployed, and also not participating in the labor force.

Indicators of the overall business environment and responses by surveyed entrepreneurs point to barriers—especially the lack of access to finance—to expanding self-employment. These barriers are both country-specific and specific to Roma. The World Bank's Doing Business survey shows that of all the five countries, starting a business is most difficult in the Slovak Republic and the Czech Republic (World Bank 2011). These findings may help explain why Roma in these two countries have lower self-employment rates than in the others. However, lack of start-up finance is highlighted as a particular challenge by entrepreneurs in all of the countries, along with a general lack of customers and licensing difficulties.

In addition, among marginalized Roma households, savings are virtually nonexistent and indebtedness is high (World Bank 2012d). In Bulgaria, Hungary, and Romania, fewer than 4 percent of Roma households have savings, while in the Czech Republic and the Slovak Republic, these numbers go up to 13 and 9 percent, respectively. Debt is of particular concern in Hungary and the Czech Republic, where as much as 45 and 33 percent of marginalized Roma have utility bills in arrears. As a consequence, many Roma households turn to formal and informal financial providers: 20–40 percent of Roma households are currently borrowing or borrowed in the past from financial providers. In comparison, less than 20 percent of the general population has a formal financial loan. In addition, a substantial share of these loans are contracted with informal providers, who are likely to charge very high interest rates—in the Czech Republic and Bulgaria, as much as half of the loans are taken up with informal lenders.

Microcredit is unlikely to substantially raise employment rates among the Roma unless it is accompanied by a comprehensive approach to financial inclusion. Not many microfinance lenders target start-up businesses in general, and even fewer are reaching burgeoning Roma entrepreneurs. The microlending challenges facing the recent Hungarian Kiútprogram microcredit pilot program offer an important example in this regard (see box 3.7). Interesting to note is how Kiútprogram has employed a comprehensive approach that includes considerable support with tax and business registration, as well as business training.

Box 3.7 Kiútprogram ("Way Out Program"), Hungary

The Kiútprogram is a social microcredit initiative aimed at enabling the unemployed in deep poverty—primarily, but not exclusively Roma—to become self-employed. To achieve this, the Kiútprogram provided participants with financial services (importantly, unsecured microloans) and related social services, from counseling to physically escorting applicants to local municipalities to register their businesses.

Fieldworkers provided a multitude of services, including help with developing the business plan, registering the business, and accounting. The fieldworkers' workload was larger than originally anticipated; they had to personally meet the clients at least once a week and provide continuous technical assistance to the business operation.

Results of the Kiútprogram indicate that facilitating the creation of sustainable enterprises required intensive intervention by well-trained fieldworkers familiar with social work, lending, and business. The program focused on participants' employment (including self-employment) outcomes rather than profitability for the lender. It showed the potential to significantly increase participants' inclusion and economic empowerment by demonstrating their commitment to break out of poverty and operate a business as a profitable investment in the formal economy.

Source: World Bank 2013.

Focusing on Hard-to-Place Job Seekers: Challenges Facing the Active Labor Market Programs and the Public Employment Services Centers

The main challenge faced by PESs in the five countries will be to systematically implement measures to include hard-to-reach job seekers (including Roma), and to refine some marginal elements to ensure that Roma job seekers' specific needs are addressed (see box 3.8). Incompletely implementing effective activation policy can pose substantial risks to the prospects of the disadvantaged and long-term unemployed, in particular those who suffer from severe forms of social exclusion, skill deficiencies, and discrimination.

Improving Active Labor Market Programs and Social Protection Schemes to "Make Work Pay"

The five Central and Eastern European countries significantly differ in terms of what fraction of their GDP is spent on active labor market programs. Most, however,

---

Box 3.8 Public Employment Services Centers: Their Main Constraints in Reaching Out to Marginalized Roma

In May 2014, the World Bank organized a workshop titled "Roma Inclusion Mobile Innovation Lab" (RIMIL). Hosted by the Fundación Secretariado Gitano in Madrid, Spain, the event convened senior public officials who deal with Roma activation across seven CEE countries (Bulgaria; the Czech Republic; Hungary; Macedonia, former Yugoslav Republic of; Romania; Serbia; and the Slovak Republic).[a]

Participants identified several main factors that constrain Roma populations in accessing productive employment in their respective countries. These included the Roma's social and economic background; their lack of education and skills; the geographical areas in which they live; discrimination; lack of information job opportunities; and demotivation.

They also discussed the main challenges that institutions (mainly PES) face in incorporating Roma populations in ALMPs. Among the most crucial highlighted were

- Local providers' lack of capacity, especially in problematic areas, to reach the most disadvantaged (the Czech Republic, Hungary, Serbia, the Slovak Republic);
- Language constraints and limited skills and education (Bulgaria, Romania);
- Lack of motivation to register (Macedonia, former Yugoslav Republic of; Serbia) and lack of personal documentation needed to register (Serbia); lack of case-management systems and low intersectoral integration (the Czech Republic, Serbia);
- Weak usage of ethnic data in targeting and in monitoring (Hungary, the Slovak Republic);
- Institution's lack of cultural sensitivity toward Roma, and employer discrimination (Hungary; Macedonia, former Yugoslav Republic of); and
- A set of issues believed to be "specific" to Roma job seekers, for example, lack of motivation (Bulgaria, the Slovak Republic); tendency to be engaged in informal work to retain social benefits (Romania); or a tendency to be discouraged by low salaries.

a. For more information, see http://www.worldbank.org/en/results/2014/06/13/promoting-access-to-productive
-employment-for-marginalized-roma. RIMIL 2014.

---

tend to focus on direct job creation and employment incentives (see table 3B.4 at the end of the chapter). Direct job creation encompasses public works programs, which represent one of the major programs that reach marginalized unemployed Roma. Employment incentives include grants and subsidies paid by the government to prospective employers to promote hiring hard-to-place job seekers (subsidies for social security and health insurance, for instance). Training, on the other hand, scores relatively low on the preference list of the five countries studied here.

Public workfare programs are the most frequent ALMPs to reach Roma job seekers (Messing et al. 2013). In the Slovak Republic, activation works are the key program for involving Roma (World Bank 2012c), although exact data or even estimations on the actual ethnic distribution of participants are not available. In Hungary, Csoba and Nagy (2012) estimate that 18 percent of ALMPs recipients are Roma, 84 percent of which are involved in public works. As a comparison, 45 percent of non-Roma beneficiaries are receiving training, and only 48 percent are engaged in workfare programs. While public employment programs in the Slovak Republic provide positive incentives (participants' welfare income is topped up), the Hungarian case displays a negative stimulus (those who do not participate lose their entitlement to welfare allowances).

On the other hand, few Roma job seekers are engaged in employment incentives schemes or training programs. Csoba and Nagy (2012) show that only 4 percent of Roma ALMP recipients made use of this measure, while the proportion among non-Roma was almost double in Hungary. Similarly, Roma appear to be largely uninvolved in training programs. Evidence from Hungary shows that lack of information, discrimination, and preference for the most employable, and so on all result in Roma's low participation in training programs (Csoba and Nagy 2012). Evidence from the Bulgarian Longitudinal Inclusive Society Survey (BLISS) indicates that Roma are significantly less likely to participate in training programs (1.4 percent versus 6.9 percent, for non-Roma), with lack of awareness of suitable training being the main reason for not participating (43.6 percent) (World Bank, forthcoming).

When programs are targeted, they focus on economically and socially disadvantaged groups. Marginalized Roma job seekers are well represented in these, as they usually come from economically depressed areas and face special employment barriers, low education, limited vocational skills, and often long-term unemployment. In Hungary, Romania, and Bulgaria, the ALMPs' target populations include various categories of vulnerable groups such as youth, long-term inactive women, and others. As a large proportion of Roma fall into these groups, such programs reach out to a relatively larger share of Roma, even if they are not directly targeted.

Employment regulations can also play an important role for Roma labor market inclusion. For example, a recent reform of atypical contracts in the Slovak Republic has likely impacted the ability of disadvantaged Roma workers to access formal employment (see box 3.9).

Furthermore, a common challenge across countries in building an effective social protection policy framework is to adequately balance protecting the most

---

Box 3.9 Reforming Atypical Contracts in the Slovak Republic

Atypical labor contracts usually regulate employment relationships that do not conform to the characteristics of dependent employment. The Slovak Republic has a variety of atypical contracts, which are fixed-term (up to one year) and are used mainly for small jobs. More than three-quarters of people whose employment is regulated by these contracts earn less than €150 monthly—less than half of the minimum wage of €352 in 2014. Compared to standard employment contracts, they offer more flexibility, mainly due to relatively easier hiring and firing procedures, as well as limited worker protection and low social security contributions (a social contribution rate of 1.05 percent compared to 48.6 percent in standard employment contracts). Such limited protection created increasing concern in the public debate.

In response to these concerns, in 2013 the government raised social and health contributions to the same level as regular employment contracts and made the contracts subject to minimum wage regulations. The provisions led to a rapid and immediate decline in the use of these contracts. This reform transferred the full payroll tax burden on to workers regardless of their income. In particular, workers with labor productivity below the minimum wage have been hit hard. Because marginalized Roma are typically poorly qualified for well-paying jobs, they are particularly likely to be affected by these changes. Options to limit the adverse impact on low-skill workers include tax exemptions for them.

Source: Goliaš 2014.

---

vulnerable groups while encouraging activation or labor market integration for those with work capacity. "Making work pay" entails designing active labor market and social assistance policies in such a way that low-income groups and hard-to-place job seekers are not involuntarily incentivized to stay out of employment. This has been found to be the case in countries such as the Slovak Republic and the Czech Republic (see box 3.10).

Jobseeker Profiling and Service Differentiation

Profiling clients at registration would allow services to be better tailored to job seekers' needs, particularly hard-to-place job seekers who need intensive guidance and followup from PES. Rather than spread time equally across all job seekers, PES staff could focus on those hardest to place. The previous sections showed that marginalized Roma are particularly outside of the labor market: Long-term unemployed and discouraged inactive Roma make up a large part of the working-age population. They have lower educational attainment, lower skills levels, and limited exposure to training programs. A good statistical profiling model would not only involve hard factors (such as formal qualifications, prior work experience, and length of unemployment) but also soft factors (such as motivational issues and health and social networks) and external factors (local labor market conditions and demand assessment).

In the case of Bulgaria, social assistance and labor offices have less capacity and time to provide psychological services and social-pedagogic guidance to

Box 3.10 Making Work Pay for Vulnerable Roma

A recent report that aimed to assess the extent to which the current systems of social assistance and labor market programs address unemployment and poverty in the Slovak Republic concluded that some perverse incentives are embedded in the design of social assistance, and these may be preventing vulnerable groups from engaging in formal employment.

The Slovak Republic's main social assistance benefit is the benefit in material need (BMN), for which all families whose incomes fall below the subsistence minimum qualify. Other social assistance schemes include family and disability benefits. Despite the popular perception that the Roma are the main beneficiaries of the BMN, only about a third of households that receive the BMN are of Roma origin. Although the statistical analysis was not conclusive with regards to the impact of the BMN on work incentives, an analysis of theoretical effects of the tax-benefit system indicate that disincentives might exist, especially for part-time, low-paying work.

In addition, existing instruments to make work pay—such as the activation allowance of €63.07 per month for those who become employed after experiencing long-term unemployment; the employee tax credit of €50.34 (maximum) annually; and a child credit of €20 per child per month—are not sufficient and largely ineffective. Finally, opportunities to increase social benefits through activation programs, such as municipal works, weaken the incentives to take up "real" jobs.

Source: World Bank 2012c.

Box 3.11 Job Seeker Profiling—Germany

A good example of jobseeker profiling comes from Germany, which identifies four groups of job seekers: (a) "market clients" that are closest to the labor market; (b) "clients for counseling and activation" that need job search assistance; (c) "clients for counseling and support" that need designated programs; and (d) "clients in need of supervision" that are furthest from the labor market and need special attention. Under the German system, training is limited to the first group and to top job seekers from the second group—those who have at least a 70 percent chance of finding a job after the training. Job creation measures and public employment are only available for the fourth group of clients. Traditional active labor market programs are targeted to groups two and three. This targeting has helped reduce caseloads as well as spending.

Source: Jacobi and Kluve 2006.

vulnerable groups, or to guide employers in hiring vulnerable groups. Refocusing social workers' job duties and increasing staff in social assistance and employment offices would be a prerequisite for improving the situation. Examples of mainstreamed job profiling include the Netherlands and Germany (see box 3.11), where the hardest-to-place individuals receive intensive counseling and can participate in special programs that focus on raising employability.

Individual Action Plans

Individualized actions plans should be developed for hard-to-place job seekers identified through effective profiling (see box 3.12).[4] Long-term unemployed and discouraged job seekers need individual reintegration action plans to boost their employability. An individual action plan describes a person's pathway to employment; it lays out the required training and addresses the client's multiple social needs insofar as they deepen labor market exclusion (including Roma-specific constraints such as poor health, indebtedness, or limited availability of child care). In such cases, a combination of outreach activities must be implemented, including regular follow-up with the jobseeker; adapted training (literacy, soft skills, drafting a CV); providing social and psychological help; and (if needed) medical follow-up. The individual action plan can also involve contracting out activation services entirely for the most difficult to place clients, based on performance-related payments to the contractors (see "Fostering Complementarities between the Public and Private Sectors," later in this chapter).

Rewarding the Placement of the Hard-to-Reach

Effectively implementing the activation agenda involves using a different operations model for the PES, one that better concentrates resources on the hard-to-place. In most PESs, labor office staff needs to be more specialized and better trained to deal with hard-to-place clients, and thus larger investments need to be made in training, retraining, and rotating staff. Such an agenda also involves providing culturally sensitive services that are centered on individuals' needs and abilities, involving dedicated advisers for minority job seekers in those areas with large minority communities (for example, Roma mediators). Some countries have also

---

Box 3.12 Job Seeker Profiling and Individual Action Plans—The Slovak Republic

In 2009, the Slovak Republic introduced a three-zone system, which profiles PES clients into three groups based on their degree of labor market barriers and their level of personal motivation. The contact officers who work in Zone I—which is essentially a self-help area—initially profile the clients. Basic placement and related services are offered in Zone II, while Zone III offers specialized counseling services and works more closely with clients to develop individual action plans. According to the profiling system, disadvantaged job seekers, who often are also recipients of the guaranteed minimum income (GMI), are put in the hardest-to-place category and offered specialized counseling and access to ALMPs.

This system helped differentiate job seekers so they could be more specifically targeted. Nevertheless, GMI recipients are not given preferential treatment with respect to placement on the labor market. Given that GMI recipients are typically less ready for jobs in the open job market, the end result is that treating all PES clients equally risks not investing sufficiently in GMI beneficiaries.

Source: World Bank 2012c.

---

introduced incentives for employment office staff to focus on the long-term unemployed, and reward successful placements of difficult cases (such as is done in Australia).

Service Integration with Social Welfare

Merging the traditional PES with social welfare offices or introducing integrated computer systems is likely to help reach hard-to-place job seekers. Service integration builds on the recognition that long-term unemployed, youth, and discouraged, inactive individuals typically have multiple needs that are best addressed in an integrated, one-stop shop manner (see Lechner and Wetzel 2012). In most cases, this requires close coordination between different agencies; however, agencies struggle in this endeavor. For example, a recent analysis in Bulgaria finds that cooperation between different agencies is mainly focused on administrative functions and rule enforcement rather than on labor market inclusion. This dilutes responsibilities and limits the impact of initiatives on integrating the most vulnerable into the labor market (World Bank 2014a).

Some OECD countries have merged employment service with social work functions to provide integrated services to job seekers, especially those who depend on social assistance and are out of work (see box 3.13).

Fostering Complementarities between the Public and Private Sectors

Outsourcing activation services is particularly useful in the case of highly disadvantaged job seekers, such as marginalized Roma, who require more specialized and intensive interventions. Many countries have contracted out partnerships with private sector service providers and/or community-based organizations and NGOs in order to facilitate contact between the employment office and the client, and to provide services. PESs in Germany, Australia, and the Netherlands

---

Box 3.13 Integrating PES and Social Welfare—Spain, the United Kingdom, and Germany

An example of the integrated approach comes from Spain's Personal Itinerary of Integration program, which involves cooperating with local companies to provide both orientation and training.

In the United Kingdom, Jobcentre Plus (JCP) combines the previously separate job placement and benefit administration functions into a one-stop shop for employment service and income support. In focusing on both inactive and unemployed clients, the JCP's service mix includes social work functions to address the multiple social needs of marginalized job seekers. Initial evaluations find that service integration in the JCP has had a positive impact on job entry outcomes, a neutral effect on client service outcomes (speed, accuracy, proactivity), but a negative impact on benefit-program, processing accuracy.

Similarly, Germany has sought to build organizational linkages between the Federal Labor Offices and the municipal social welfare departments that manage social assistance benefits.

Box 3.14 Outsourcing Some Services for the Hardest to Place—The Netherlands

The Netherlands outsources employment reintegration services for the unemployed who are not expected to find work within six months. The traditional public employment service continues to manage jobseeker registration, profiling, initial job referral services, and services for easy-to-place job seekers. In contrast, job seekers that are further from the labor market are redirected to the social insurance agency that handles people with unemployment insurance entitlements, or to the municipalities for those who only have access to non-contributory social assistance benefits. Both entities are then in charge of managing benefit payments and transferring job seekers to reintegration services.

Box 3.15 Public-Private Partnerships—The Dominican Republic

Juventud y Empleo in the Dominican Republic is a labor market insertion program that provides life and technical skill training combined with private sector internships. The program is demand-driven, inspired by the Jovenes model, and has two components: (a) a three-month course on life and technical skills in qualified training institutions and (b) a two-month internship or on-the-job training experience in private firms. The Ministry of Labor outsourced the provision of training services to private training institutions through a competitive bidding process.

Impact evaluations of the program have shown positive impacts on young beneficiaries' earnings (mainly hourly wages) as well as reduced risky behaviors and increased life skills. A cost-benefit analysis indicates that the cost of the program is recovered after two years (Card et al. 2011).

(see box 3.14) rely on outside partners to deliver complete services to the hardest to place. However, outsourcing is likely only effective when coupled with a performance monitoring and measurement system that allows the individual's progress finding and retaining a job to be tracked.

Similarly, in Latin America and the Caribbean, the Jovenes (youth) programs are models for public-private partnerships. These programs match job seekers with the existing demand on the labor market. By relying on competition and consultation with employers, the programs have ensured skills relevance and job placement. The model, replicated across the region, combines in-classroom with workplace training, which fosters youths' smooth transition into the labor market (see box 3.15).

The provision of services can also be contracted to NGOs that have experience working in Roma communities and are better positioned to deliver effective services that are tailored to marginalized Roma's needs. To this end, the Czech Republic launched the Social Inclusion Agency to promote innovative partnerships between public services and NGOs in select marginalized communities, and offers a new approach for promoting the employment of Roma (World Bank 2008). In Bulgaria, some labor offices successfully employ Roma mediators who are hired under the national program Activate Inactive Persons. The experience in Germany and other countries confirms that if counselors belong to the same group (such as an ethnic minority) as the unemployed, services can be delivered in a more effective way; a trusting relationship may be crucial to this achievement.

Responding to Clients' Needs

It is important that PESs progressively shift how they are regarded by Roma—they must transition away from being viewed as the formal body to which the unemployed are obliged to come once a month to register, but without providing job search support. Employment offices are required to provide a variety of services beyond administration related to the unemployed, such as job match and counseling services to provide support when people apply for vacancies. However, qualitative evidence suggests they are generally falling short of delivering on this mandate throughout the region, particularly in Bulgaria and Romania (Messing et al. 2013). PESs often function as registration counters that offer no mediation work or counseling services, which keeps the most vulnerable away from the labor market and turns labor market barriers into pervasive issues that affect all Roma job seekers. Employment offices must be regularly evaluated (via regular client surveys, for example) for how effectively they service the unemployed to ensure high-quality, focused service provision.

Lack of trust toward PESs could be addressed by having mediators work with specific groups. Previous research findings suggests that low-skilled Roma, especially those who live in marginalized areas, are reluctant to register with job centers, given the difficulties accessing the office and mistrust of the staff. Having mediators or counselors who are adequately trained to serve Roma increases service utilization and trust in the areas of health and social protection (World Bank 2014b). Similarly, Roma mediators in Hungary were found to be genuinely supportive of unemployed Roma, and generated increased levels of trust in the office among job seekers. In Bulgaria however, the Roma mediators were found to have no effect due to the fact that their appointment usually served political ends, and the person was simply not skilled for the task and had no motivation to fulfill the role (Messing et al. 2013).[5]

Performance Measurement and Impact Evaluation

Systematic performance monitoring and impact evaluation of employment programs has become widespread across many EU countries, but such measures are still few and far between in the five countries of interest.

Data on ALMPs exist most often only at a highly aggregated level—national or regional. With the exception of the Slovak Republic, essential data on ALMP implementation, such as the number of beneficiaries or the local budget, are not available at the municipality level either because such data are not recorded or because local PES branches are reluctant to share information with researchers. Local staff is usually prepared to participate in interviews about the activation programs they manage, but they often remain unwilling to provide detailed information about the actual implementation. The data on program participation and disbursement available from the labor ministries are too disaggregated to conduct meaningful analysis. In Hungary and the Slovak Republic, data collection about job seekers is somewhat sophisticated, but its use is restricted to the agencies and ministries.

When data are available, their quality is often poor. Programs are typically rated as successful based on outputs—such as the number of program participants—rather than outcomes—such as the proportion of participants employed 6 months after the end of the training. Implementing agencies lack data on the number of dropouts, successful graduates, beneficiaries who found a job, the type and adequacy of the jobs offered, and so on. With a better data availability, measurement and evaluation should shift from process evaluation to impact assessment. The goal of ALMPs is to reinsert unemployed and out-of-the-labor-force individuals into the labor market, and so program assessments should focus on tracking the outcomes of their services and match them to job seekers' characteristics in order to figure out which measures are likely to be the most efficient for each vulnerable group. For example, such targeting systems are in place in Canada, Germany, and Denmark.

In addition to the general problem of limited data, one of the most important obstacles to assessing the success—or failure—of current ALMPs with respect to Roma integration is the lack of available data on Roma participation in such programs. Most countries do not collect information regarding the ethnic affiliation of their beneficiaries. It is thus impossible to discern the actual number or share of Roma beneficiaries in individual reprogramming, or to compare their outcomes to other job seekers. Even the few existing Roma-targeted employment programs do not have data about the ethnic composition of their recipients; they are considered Roma because the priority target group is Roma, or because the implementing agency is an organization that works with the Roma community. As a consequence, it is difficult to draw conclusions about the impact these programs have on the labor market inclusion of Roma communities.

As mentioned earlier, evidence-based management relies more on absorption assessments and process evaluation rather than on the evaluation of participants' outcomes. Evidence-based policy is applied inconsistently, and typically only at the national level. Programs are judged by their demand and their absorption capacity. Net impact assessments are sometimes conducted, but their conclusions have less bearing on the decision to continue, modify, or cancel a program. The lack of evidence-based policies and programs make it difficult to assess local disparities and specificities. One attempt to rigorously evaluate ALMPs in Hungary was led by Adamecz et al. (2013) (see box 3.16). Similarly, but not limited to employment, Briciu and Grigoriaș (2011) conducted an impact evaluation, the prime objective of which was to measure the real impact that health workers had on improving Roma access to health services—access to social services and basic health care, use of contraceptive methods, and access to health services for mothers and children.

Box 3.16 Evaluating Active Labor Market Program Measures—Hungary

This evaluation focused on two Active Labor Market Program measures, the Improvement of Employability of the Disadvantaged and the One Step Ahead! programs, which targeted vulnerable job seekers (including but not limited to Roma) and sought to answer two questions: (a) how effectively the programs actually reached those Roma who belonged to their target groups; and (b) whether program participation increased the probability of finding a job. While both programs significantly increased the labor market potential of the participants, no specific conclusion could be reached regarding Roma, as individual ethnicity data was not available. Without this, it is impossible to evaluate how effectively the programs reached Roma within the group of beneficiaries.

Source: Adamecz et al. 2013.

Directions for Policy

To efficiently include marginalized Roma in the labor market, governments will need to put in place systemic reforms to reach hard-to-place job seekers as well as change the design of some programs, to avoid leaving disadvantaged Roma behind.

Given the widespread functional illiteracy among Roma in marginalized localities, second-chance education and literacy programs should become core pieces of any labor market initiative focused on Roma inclusion. Governments should simultaneously put in place systems to detect at-risk groups early on and give them prioritized and individualized attention. In particular, youth could benefit from career counseling and professional orientation programs offered at school. In addition to being Roma-sensitive—that is, adequately taking into account the specific challenges faced by young Roma job seekers—these counseling services should be gender-sensitive by responding to the particular needs of young Roma women who need to juggle household tasks, child care, and employment.

ALMPs should concentrate spending and human resources away from skilled secondary school and university graduates and toward low-skilled and disadvantaged job seekers. As most skilled individuals are highly likely to be able to find employment without much support from PES, resources could be shifted to the disadvantaged, the low-skilled, the long-term unemployed, and others who have trouble finding employment on their own.

Public works programs should remain an important intervention, especially for unskilled Roma and those in low labor-demand regions, although such programs require modifications. In particular, they should involve strategic vocational skill upgrading through training, in addition to transmitting work habits and experience. In this respect a public works assignment should have a built-in program to formally identify training needs for each client, as well as an agreed training plan linked to the national qualifications framework.

Finally, training and retraining programs should be better linked to actual employment and build on client choice. Retraining programs on average appear to not have had results for jobless Roma. Successful programs should ideally be closely linked to actual employment and take account of the skills needed in the labor market. If not linked to employers' needs and clients' choices, they risk wasting spending and undermining beneficiaries' motivation.

Annex 3A: Spotlight on Chile Solidario as an Example of an Integrated Approach

Chile Solidario is internationally regarded as an example of successful integration among the many sectors and services that are involved in the provision of support to the most vulnerable and marginalized populations. The experience of Chile Solidario indicates that social intermediation programs can be effective tools for reaching the extreme and chronic poor, including marginalized Roma populations in CEE. However, to be effective, such programs should be designed to respond to clearly identified challenges, tailored to local capacity and conditions, and well integrated within existing institutions and programs.

How Was Chile Solidario Born?

Poverty reduction in Chile was substantial throughout the 1990s, not only as a result of continued and high economic growth, but also because of significant improvements in social policies. Between 1989 and 1996 poverty fell from 38.6 percent to 23.2 percent; that is, 15.4 percentage points in 6 years (about 40 percent reduction). However, while poverty rates continued to decline, extreme poverty stagnated, affecting around 5.6 percent of the population.

What made extreme poverty more difficult to eradicate? Based on the information available in the National Survey for Socioeconomic Characterization (Encuesta de Caracterización Socioeconómica Nacional or CASEN, the official Chilean survey that measures poverty) and qualitative analyses, an assessment was performed to better understand the situation and recommend improvements of existing social policies aimed at targeting the extreme poor. The analysis indicated that:

- *Intra-poor targeting had limited effectiveness.* Extremely poor families had proportionately fewer benefits than poor families and the benefits were concentrated on the upper side of the poverty distribution.
- *Social programs were organized by explicit demand.* That is, people had to apply for social benefits, go to a government office, and make the necessary arrangements.
- *The information available about social benefits did not reach the poorest population.* In general, processes for applying for social benefits were complex and required the applicant to manage a lot of information, not always in a language or in a format that facilitated proper understanding.

Being Fair, Faring Better • http://dx.doi.org/10.1596/978-1-4648-0598-1

- *Extremely poor families were excluded from social and community networks, isolated even within their own communities.* This was particularly the case for women.
- *Social interventions (programs, benefits) were being targeted at the individual level, with little coordination among them.* Different programs were not coordinated at the family level, leading to duplication and inefficiencies.

These results allowed the identification of some potential policy options that were reviewed for the design of Chile Solidario are summarized in table 3A.1.

The Design of Chile Solidario

Chile Solidario was designed to reorient existing institutional capacity toward social interventions that were perceived to have the highest impact on eradicating extreme poverty. As such, Chile Solidario was not designed as a specific program or social benefit, but rather as "a management model based on the articulation of institutional and local networks to provide social protection to the poorest families."

The initiative's central objective was thus to improve the coordination mechanisms for the delivery of integrated services to support families in extreme poverty. Rolled out in 2002 and fully phased in by 2005, the program provides

Table 3A.1 Policy Options for the Design of Chile Solidario

Policy options	Purpose	Implications for institutions
Addressing extreme poverty only through monetary family income (includes cash transfers provided by the government).	Families have an income level that would allow them to at least achieve the value of the poverty line, mainly through the provision of cash transfers.	Focus on tax collection and/or reallocation of existing resources (programs), in order to finance the family income supplement.
		Provide administrative mechanisms to implement and deliver a direct subsidy to families using the payment systems available.
Addressing extreme poverty through guaranteed benefits and preferred access to social services network.	Reorganization of available resources, ensuring that each institution prioritize the poorest. Guaranteed provision of benefits to all those who meet the requirements; and/or Preferential access based on availability of benefits and service delivery capacity.	Standardization of targeting criteria and eligibility across programs. Overcoming good targeting of each program through targeting various programs at members of the same family.
Addressing extreme poverty in a decentralized and personalized manner.	Reverse the logic of a centralized administration and service provision through a management model where regional and local institutions (subnational) assume a strategic role (coordinator and provider).	Design new services to allow a direct and regular contact with extreme poor families, in order to match demand with the available supply.

individuals and families in extreme poverty and vulnerability (5 percent of
Chile's poorest families) with social protection coverage for five years, and aims
to help beneficiaries access and effectively use the social services network in an
autonomous manner.

The key specific goals and defining features of the intervention included:

- Improve outreach to potential beneficiaries, through for instance strengthened
  institutional arrangements to facilitate entry (single entry point) and adjustments to services.
- Engage beneficiaries in the process, through the use of social workers and the
  methodology based on a contract and specific family plan, and through follow
  up (such as family visits), implementing a task-centered approach.
- Offer support to families to learn about and use existing services and benefits,
  including cash transfers.

How Does the Program Work?

Participation in Chile Solidario is voluntary and formalized through the commitment to work toward achieving measurable goals. The entry point to the system
is a psychosocial support service (Programa Puente), provided by a family counselor for two years; it uses a methodology based on family visits, information, and
guidance (such as referrals to social services and benefits).

The family and the social worker prepare a family-specific development plan
together, in order to identify and prioritize problems and to develop a strategy
for overcoming them. The plan is detailed around measurable objectives for both
the institutions and the beneficiaries to achieve, structured around 53 "minimum
quality of life" conditions along 7 dimensions: identification, health, education,
family dynamics, housing, work, and income.

This set of expected results allows the linkage between the demand and the
supply in a practical manner. Participating households know from the beginning
on which of the 53 expected results they need to work and concentrate their
efforts, while the supply-side (a variety of providers) knows the amount of
demand in each locality and how many and which of the expected results are
under the responsibility of each provider. In that context, the social worker can
operate as a connector linking demand and supply. Without specific and clear
expected results at the household level (the same applied for communities), it is
very difficult to integrate social services.

The psychosocial support component, a type of caseworker relationship, is
one of the main innovations of Chile Solidario. This component is complemented by a family cash transfer (flat amount per family), called *Bono de
Protección Familiar*, delivered on a monthly basis, preferably to a woman, and
which is intended to help finance the costs associated with access to services. The
value of the transfer decreases over time, given that the transaction costs are
deemed to be higher at the outset of the process.

For all families covered by Chile Solidario, benefits are legally guaranteed
to the extent that they meet the requirements and take the necessary steps

to activate the benefits. Although most of the benefits guaranteed under the program existed before the creation of Chile Solidario, they were operating based on an application process and a specific quota of benefits for each municipality.

In addition to the guaranteed benefits, families covered by the program have preferential access to a number of social programs available and related to the seven dimensions along which the expected results are organized. Preferential access is enabled through interagency agreements that provide conditional transfers to service providers, based on results.

The Psychosocial Support Component

A family support component is the central pillar of any social intermediation program, and therefore needs to be properly developed and implemented. Psychosocial support is key to help households acquire the skills they need to autonomously participate in the welfare, education, and health systems available to them.

Well-trained and qualified social workers are the backbone of such family support component, which is usually delivered through regular family visits. Family support responds to the need of providing families with a personalized service, and establishing a relationship of trust, developing greater self-confidence and self-efficacy of beneficiaries to successfully face the challenges of access and permanence in the network of social protection services.

The psychosocial support service adopts a methodology focused on: (a) achieving minimum conditions that the family has to fulfill in order to enter and remain in the program; (b) maintaining and strengthening these minimum conditions; and (c) developing family dynamics and personal skills that promote effective strategies to address the risks to which they are exposed.

The psychosocial support service revolves around the figure of a professionally trained family counselor who plays a crucial role in connecting the family and the local network of social services. The family counselor will visit the families that sign a required participation agreement regularly at home and refer them to local social services. Chile Solidario provides regular training to family counselors, whose performance is also evaluated twice a year.

In this model, the family counselor is not a family representative but enables the family to act effectively in the network. At the same time, the counselor works with service providers to promote adequate and timely connections. The family counselor position was created by Chile Solidario as a new job at the municipal level. While 36 percent of the family counselors are open-ended municipal personnel, mainly in the area of social assistance, the remaining 64 percent are new municipal positions.

All families that conclude the stage of psychosocial support automatically enter a phase of monitoring and tracking the minimum conditions, a process that is done administratively through the Integrated Social Information System (Sistema Integrado de Información Social, or SIIS). Along this three-year period, families keep guaranteed benefits and preferential access to social programs, and *Bono de Proteccion* (protection bonus) is replaced by *Bono de Egreso* (exit bonus) during 36 months, operating as a "prize" to the completion of the first stage.

Systems Management

Since Chile Solidario is a management model, it was necessary to develop a set of tools that allowed a systemic operation.

- *Interagency coordination* is a central tool for systemic management. It entails both horizontal coordination (between institutions) and vertical coordination (between levels of government administration). Chile Solidario management occurs at the local level, where the constant contact with the families of the system is maintained and an articulated set of available services should be provided to the population covered. The national system coordination process focuses on the articulation and coordination of resources (programmatic, managerial, and financial) necessary for effective and efficient local implementation. The Ministry of Planning is responsible for the national coordination of Chile Solidario.[6] Regional coordination is focused on the effectiveness of interagency agreements at the regional and local levels, ensuring a good match between demand and supply of services and supporting municipalities in managing the available supply for their beneficiaries. In all cases, the coordination process is based on concrete results, expressed as the quality of life minimum conditions, and interagency coordination is based on the seven dimensions along which minimum conditions are organized.

- *Information management* through the SIIS collects and administers data about families and their members and the trajectory of the individual and the family in Chile Solidario. The SIIS is the device that allows calculating the demand for services and monitoring the available supply, psychosocial support, and changes in beneficiary families' living conditions. The information managed through the SIIS is a key input for the decision-making process of annual budget and programmatic decisions, both for the national coordination of Chile Solidario and for institutions that provide services to the population covered by the system.

- *Subnational management* is based on annual work plans, both at the regional and local levels, and a mechanism to transfer implementation resources to municipalities. The system had been gradually decentralized to municipalities for the provision of programs managed through Chile Solidario in order to ensure greater relevance and timeliness of services. This process was done through annual implementation agreements of specific services based on quality standards set by the system.

- *Financial management* occurs through a budgetary mechanism of conditional transfers to institutions that provide services and benefits to the population covered by Chile Solidario. Resources are transferred based on annual interagency agreements establishing coverage and performance goals to each provider institution, including auditing and accountability mechanisms. Resources are nominated for beneficiaries covered by Chile Solidario and therefore cannot be used for other purposes. Institutions' performance is binding with the process of the annual budget debate in Congress. In fact, this is the mechanism that facilitates and strengthens the role of the system coordination and aligns provider institutions in the availability of supply to beneficiary households.

What Have Been the Results of the Initiative?

According to information available at the end of 2013, the Chile Solidario system covered a total of 340,875 families for the complete committed period of five years. By the same date, another 81,209 families were being covered by the system in different stages. Since 2006, based on the same intervention strategy, other extremely vulnerable target groups were incorporated into the system, including homeless individuals, the elderly living alone, and children dependent on adults in prison. Between 2002 and 2012, the effective coverage[7] of Chile Solidario increased to 482,558 families, and therefore about 2 million individuals were covered by the system during its years of operation.[8]

Chile Solidario was successful in providing social protection coverage to the country's poorest families. The system also achieved high rates of effectiveness in meeting the minimum quality of life conditions of participating families. Impact evaluations showed that the greatest impact materializes in the first two years of participation in the system, when families receive psychosocial support. The system was found to have the following results:

- An increase in the number of people accessing government subsidies, ranging from 2 to 20 percent, and improvements in school attendance and health care.
- Greater enrollment in programs designed to help people find and keep jobs.
- A positive effect on employment for male household heads ages 51–65 (a 2–3 percent increase in the likelihood that they would have a job with a labor contract).
- For spouses who took advantage of the jobs services, which included training, a corresponding increase in employment, or in income from employment. This is particularly relevant given the low percentage of women participating in the labor market.
- An increase of 4–6 percent in take-up of the jobs services.
- Higher total household income, especially in rural areas.
- Better access to municipal programs to help families protect their homes from rain and cold.
- Improvement in access to adequate sewage systems and to a legal housing situation in the long run.
- An increase of 3.5–7 percent in the rate of home ownership or rental of the house in which families live.

Participation in the program also appears to have positive psychosocial effects, including better perceptions of the future, increased self-efficacy, increased self-confidence, and fewer symptoms of depression.

The experience of Chile Solidario indicates that social intermediation programs can be effective tools for reaching the extreme and chronic poor, including marginalized Roma populations in CEE. However, to be effective, such programs should be designed to respond to clearly identified challenges, tailored to local capacity and conditions, and well integrated within existing institutions and programs. The methodology of Chile Solidario needs to be adapted to each population, given their particular characteristics and needs. In the case of marginalized Roma in CEE, special attention should be paid to cultural aspects of Roma people in each country as well as non-Roma's perceptions about them. The intervention methodology would require a careful customization, taking into account the availability of services for Roma and non-Roma populations, the current mechanisms to access those services and potential changes needed to ensure effective access, and cultural changes required within the institutions that provide social services to these populations. An in-depth analysis of coping strategies and styles used by Roma populations in each country—as well as openness of services providers—would be needed to ensure appropriate adaptations and adjustments of the psychosocial support methodology.

Annex 3B: Employment Data Regression Tables

Table 3B.1 Roma Probability of Being Employed, by Gender, Age, and Educational Level

	Bulgaria	Czech Republic	Hungary	Romania	Slovak Republic
Roma	−0.028	−0.077***	−0.094***	0.004	−0.059***
	(0.021)	(0.019)	(0.019)	(0.020)	(0.018)
Male	0.044***	0.074***	0.038***	0.092***	0.060***
	(0.015)	(0.013)	(0.014)	(0.014)	(0.014)
Age	0.013***	0.005	0.006*	0.018***	0.006*
	(0.003)	(0.003)	(0.003)	(0.003)	(0.003)
Age square	−0.000***	−0.000***	−0.000***	−0.000***	−0.000**
	(0.000)	(0.000)	(0.000)	(0.000)	(0.000)
Child < 6 years	0.010	−0.011	−0.006	0.005	0.009
	(0.016)	(0.013)	(0.015)	(0.015)	(0.015)
Education (omitted: none)					
Lower basic	−0.036	−0.051	0.042	−0.007	0.007
	(0.025)	(0.040)	(0.041)	(0.020)	(0.040)
Upper basic	−0.012	−0.077**	0.035	−0.027	−0.019
	(0.024)	(0.037)	(0.039)	(0.020)	(0.038)
Lower secondary	0.050	0.102***	0.105**	0.015	0.057
	(0.036)	(0.039)	(0.049)	(0.031)	(0.041)
Upper secondary	0.071**	0.168***	0.104**	0.037	0.116***
	(0.030)	(0.045)	(0.043)	(0.030)	(0.045)

table continues next page

Being Fair, Faring Better • http://dx.doi.org/10.1596/978-1-4648-0598-1

Table 3B.1 Roma Probability of Being Employed, by Gender, Age, and Educational Level *(continued)*

	Bulgaria	Czech Republic	Hungary	Romania	Slovak Republic
Tertiary	0.153***	0.156***	0.246***	0.124**	0.192***
	(0.052)	(0.059)	(0.068)	(0.053)	(0.061)
Years unemployed	−0.188***	−0.175***	−0.150***	−0.161***	−0.114***
	(0.005)	(0.005)	(0.005)	(0.004)	(0.005)
Rural	0.049***	−0.106**	0.003	0.014	0.046***
	(0.014)	(0.047)	(0.014)	(0.014)	(0.015)
Constant	−0.070	2.656***	0.282	0.406**	1.539
	(0.478)	(0.997)	(0.976)	(0.205)	(1.126)
Regional fixed effects	Yes	Yes	Yes	Yes	Yes
R^2	0.479	0.567	0.399	0.459	0.323
Number of observations	2,454	2,483	2,571	2,605	2,553

Note: Restricted to working-age population (ages 15–64).
* P <0.10; ** P <0.05; *** P <0.01.

Table 3B.2 Labor Market Participation for Roma and Non-Roma Neighbors

	Bulgaria	Czech Republic	Hungary	Romania	Slovak Republic
Roma	−0.019	−0.020	−0.041	−0.005	−0.003
	(0.026)	(0.026)	(0.025)	(0.026)	(0.026)
Male	0.065***	0.154***	0.126***	0.128***	0.122***
	(0.017)	(0.017)	(0.019)	(0.017)	(0.019)
Age	0.006	−0.005	−0.003	0.021***	0.016***
	(0.004)	(0.005)	(0.005)	(0.004)	(0.005)
Age square	−0.000	0.000	0.000	−0.000***	−0.000***
	(0.000)	(0.000)	(0.000)	(0.000)	(0.000)
Child <6 years	−0.055***	−0.082***	−0.072***	−0.013	−0.130***
	(0.019)	(0.017)	(0.019)	(0.018)	(0.020)
Years unemployed	−0.145***	−0.144***	−0.145***	−0.147***	−0.088***
	(0.006)	(0.006)	(0.006)	(0.005)	(0.007)
Rural	0.023	−0.062	0.030	−0.024	−0.000
	(0.017)	(0.064)	(0.019)	(0.017)	(0.021)
Education (omitted: none)					
Lower basic	0.009	0.073	0.046	0.008	0.242***
	(0.028)	(0.054)	(0.056)	(0.023)	(0.056)
Upper basic	0.019	0.142***	0.064	0.030	0.325***
	(0.027)	(0.049)	(0.054)	(0.023)	(0.052)
Lower secondary	−0.007	0.235***	0.109	0.091**	0.278***
	(0.041)	(0.051)	(0.067)	(0.037)	(0.056)
Upper secondary	0.057	0.275***	0.138**	0.043	0.230***
	(0.035)	(0.058)	(0.058)	(0.036)	(0.061)
Tertiary	0.053	0.273***	0.209**	0.171***	0.357***
	(0.060)	(0.075)	(0.089)	(0.066)	(0.090)

table continues next page

Table 3B.2 Labor Market Participation for Roma and Non-Roma Neighbors (continued)

	Bulgaria	Czech Republic	Hungary	Romania	Slovak Republic
Constant	0.489	−0.836	−0.668	1.616***	4.286***
	(0.558)	(1.270)	(1.259)	(0.251)	(1.546)
Regional fixed effects	Yes	Yes	Yes	Yes	Yes
R^2	0.312	0.397	0.355	0.415	0.199
Number of observations	2,112	2,082	1,965	2,236	2,229

Note: "Labor market participation" is defined as working-age individuals (ages 15–64) who are either employed or unemployed, looking for work, and ready to accept a job offer. The sample is restricted to working-age individuals who are not in school or training, and did not retire early.
* $P <0.10$; ** $P <0.05$; *** $P <0.01$.

Table 3B.3 Blinder–Oaxaca Decomposition of the Gap in Employment for Roma versus Non-Roma

	All, simple	All, complex
Bulgaria	21	21
Czech Republic	36	40
Hungary	37	36
Romania	14	15
Slovak Republic	42	43

Source: UNDP, World Bank, and EC 2011.
Note: Simple controls include gender, age, and education level. "Complex" controls include all of the "simple controls" as well as living in a rural versus urban environment, and the region of residence.

Table 3B.4 Budget Allocation for and Participation in Labor Market Programs, 2012

	Budget					Number of participants				
	Bulgaria	Czech Republic	Hungary	Romania	Slovak Republic	Bulgaria	Czech Republic	Hungary	Romania	Slovak Republic
Training	11	19	3	7	1	3,687	N/A	15,351	19,347	265
Employment incentives	6	32	127	32	58	3,017	3,581[a]	241,897	31,970	28,668
Supported employment and rehabilitation	1	143	N/A	N/A	35	333	35,960[a]	N/A	N/A	11,163
Direct job creation	59	27	455	5	6	18,445	6,669	63,023	2,812	11,618
Start-up incentives	2	3	5	0	34	N/A	3,516	1,836	N/A	23,701
Out-of-work income maintenance and support	183	366	408	215	182	120,972	104,472	271,365	165,808	42,521

Source: EuroStat 2014, latest year available.
Note: Budget is in million euros.
a. Data for 2011.

Two different model specifications used in a Blinder-Oaxaca decomposition analysis are summarized table 3B.3. According to these models, the gap in employment between Roma and non-Roma is explained mostly by differences in endowments, including differences in age and education level. This means that according to these models, if Roma were to have the same endowments as their non-Roma neighbors, there would only be a small a gap in employment. The simple and complex models present estimates of the unexplained part of the gap: these models compare the actual gap in employment to the gap that would be predicted based on a model in which ethnicity as well as the specified background characteristics are taken into account. In these models, 15–40 percent of the gap in employment between Roma and non-Roma remains unexplained, and at least part of this gap could thus be attributed to discrimination in the job market. The employment gap is larger in the Slovak Republic, Hungary, and the Czech Republic, and quite low in Bulgaria and Romania.

Notes

1. The report, which uses data from the EU Statistics on Income and Living Conditions survey, focuses on Bulgaria, Estonia, Greece, Lithuania, Hungary, and Romania.

2. With the exception of the Czech Republic, where a small share of Roma workers are engaged in the agricultural sector because the Roma population is largely urban.

3. See the annex for a complete discussion on the Blinder–Oaxaca decomposition.

4. For a more detailed discussion, see Loxha and Morgandi (2014).

5. Hiring coordinators of Roma origin can have a counterproductive effect, with only the more employable Roma being offered services. Messing et al. (2013) found that Roma coordinators with a good knowledge of the local Roma society seemed to select "better" applicants for jobs as opposed to those who were in the most vulnerable situations. The mediator selected those applicants who had a greater chance of remaining in the program and those with whom the employer or trainer would more likely be satisfied.

6. In 2011, an institutional change replaced the Ministry of Planning with the Ministry of Social Development.

7. Effective coverage includes those families who followed the whole intervention process of Chile Solidario, and therefore are not included in families that refused to participate and those that did not complete the stages of the system.

8. In May 2012, Law No. 20,595 was approved. It created the "Ethical Family Income," which provides unconditional and conditional cash transfers to families who live in extreme poverty. Although the Chile Solidario Law was not derogated, in fact the new law established a closing date for being enrolled in Chile Solidario.

References

Adamecz, A., B. Czafit, K. Bördős, E. Nagy, P. Lévai, and Á. Scharle. 2013. *Roma Inclusion and Impact Evaluation of Two Mainstream EU-Funded Active Labour Market Programmes*. Report, Budapest Institute, Budapest.

Almeida, R., J. Arbelaez, M. Honorati, A. Kuddo, T. Lohmann, M. Ovadiya, L. Pop, M. Sanchez Puerta, and M. Weber. 2012. "Improving Access to Jobs and Earnings Opportunities." Social Protection & Labor Discussion Paper 1204, World Bank, Washington, DC.

Asenov, R., I. Tomova, S. Cherkezova, and L. Stoychev. 2014. "Drivers of Labor Market Discrimination of Roma in Bulgaria." [Fieldwork]. Washington, DC: World Bank.

Briciu, C., and V. Grigoraş. 2011. *Evaluarea impactului programului de mediere sanitară*. Centrul Romilor pentru Politici de Sănătate–SASTIPEN, Bucharest.

Card, D., P. Ibarrarán, F. Regalia, D. Rosas-Shady, and Y. Soares. 2011. "The Labor Market Impacts of Youth Training in the Dominican Republic." *Journal of Labor Economics* 29 (2): 267–300.

Csoba, J., and Z. Nagy. 2012. "The Evaluation of Training, Wage Subsidy and Public Work Programs in Hungary." In *The Hungarian Labour Market*, edited by K. Fazekas and G. Kézdi. Budapest: MTA KTK, OFA.

ERRC (European Roma Rights Centre). 2005. *The Glass Box: Exclusion of Roma from Employment*. Report, European Roma Rights Centre, Budapest.

Eurostat. 2014. *Labor Market Policy—Expenditure and Participation*. Report, Eurostat, Luxembourg. http://ec.europa.eu/eurostat/about/overview.

Goliaš, P. 2014. "Reforming Non-standard Contracts in Slovakia." Presentation at the 2014 Conference on Dual Labour Markets, Minimum Wage and Inequalities, Warsaw, October 8.

Jacobi, L., and J. Kluve. 2006. "Before and After the Hartz Reforms: The Performance of Active Labor Market Policy in Germany." IZA Discussion Paper 2100, Institute for the Study of Labor, Bonn.

Kahanec, M. 2014. "Roma Integration in European Labor Markets." *IZA World of Labor* 2014 (39): 1–10.

Lechner, F., and P. Wetzel. 2012. "EEO Review: Long-Term Unemployment. Austria, European Employment Observatory." European Employment Policy Observatory. www.eu-employment-observatory.net.

Loxha, A., and M. Morgandi. 2014. "Profiling the Unemployed. A Review of OECD Experiences and Implications for Emerging Economies." Social Protection and Labor Discussion Papers 91051, World Bank.

Messing, V., B. A. Bereményi, L. Kurekova-Mytna, J. Konsteková, A. Pamporov, and F. Pop. 2013. "From Benefits to Brooms: Case Studies Report on the Implementation of Active Labor Market Policies for Roma at Local Level." Working Paper 19.3, NEUJOBS.

Research Institute for Quality of Life. 2010. *Legal and Equal on the Labour Market for the Roma Communities: Diagnosis of the Factors Influencing the Employment Rate of the Roma Population in Romania*. Report, Soros Foundation, Bucharest.

Revenga, A., D. Ringold, and W. M. Tracy. 2002. *Poverty and Ethnicity. A Cross-Country Study of Roma Poverty in Central Europe*. Washington, DC: World Bank.

RIMIL (Roma Inclusion Mobile Innovation Lab). 2014. "Promoting Access to Productive Employment for Marginalized Roma." Workshop, Madrid. http://www.worldbank .org/en/results/2014/06/13/promoting-access-to-productive-employment-for -marginalized-roma.

Salner, A. 2013. "Background Note Employing Marginalized Slovak Roma at US Steel Košice—Lessons from the First Ten Years." Mimeo, World Bank, Washington, DC.

Social Observatory, University of Bucharest. 2010. "Social Inclusion Barometer." Survey, University of Bucharest.

UNDP (United Nations Development Programme), World Bank, and EC (European Commission). 2011. *Regional Roma Survey*. Report, UNDP, World Bank, and EC, New York.

World Bank. 2008. *Czech Republic: Improving Employment Chances of the Roma*. Report 46120 CZ, World Bank, Human Development Unit, Europe and Central Asia.

———. 2011. *Doing Business 2011: Making a Difference for Entrepreneurs*. Washington, DC: World Bank.

———. 2012a. *Implementing the Benefit in Material Need in the Slovak Republic*. Washington, DC: World Bank.

———. 2012b. *Promoting Access to Quality Early Childhood Development for Roma Children in Eastern Europe*. Washington, DC: World Bank.

———. 2012c. *Protecting the Poor and Promoting Employability. An Assessment of the Social Assistance System in the Slovak Republic*. Report, World Bank, Washington, DC.

———. 2012d. *Reducing Vulnerability and Promoting the Self-Employment of Roma in Eastern Europe Through Financial Inclusion*. Working Paper No. 72331, World Bank, Washington, DC.

———. 2013. *World Development Report 2013: Jobs*. Washington, DC: World Bank.

———. 2014a. "Activating and Increasing Employability of Specific Vulnerable Groups in Bulgaria—a Diagnostic of Institutional Capacity." Mimeo, World Bank, Washington, DC.

———. 2014b. *Diagnostic and Policy Advice for Supporting Roma Inclusion in Romania*. Report, Washington, DC: World Bank.

———. 2014c. *Gender Dimensions of Roma Inclusion*. Report, World Bank, Washington, DC.

———. 2014d. *Portraits of Labor Market Exclusion*. Report 91883, World Bank, Human Development Unit, Europe and Central Asia.

———. Forthcoming. *Results from BLISS*. Report, World Bank, Washington, DC.

CHAPTER 4

Improving Living Conditions to Grow, Learn, Participate, and Earn

Kosuke Anan, with input from Carmen de Paz Nieves and
Paula Restrepo

Summary

Access to adequate living conditions is critical to attaining equality of opportunities for marginalized Roma in Central and Eastern Europe (CEE). Lack of access to basic infrastructure, connectivity to social services, and markets hamper one's opportunity to grow, learn, stay healthy, be productive, and take part in social and economic life. The majority of Roma in the five new member CEE countries studied, however, continue to live in very poor conditions (figure 4.1 presents some of the most salient facts about living conditions for Roma in marginalized communities). A significantly larger proportion of Roma—between 32 percent of Roma in the Slovak Republic and 17 percent in the Czech Republic, as opposed to 3 and 5 percent of non-Roma, respectively—live in dilapidated houses or slums. In addition, as much as 72 percent and 83 percent of Roma households in Romania do not have access to improved water sources and sanitation, respectively.

The level of formality (that is, whether property and land documents exist), segregation, and settlement history influence the diverse characteristics of Roma's living conditions, and the challenges associated with these. Common features of disadvantaged Roma communities include: (a) low-quality urban blocks of flats or former workers' colonies; (b) urban slum areas; (c) modernized urban social housing; (d) dilapidated urban buildings in historical city areas; (e) rural and periurban informal settlements; and (f) traditional rural settlements. These communities generally face challenges in meeting a combination of the following needs: (a) access to basic community services; (b) safe location; (c) accessible and well-connected communities; (d) access to adequate housing; (e) spatial integration; and (f) tenure security.

The wide diversity of Roma communities requires tailored solutions to respond to the unique combination of gaps each community faces. The selection of interventions should be based on an adequate assessment of the community's specific needs and with the active involvement of the community.

Funding should be made available on a flexible and customizable basis, instead of prescribing one-size-fits-all solutions across a country or region. Interventions often require activities to be integrated, and these should address both supply- and demand-side bottlenecks (both service providers' and users' bottlenecks) in order to ensure sustainability. For example, improving physical housing conditions, basic infrastructure, and services (community roads, sewerage, wastewater treatment plants, water, electricity, community centers, schools, clinics, and so on) needs to be complemented by other activities that help overcome some of the key barriers faced by marginalized Roma. These include investing in (a) service users' awareness and capacity; (b) affordability of services; (c) maintenance and operation capacity; (d) costs associated with accessing the services; (e) eligibility to access the services (such as through civil documentation); (f) social integration (combatting discrimination and distrust); and (g) facilitating civil documentation.

Figure 4.1 Notable Facts about Living Conditions among Roma

Over 80% of rural Roma households in Bulgaria lack access to improved sanitation.

About a quarter of Roma in the Czech Republic live more than 1 kilometer from the nearest bus stop.

Over 50% of Roma who live in rural, predominantly Roma neighborhoods in Hungary lack access to improved sanitation.

Between 72% and 85% of Roma households in Romania do not have access to improved water sources and sanitation, respectively.

In the Slovak Republic, 30% of Roma live in low/poor quality housing.

Source: UNDP, World Bank and EC 2011.

Adequate Living Conditions Matter for Equality of Opportunity

Access to adequate living conditions is critical if Roma children in CEE are to attain equality of opportunity. Lack of access to basic infrastructure (such as running water, electricity, sewerage, or septic tanks), connectivity to social services (such as schools and health care) and markets (including job markets) can all hamper a child's opportunity to grow, learn, stay healthy, be productive, and take part in social and economic life later on. Lack of access often takes the form of inadequate transportation and roads; lack of protection from hazards and violence; and inadequate housing conditions. Living conditions, therefore, not only determine the prospects of the adult Roma population, but also and particularly those of future generations.

Lack of access to clean water and sanitation can have important repercussions on health, especially for children who may be more susceptible to suffering from infectious diseases, such as diarrhea. For example, persistent diarrhea leads to malnutrition, which can permanently reduce a child's lifelong cognitive development and also has detrimental effects on the ability to learn and be productive in adult life. Water that is contaminated with arsenic, lead, and other hazardous chemicals (such as pesticides and herbicides) can also have irreversible effects on a child's health and development. The inability of a child to regularly attend preschool or school due to illness, along with commuting challenges and safety concerns, undermines opportunities to receive education.

Lack of adequate housing that is quiet, sufficiently lit, and protected from extreme temperatures can also obstruct a child's ability to study, thus impeding her learning achievements. Indeed, gaps in living conditions likely undermine Roma children's chances to grow up in a healthy environment, which in turn will negatively affect education outcomes (see box 4.1). The persistence of these gaps not only bears significant individual costs, but social ones, too. The observed health-related vulnerabilities for marginalized Roma and gaps in outcomes vis-à-vis the non-Roma partly reflect the poorer living conditions among the former.[1]

The interaction between access to adequate housing and progress in schooling, good health and access to jobs has long been recognized, including in the European Union (EU) Framework for National Roma Integration Strategies, which identifies these as four critical areas for achieving the social inclusion of marginalized Roma. This chapter, which mainly covers housing and basic infrastructure, argues that adequate living conditions are vital to improving marginalized Roma's access to employment, education, and good health.

This chapter presents the key types of communities in which marginalized Roma live, and offers an analysis of living conditions in those communities. It then presents options for addressing the gaps and discusses measures to increase the interventions' effectiveness and sustainability.

Box 4.1 Implications of Living Conditions for Health and Education Outcomes

There is growing consensus that people's physical environment has important implications for development outcomes, such as health or education. This is particularly the case for children, as families and residences modulate their behavior and access to experiences and opportunities more strongly (Boardman 2004; Bronfenbrenner and Morris 1998; Capon 2007; Gephart 1997; Lavin et al. 2006; and New South Wales Department of Health 2009).

The home in which they live appears to have a significant impact on children's health status and educational attainment. Overcrowding, for example, has been linked with psychological problems or worsening academic achievement regardless of a family's socioeconomic status (Evans and Saegert 2001; Solari and Mare 2012). This can have effects that may persist throughout life, affecting future opportunities and well-being (Breysse et al. 2004; Solari and Mare 2012). Improvements to housing conditions, such as replacing dirt floors with cement ones, is found to not only significantly improve residents' health conditions (particularly by reducing diarrhea, anemia, and parasitic infestations) but to also significantly reduce depression and perceived stress (Cattaneo et al. 2009).

Living in extremely poor neighborhoods or with deteriorating physical features can also have a negative effect on health outcomes and general well-being—as measured by mortality, child and adult physical and mental health—and on health behaviors, mainly through reductions in physical activity, increased anxiety, and social disorders (CABE Space 2005; Ellaway, Macintyre, and Bonnefoy 2005; Ellen and Turner 2003; Ellen, Mijanovich, and Dillman 2001; Kawachi and Berkman 2003; Macintyre, Ellaway, and Cummins 2002; Macintyre and Ellaway 2003a, 2003b; Semenza 2003; Weich et al. 2002).

People who live in the most deprived areas of the United Kingdom and the United States, for example, are found to have the highest illness rates, and are more likely to report depression and show a higher incidence of coronary heart disease (Berry 2007; Boyle, Norman, and Rees 2004; Roux Diez et al. 2001). Mixed-income neighborhoods, in turn, are linked to health benefits for disadvantaged groups (Lund 2002; Dekker and Bolt 2004).

Children who live in "unsafe" or socioeconomically disadvantaged neighborhoods may be exposed to greater risks of developing mental and behavioral problems, including hyperactivity, aggression, or withdrawal, and adolescents may be more likely to use drugs, engage in delinquent behavior, or become pregnant (Brooks-Gunn et al. 1997a, 1997b; Flournoy and Yen 2004; Jencks and Meyer 1990; Leventhal and Brooks-Gunn 2000, 2003).

In addition, school readiness, high school graduation rates, educational achievement, and even later annual earnings tend to be higher in socioeconomically advantaged neighborhoods (Brooks-Gunn et al. 1993; Clark 1992; Connell and Halpern-Felsher 1997; Ensminger, Lamkin, and Jacobson 1996; Galster et al. 2007).

The Majority of Roma Currently Lives in Poor Conditions

While not all Roma are poor or marginalized, the majority in new member CEE countries live in poor conditions. At the same time, not all marginalized Roma face similar challenges or share the same gaps. Conditions are different in urban and rural areas, and the level of formality (that is, whether property and land documents exist), segregation, and the history of a settlement, influence the nature and characteristics of the challenges marginalized Roma face.

While not exhaustive, and acknowledging that the exact circumstances and conditions may vary across countries and settlements, box 4.2 lists some of the common typologies of communities in which marginalized Roma generally live in CEE countries.

These different typologies of disadvantaged communities share similar challenges, which can generally be classified into the following seven common categories: (a) lack of access to basic community services; (b) unsafe neighborhoods;

Box 4.2 Key Common Types of Disadvantaged and Marginalized Communities[a]

Low-quality urban blocks of flats or former workers' colonies

These low-quality housing facilities were built during the socialist regime for the workers of large enterprises. Most often, these buildings are concentrated in one or two low-quality blocks of flats. Main problems include massive overcrowding, which puts serious pressure on the block installations, and overdue payments for basic services (electricity, water, sewerage, and garbage collection). Usually these apartments include only one small room that is overcrowded by a large family. Common spaces and installations—for example, electricity, sewerage, water, and so forth—are often damaged. Utility supply infrastructure tends to be limited. In some cases, a hydrant may be the single source of water for the whole neighborhood.

Urban slum areas

These slum areas are often found in old neighborhoods at the outskirts of towns and cities with very poor communities that include Roma and non-Roma. These have grown larger since 1990. In addition to low-quality housing, many additional improvised shelters have been put together over time, either in the courtyards of the old houses or on public areas. These shelters are typically made of plastic and paperboard, with some wooden framing. Houses and shelters are very small, but accommodate large families with many children. Not all urban slums consist of such old neighborhoods. Some were developed in the early 1990s by locals who lost their apartments because of overdue debts to utility providers. Some slums have virtually no infrastructure; others, for example, have just one tap that supplies water for the entire area. In other areas, the infrastructure is developed along the main street but is not available in the rest of the area (not even electricity). As a result, many such areas are unsanitary and highly exposed to natural hazards such as heavy rain or flooding. Informality (lack of property and land documents) is common, and slum residents claim they are highly exposed to the discretionary actions of powerful gang leaders in the area. While some slums can be peaceful and quiet, particularly in the old neighborhoods, others can be unsafe.

box continues next page

Box 4.2 Key Common Types of Disadvantaged and Marginalized Communities[a] *(continued)*

Modernized urban social housing

Modern social housing units were often developed through integrated projects, which combined large investments in new buildings with infrastructure and a series of social interventions. Areas of modernized social housing are well endowed with infrastructure and utility services (sometimes better than the rest of the urban areas) but accommodate poor people in difficult social situations that are eligible for these houses. Paying for utilities remains a considerable challenge for many poor residents. The monthly bill for just one utility (usually electricity) is often larger than a family's income, and the situation is unsustainable for many residents who cannot afford to live and maintain the house. Modernized social housing can also deepen segregation when it is located outside of the city, away from where the residents have lived and grown up. It is also often exposed to many natural hazards.

Low/poor quality urban buildings in historical city areas

Old individual houses in some historical city areas were nationalized and assigned to families during the socialist period. Homeless people also illegally occupied some after 1990, especially those in a very poor condition. These are old neighborhoods where inhabitants have lived for more than 30 years. Except for the fact that these communities are located in urban central areas, to a large extent their living conditions resemble those in the slum areas. Because the location of such houses is highly attractive for investors and the houses have high market potential, the former owners (or their inheritors) or local authorities often try to recuperate these properties, sometimes by evicting the occupants. Some people are allowed to stay in ruined buildings but are not given documents that identify them as tenants of that address, given that the building was administratively registered as "destroyed." This means that the resident cannot get a job and has no right to medical care or social benefits.

Rural and periurban informal settlements

Informal settlements in rural and periurban areas usually constitute relatively smaller communities of 20–30 households. These informal settlements have often grown out of traditional settlements in the nearby public land, with the formation and growth of new families. The houses typically have one to two rooms and are of relatively poor structural quality, made with adobe, wood, and tin sheets. Sanitation is extremely poor; many households might share a single pit latrine. Similarly, there might be a shared well for water. Younger and larger families usually occupy these areas. Typically, young adults are unemployed and live on informal economy activities (such as metal/garbage collection) or work as day laborers. These settlements could be very isolated and have limited access to social services and markets.

Traditional rural settlements

There are old settlements in rural areas where Roma families have lived for decades, and sometimes over generations. Generally, houses located in these rural traditional settlements are of relatively decent quality, but some are of low/poor quality. Infrastructure (water, sanitation, electricity) in these settlements may be minimal or nonexistent. During the socialist regime, residents were mainly employed by local cooperatives or national enterprises in

box continues next page

Being Fair, Faring Better • http://dx.doi.org/10.1596/978-1-4648-0598-1

Box 4.2   Key Common Types of Disadvantaged and Marginalized Communities *(continued)*

nearby towns, many of which disappeared after 1990. Access to the job market is limited in many of these settlements, and many families practice semi-subsistence agriculture. Limited income typically comes from the informal economy in a nearby town, day labor in the agriculture sector, and social assistance.

a. These typologies largely draw on the types of disadvantaged and marginalized areas identified through qualitative research conducted for the 2014 Atlas of Urban Marginalized Areas in Romania and for the housing chapter of the 2014 Diagnostics and Policy Advice for Supporting Roma Inclusion in Romania. The study defined "disadvantaged areas" as those that have disadvantages in one or two dimensions of human capital, employment, or living conditions. The areas that have gaps in all three dimensions are defined as "marginalized." It was also informed by "A Review of 36 Projects Improving Roma Living Conditions in Bulgaria, the Czech Republic, France, Hungary, Italy, Romania, Slovakia, Spain, and the United Kingdom" (World Bank 2014d).

Table 4.1   Common Needs of Disadvantaged and Marginalized Communities[a]

Type of disadvantaged/marginalized community	Main common needs faced by residents
Low-quality urban blocks of flats or former workers' colonies	Access to basic community services
	Access to adequate housing
Urban slum areas	Access to basic community services
	Safe location
	Access to adequate housing
	Spatial integration
	Tenure security
Modernized urban social housing	Accessible and well-connected communities
	Spatial integration
Low/poor quality urban buildings in historical city areas	Access to adequate housing
	Tenure security
Rural and periurban informal settlements	Access to basic community services
	Accessible and well-connected communities
	Access to adequate housing
	Spatial integration
	Tenure security
Traditional rural settlements	Access to basic community services
	Accessible and well-connected communities
	Spatial integration

a. Residents may face needs not listed for the type of their community.

(c) limited accessibility; (d) inadequate housing; (e) spatial segregation; and (f) lack of tenure security. Table 4.1 summarizes them.

The Regional Roma Survey (RRS) data do not allow disaggregating the Roma population according to the above typology in each country. The RRS data, among others, lacks adequate and objective information about the formality of tenure, population density, housing conditions, and accessibility to social infrastructure. In the future, it could be valuable for governments to collect such data, which would allow (a) estimating the size of the population in each type of disadvantaged community and (b) further analyzing the relationship between the type of disadvantaged community (or its attributes) and the type and level of vulnerability and well-being experienced by its residents.

Limited Access to Basic Community Services

Roma households across CEE countries generally have lower access to basic services compared to their non-Roma neighbors, as shown in figure 4.2. Limited access is linked to a variety of factors, including the informality of Roma settlements, discrimination, overdue utility payments accrued by former tenants, or lack of financial resources for installing and maintaining amenities. These factors can interact in different ways depending on context. For example, an entire block of flats might have its electricity cut off from time to time due to historical debt, or due to nonpayment by some residents (see World Bank 2014c).

There is a high variation across the five countries in basic service coverage. This reflects in part their different levels of development, how broad coverage is nationwide (the scale effect in the HOI terminology used in chapter 1), and how skewed this coverage is across different groups (Roma/non-Roma; rural/urban—the dissimilarity effect in the HOI terminology). In Romania, as much as 72 percent and 85 percent of Roma households do not have access to improved water sources[2] and sanitation,[3] respectively. This likely has significant effects on their health, income, and education, as it implies the additional burden of collecting water. While a large share of non-Roma neighbors in Romania also lack access to improved water sources and sanitation, even compared to Roma in other countries, the gap between Roma and non-Roma is still considerably wide in Romania and warrants attention. In Bulgaria, instead, while 95 percent of Roma have access to improved water, more than three-quarters (77 percent) do not have access to improved sanitation. In the Slovak Republic, approximately two-thirds of Roma

Figure 4.2 Roma versus Non-Roma Access to Water Source and Improved Sanitation

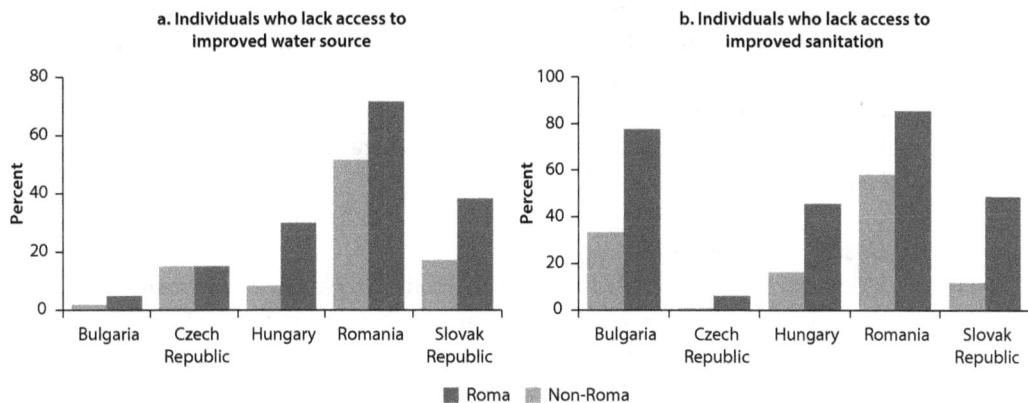

a. Individuals who lack access to improved water source

b. Individuals who lack access to improved sanitation

Roma   Non-Roma

Source: UNDP, World Bank, and EC 2011.
Note: "Improved sanitation" is defined as having a toilet and a shower or bathroom inside the dwelling.

Figure 4.3 Rural versus Urban Roma Access to Improved Water Source and Sanitation

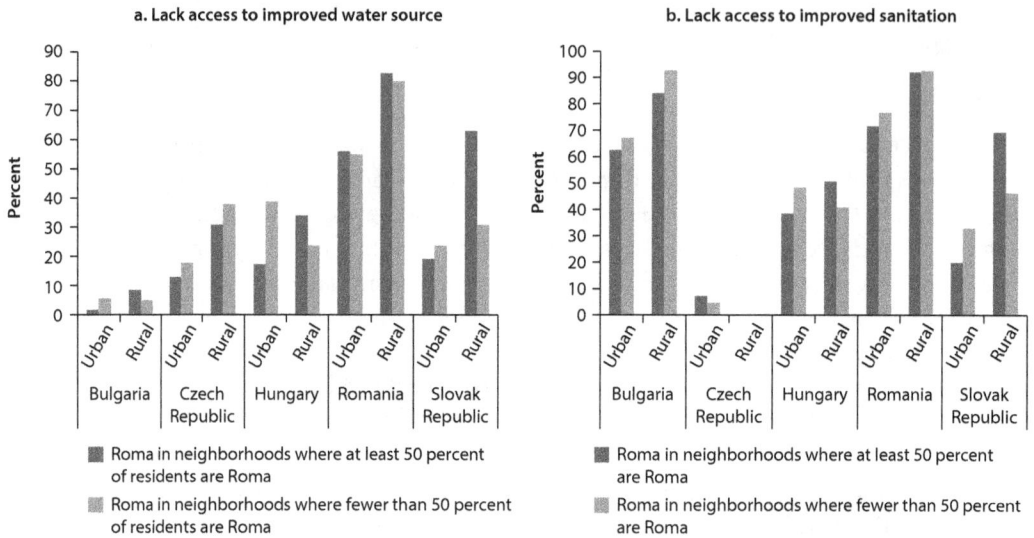

a. Lack access to improved water source

b. Lack access to improved sanitation

Roma in neighborhoods where at least 50 percent of residents are Roma

Roma in neighborhoods where fewer than 50 percent of residents are Roma

Roma in neighborhoods where at least 50 percent are Roma

Roma in neighborhoods where fewer than 50 percent are Roma

Source: UNDP, World Bank, and EC 2011.

from rural areas who live in Roma-predominant neighborhoods[4] do not have access to an improved water source or improved sanitation (figure 4.3).

According to the RRS, irregular or no collection of solid waste is also a problem for a large share (between one-fifth and above one-third) of Roma families in Romania, Bulgaria, and the Slovak Republic, especially in segregated areas. Finally, the majority of Roma households report using wood as the main source of energy for cooking in Bulgaria, the Slovak Republic, and Romania.

The share of Roma people who use wood as their main source of heating is even higher in Hungary. In general, a large share of the population in the five countries spends a considerable proportion of their household expenditure on heating, and many Roma appear to suffer from high heating costs. Close to 90 percent of Roma in Hungary restrict themselves when heating their dwelling, and 58 percent of Roma do so in the Czech Republic. While more research is needed, it is likely that energy poverty is a relevant dimension for marginalized Roma households, especially in countries where temperatures drop during the winter.

Unsafe Neighborhood

Many communities in which marginalized Roma live have safety issues. Violence, the risk of natural disasters, the presence of hazardous materials, and/or lack of clean and safe public spaces often prevent community members from accessing adequate housing, employment, education, or health services. Impoverished urban neighborhoods are often characterized by high crime rates, and informal settlements are especially prone to organized crimes associated with prostitution, drug dealing, and petty crime, as in most urban slums. Some communities—those that grew without formal planning or as the result of people occupying abandoned settlements or structures—are located in disaster-prone areas (landslides, floods) or areas exposed to manmade hazards (such as toxic waste). All of these safety risks hamper the ability of residents to take part in social and economic life, and can have irreversible impacts on children's development. In Bulgaria, for example, safety concerns lead both girls and boys to drop out of school early, especially in urban areas (such as Sheker Mahala), where the fear of ethnicity-motivated violence is strong (World Bank 2014a).

Limited Accessibility

It is a challenge for many Roma communities to reach markets, centers of employment, and social amenities. Limited accessibility is often due to poor access roads or pathways, poor connection to public transportation, and/or unreliable public transit. Between about a quarter and a third of Roma live more than 1 kilometer away from the nearest bus stop, while about half of Roma live more than 10 kilometers from the nearest city centers in the five countries studied (except for the Czech Republic, where 98 percent of surveyed Roma live in urban areas) (see figure 4.4). While the distance from public transportation and the nearest city is not an adequate indicator for measuring communities' connectivity, it can be used as a proxy. In Bulgaria, a greater share of Roma in Roma-predominant neighborhoods live away from the nearest bus stop, compared to Roma in non-Roma predominant neighborhoods, while the opposite is true for Hungary (see figure 4.5). In the Czech Republic, although the majority of Roma live in urban areas, about a quarter live more than 1 kilometer from the nearest bus stop. More than 60 percent of Roma from the rural areas of Bulgaria, Hungary, Romania, and the Slovak Republic live more than 10 kilometers from the nearest city center.

Figure 4.4 Roma Limited Access to Urban Opportunities Measured by Proximity to Bus Stops and City Centers

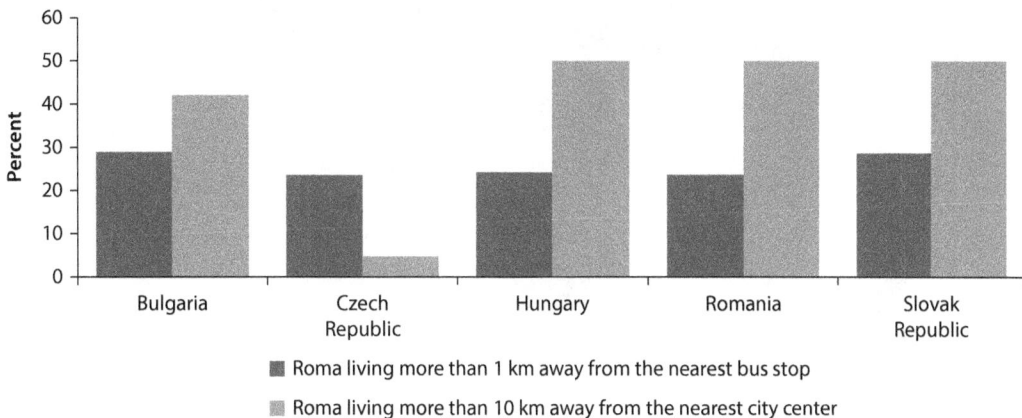

Source: UNDP, World Bank, and EC 2011.

Figure 4.5 Urban versus Rural Roma Disparities in Connectivity Measured by Proximity to Transportation Hubs and City Centers

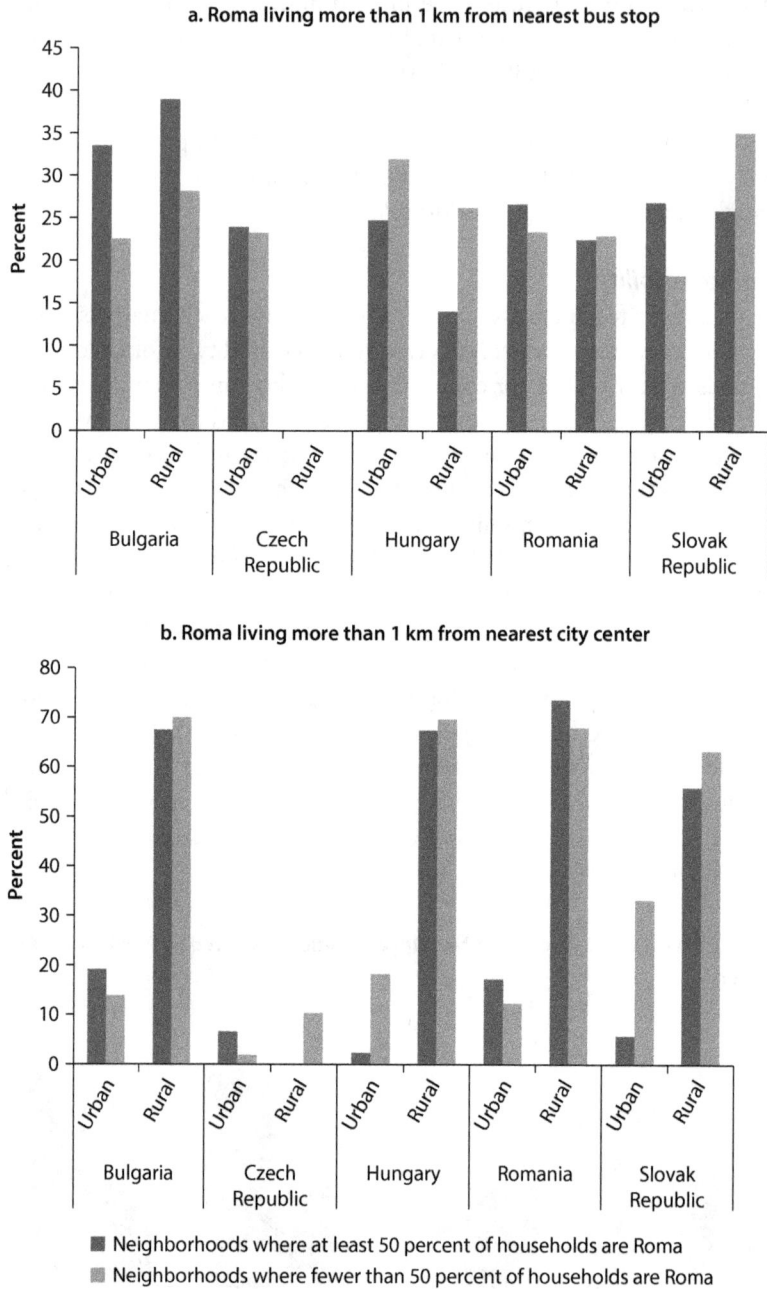

a. Roma living more than 1 km from nearest bus stop

b. Roma living more than 1 km from nearest city center

■ Neighborhoods where at least 50 percent of households are Roma
■ Neighborhoods where fewer than 50 percent of households are Roma

Source: UNDP, World Bank, and EC 2011.

Long commutes appear to discourage marginalized Roma students from attending secondary school, especially during winter. The following quote by a Roma boy from Vesselinovo, Bulgaria, also illustrates how connectivity affects schooling: "When I don't have money for the bus, I get on my bike and I go to town because I don't want to interrupt my schooling. My mother is worried that I may get hit by a car. It is better when we have money because I get on the bus, and it takes me there. But you have to have 5 leva every day for that. If the bike breaks, that's it with the school" (World Bank 2014a, p. 49). As discussed in the employment chapter, distance from centers of employment and transport costs add to the challenge of finding jobs for many Roma, especially when these are low paying.

Lack of Access to Adequate Housing

There is a need for adequate housing when units are either overcrowded,[5] dilapidated, not structurally safe, or not well insulated or ventilated, among other problems. As shown in figure 4.6, a significantly larger proportion of Roma— between 30 percent in the Slovak Republic and 35 percent in Hungary, as opposed to 5 and 11 percent of their non-Roma neighbors, respectively—live in low/poor quality housing.[6]

Overcrowding tends to be more common in urban areas, which—in addition to historical city areas and informal settlements in rural and periurban areas—commonly feature low/poor quality housing conditions. In Bulgaria, Romania, and the Slovak Republic, the share of Roma who live in low/poor quality housing is higher in rural areas compared to urban ones, while the opposite is true in Hungary (see figure 4.6). In Romania, low incomes and the inability to afford or access decent quality market-based housing[7] relegate many Roma to living in overcrowded conditions, slums, old and poorly maintained multistory housing (which was formerly workers' housing during the Communist period), or social housing units that have inadequate infrastructure.[8] Some two-thirds of Roma households surveyed in Romania live in dwellings

Figure 4.6 Roma versus Non-Roma Residing in Low- or Poor-Quality Housing

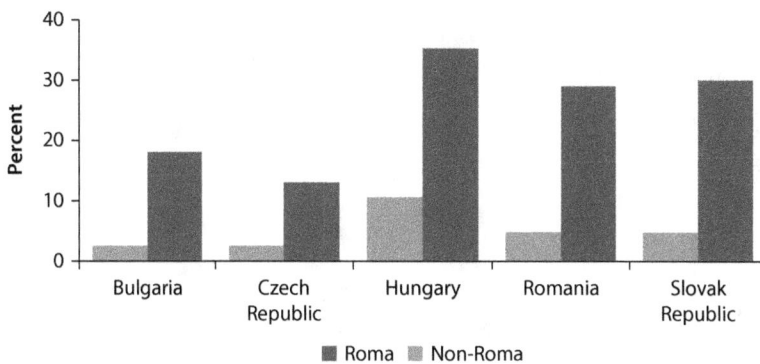

Source: UNDP, World Bank, and EC 2011.

with more than two people per room; while only about a quarter of nearby non-Roma households experience this level of overcrowding (UNDP, World Bank, and EC 2011).

Spatial Segregation

Spatial or residential segregation[9] often perpetuates marginalization by creating disadvantages, such as inferior access to basic infrastructure, social services (including education), and economic opportunities. While not an accurate measure of spatial segregation, figure 4.7 shows the percentage of Roma in the five CEE countries who live in neighborhoods where the dominant ethnicity is Roma, as a measure of Roma concentration in certain neighborhoods. More than half of Roma live in Roma-predominant neighborhoods in the Czech Republic, Romania, and the Slovak Republic, and even in Bulgaria, where the share is smallest, close to a third of Roma live in Roma-predominant neighborhoods. Spatial segregation is highly correlated with early school-leaving, low labor market participation rates, and costly access to other services (public transport, health facilities, and so on). The persistence of this phenomenon, however, does not seem to be voluntary; a majority of the surveyed Roma—between 68 percent in Bulgaria and 84 percent in Hungary—expressed a preference to live in a mixed neighborhood.

Spatially segregated neighborhoods often continue to expand as new generations of young adults who cannot find opportunities to participate in social and economic life outside the neighborhood stay in the community and start families. Segregation thus tends to be passed from one generation to the next. Some projects aimed at improving Roma living conditions can also lead to further segregation. For example, projects that resettle Roma families from informal settlements in precarious conditions to areas with a new social housing complex built to exclusively accommodate Roma families could improve their housing, but might result in further concentration and physical isolation

Figure 4.7 Roma Residing in Roma-Predominant Neighborhoods

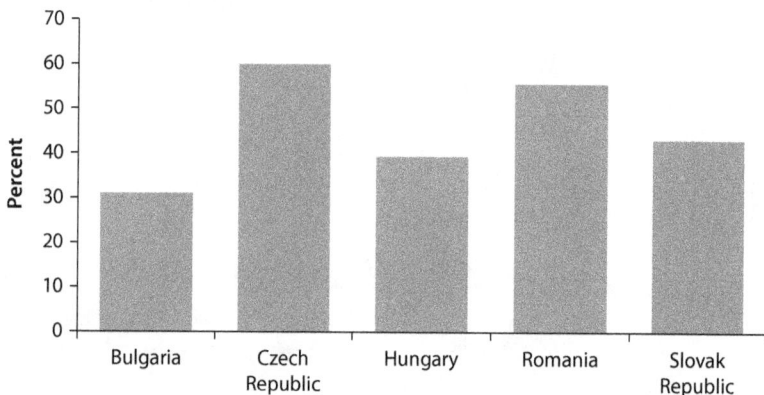

Source: UNDP, World Bank, and EC 2011.

from the rest of society. In this context, it is also important to note that in-situ social housing interventions in segregated areas, especially those that involve the construction of additional (social) housing blocks, could also reinforce spatial segregation.

Tenure Security

A large share of Europe's Roma population lives in informal settlements. The law does not formally recognize their rights regarding land, housing structures, and physical improvements made to these settlements. While precise data does not exist, the National Agency for Cadaster and Land Registration (Agentia Nationala de Cadastru si Publicitate Imobiliara, or ANCPI) of Romania estimates that in the 50 rural administrative-territorial units where systematic land registration was planned under a project supported by the World Bank, about two-thirds of Roma households had no property documents for the land and buildings they possessed.[10] Such informality contributes to and perpetuates marginalization because it may deny access to basic infrastructure, social services, and credit; generates uncertainty about property rights; and curtails economic opportunities.

One further disadvantage of informality is the possibility of eviction. It also creates difficulties for accessing social protection benefits, which are often accessed by place of legal residency, creating additional vulnerabilities for Roma women and children as they lack access to legal protection and social services in the case of separation or abandonment. In addition, even when basic infrastructure (for example, water and sanitation, electricity) and social services (education and health care) are available in the neighborhoods, if Roma do not have formal property rights they might not be able to access these services. In the Slovak Republic, for example, families who lack formal tenure (lease/ownership) are not eligible to receive housing allowances. Although data about tenure status are not available, in 2004 about one-third of Roma households in separated/segregated communities in the Slovak Republic occupied dwellings built without proper planning permissions (that is, informal), and were not eligible for a housing allowance (Staniewicz 2009).

Dealing with the Heterogeneity of Roma Communities and Needs

Options for Improving Roma's Living Conditions

The wide diversity of Roma communities requires needs assessments and tailored solutions to respond effectively to the different gaps they face. The selection of such interventions should be based on an adequate assessment of the community's specific needs, and its active involvement (see table 4.2). Funding should be made available on a flexible and customizable basis, instead of prescribing one-size-fits-all solutions across a country or a region. While common overall objectives and strategies can be shared, each community should be given flexibility regarding how to pursue them. Uniformly applying specific types of investments risks making interventions less relevant and not cost-effective.

Table 4.2 Options for Potential Interventions to Address Poor Living Conditions among Roma

Needs	Intervention options	Variants/activities
Physical/spatial needs		
Access to basic community services	Neighborhood upgrading	Rural/semirural neighborhood upgrading (expanding basic services to neighborhoods—investing in decentralized sanitation systems, electricity, and improvement of water supply networks and/or expanding solid waste collection using community collection points)
		Urban neighborhood upgrading (expanding basic services through centralized solutions—existing municipal services are expanded to cover the neighborhood)
Safe location	Public safety programs for crime and violence prevention	Basic services and simple environmental design interventions such as street lighting, public telephones, and improved street layout
		Community crime mapping and diagnostics
		Situational prevention interventions using Crime Prevention through Environmental Design principles
		Mediation and conflict resolution programs that serve to build confidence among rivals and establish community codes of conducts, among others
		Social prevention programs that address the causes of crime and violence (these can include long-term parenting skills programs and early childhood education programs and cultural programs; job training programs with at-risk adolescents, before and afterschool programs, programs to prevent domestic and gender-based violence, and educational programs in conflict resolution)
	Resettlement and livelihood restoration	Relocating households to safe areas and/or transforming some of these to other uses—such as linear parks—to avoid households from returning or other households from settling in (providing housing and basic services after relocation may be pursued through the activities presented for addressing adequate housing and access to basic community needs mentioned above)
		Livelihood restoration (skills training, employment service, life skills training)
Accessible and well-connected communities	Improving neighborhood connectivity and social infrastructure upgrading	Rehabilitating access roads
		Improvements in the coverage and reliability of public transportation
		Construction, rehabilitation, extension, or improvement of permanent social infrastructure (such as schools, health care facilities, community centers)
		Upgrading equipment for mobile social service units (such as mobile health units)
Spatial integration	Desegregation	Additional rental housing in mixed-income neighborhoods
		Subsidized rentals (and rental allowances) in mixed-income neighborhoods
		Disadvantaged/marginalized communities can also be integrated through improved neighborhood connectivity (see above)
Adequate housing	Housing improvements	Improving existing housing structures
		Technical assistance to improve or expand housing
		Financial/material assistance to improve or expand housing
	Additional housing	Increasing housing supply
		Incremental housing

table continues next page

Table 4.2 Options for Potential Interventions to Address Poor Living Conditions among Roma *(continued)*

Needs	Intervention options	Variants/activities
		Assisted self-construction
		Municipal property management
		New housing construction
		Housing construction (public housing)
		Making existing housing units available to the community—brokering supply and demand
		Subsidized rental housing
		Densification through social housing schemes
		Increasing housing supply
		Additional rental housing
		Subsidized rentals
Nonphysical/ immaterial needs		
Tenure security	Land regularization/ titling registration schemes	Inventories of land ownership
		Developing information campaigns and mechanisms for public consultation
		Formal verification of field, legal, and administrative procedures for transfer
		Extensive public communication to ensure benefits and costs of titling are well understood
		Titling program
		Land surveys
		Register and cadaster searches
		Verifying occupancy information and providing technical assistance to eligible beneficiaries

It is also important to target poor and/or marginalized Roma, rather than Roma in general, so that the interventions reach the maximum number of poor and marginalized who experience social exclusion and poor living conditions. In the past, a number of projects, particularly those on social housing, sometimes targeted relatively better off Roma, those who could afford rent and utilities. Such initiatives are likely to leave behind the most disadvantaged Roma and could further marginalize them. In targeting poor and marginalized Roma, following the principle of "explicit but not exclusive targeting" would ensure that non-Roma who face similar disadvantages as Roma will not be excluded from the interventions. These targeting principles not only ensure that interventions reach the groups that need them the most, but also prevents generating negative perceptions about the interventions, which could stigmatize Roma as unfair beneficiaries of public resources.[11] It is important to remember, however, that interventions that target marginalized areas, instead of marginalized groups, may only partially reach vulnerable people. For example, when a small settlement of Roma families is located in a generally nonmarginalized area, the settlement may not be targeted (see the Romanian example in the discussion in annex 4 Spotlight on Targeting).

Being Fair, Faring Better • http://dx.doi.org/10.1596/978-1-4648-0598-1

Promoting Access to Basic Community Services

Interventions aimed at neighborhood upgrading are required when Roma lack adequate access to basic services and/or public spaces, some of which are essential to guarantee a basic level of dignitous living. In rural/semi-rural neighborhoods with low density, investments could be made that involve decentralized sanitation systems, electricity, and improved water supply networks, and/or expanded solid waste collection using community collection points. Decentralized sanitation solutions have sometimes been applied and can involve improved pit latrines or septic tanks. In urban neighborhoods, centralized solutions—in which existing municipal services are expanded to cover the neighborhood—are generally used.

One of the most common potentially adverse consequences of neighborhood upgrading is gentrification, which can push marginalized people who live in those areas, including Roma, further out to more marginalized areas. Gentrification can especially occur when projects that involve marginalized groups are located in prime real estate (inner cities). Gentrification is not a negative outcome per se; it must only be regarded as such in this context when it renders interventions aimed at marginalized populations ineffective, often further heightening their vulnerability. As evidenced by the experiences summarized in box 4.3, gentrification's negative consequences can be addressed by taking people-focused measures to ensure that existing populations benefit from the interventions.

Safe Location

Different programs are available to address exposure to violence, natural disasters, and manmade hazards. Public safety programs could be implemented in communities with high crime rates and public safety threats (such as thefts, assaults, extortions, gender-based violence, and so on). International experience has shown that urban upgrading, which improves physical living conditions in poor neighborhoods, can also reduce crime and violence levels. Basic services and simple environmental design interventions such as street lighting, public telephones, closed-circuit televisions, and improved street layout can create safer urban spaces and enhance community integration.

These types of interventions can include (a) community crime mapping and diagnostics; (b) situational prevention interventions using Crime Prevention through Environmental Design (CPTED) principles; and (c) mediation and conflict resolution programs, which serve to build confidence among rivals and establish community codes of conducts, among others. These could be complemented by social prevention programs that address the causes of crime and violence, including long-term parenting skills programs, early childhood education programs, and cultural programs, job training programs with at-risk adolescents, before and afterschool programs, and educational programs in conflict resolution (an example is provided in box 4.4).

Projects should aim to mitigate the risks faced by communities that are located in disaster-prone areas (landslides, floods, earthquakes) or areas exposed to manmade hazards (environmental). In many cases, risk mitigation involves

Box 4.3 Addressing the Potential Negative Effects of Gentrification—Magdolna Neighborhood Social Urban Rehabilitation Project, Hungary[a]

The Magdolna neighborhood has been one of the most crowded and disadvantaged areas in Budapest. In 2007, close to 40 percent of 5,500 flats lacked a toilet, bath, or piped-in drinking water. About 60 percent of the population was estimated to be economically inactive. Public security has also been a great concern. About 30 percent of the population is Roma.

A series of measures have been implemented since 2005 to improve the neighborhood. The measures were introduced in three phases and financed by multiple sources, including the Municipality of Budapest and the European Regional Development Fund (co-funded by the state). A key innovation was to improve the existing population's living conditions, rather than just to physically remodel the neighborhood. This was important, since a failure to focus on people could have led to gentrification without benefitting the original residents.

In addition to renovating the housing stock, constructing a community center, and rehabilitating the main square, the project included the following people-focused activities:

- Organizing activities at the community center, including job search clubs, clubs for women, information technology training and access to the Internet, job fairs and exhibitions, summer camps for children, family therapies, and programs for talented children
- Special youth programs offered by street social workers
- Afterschool activities, teacher training, changes to curricula
- Vocational training designed for single mothers
- Crime prevention and public security activities
- Drug prevention programs

The local population participated in the design and implementation of the interventions, which improved their effectiveness and also contributed to increasing community members' cohesion.

Source: World Bank 2014d.
a. Unless otherwise noted, the discussion of results in the initiative presented in this chapter is not based on experimental or quasi-experimental methods. Hence, inferences about the causal impact of the interventions are not in principle warranted.

Box 4.4 Basic Urban Infrastructure Project with Public Safety Measures—Barrio Ciudad Urban Project, Honduras

This case study provides an example of how crime and violence prevention can be mainstreamed through urban design. The Barrio Ciudad Urban Project merged urban upgrading with public safety activities using a participatory approach at the community level.

At the time the Barrio Ciudad Project was being prepared, Honduras was experiencing one of the highest urbanization rates in Latin America, and also experiencing high homicide rates, which doubled between 2005 and 2010. Gang violence was common, with youth and

box continues next page

Box 4.4 Basic Urban Infrastructure Project with Public Safety Measures—Barrio Ciudad Urban Project, Honduras *(continued)*

the poor representing a disproportionate number of victims. In destitute conditions, gang membership often provided a sense of belonging and was an easy way for youth to make a living.

The project's activities developed under the Crime and Violence Prevention window include: (a) participatory creation of insecurity maps, with communities informing project design; (b) mobilizing communities, especially the youth, around violence prevention activities; and (c) improvement of selected public spaces associated with crime and violence. Under the capacity-building component, the project included activities such as vocational training, environmental management, community development, and specific training to key community actors (teachers, leaders, policemen) to prevent crime and violence. Teachers and community leaders were trained in conflict resolution and prevention. This was complemented by a temporary employment generation program.

Initial results are very promising. In the first community, where all infrastructure works and social interventions have been delivered, 85 percent of community residents reported feeling safe in their neighborhoods and 76 percent feel safe in their own homes (compared to 51 percent before). Results from the impact evaluation are expected to provide more evidence on the project's causal effects.

Source: World Bank 2014b.

---

relocating households to safe areas and/or transforming some of these areas to other uses—such as linear parks—to avoid households from returning or other households from settling in. However, relocating communities can disrupt households' livelihoods and create income shocks that can be hard for vulnerable groups to absorb. For this reason, relocation must be planned carefully to preserve or improve livelihoods.

Accessible and Well-Connected Communities

Connectivity to existing markets and social services could be improved for communities that have trouble reaching existing markets, centers of employment, and social amenities. Projects that rehabilitate access roads and/or improve the coverage and reliability of public transportation can be used to improve connectivity, but they should also take into account the community's mobility patterns so as to respond to their specific needs (an example is provided in box 4.5).

Furthermore, international experiences have shown that in addition to roads or distance, travel spaces matter. For example, Roma may face challenges in travelling through hostile communities. With regard to public transport, factors such as frequency, routes, perceived level of accessibility, and discrimination by drivers also affect connectivity.

While improving connectivity to existing markets and social amenities is important, on some occasions there is a need to extend markets and social

Box 4.5 Intervention for Increasing Connectivity—Integrated Urban Projects, Medellin, Colombia

Integrated Urban Projects (IUPs) were introduced in 2004 with the objective of providing equal opportunities to the residents of marginalized settlements in the city of Medellin, through a comprehensive approach that engaged different sectors and is based on three main pillars: (a) institutional coordination of policies and services; (b) community participation across the project cycle—from preparation to implementation—and public communication; and (c) physical transformation. This kind of intervention has been developed in more than 51 vulnerable neighborhoods in Medellin, affecting around 800,000 people.

IUPs seek to improve the living conditions of communities in a specific territory and generally include the following sectors:

- Environment—such as constructing linear parks
- Mobility and connectivity—such as developing integrated transportation systems
- Housing—such as relocating families at risk of natural disasters and project-affected households
- Education, recreation, and sports—such as rehabilitating sport units, libraries, schools, and cultural centers
- Training and employment—such as creating Enterprise Development Centers and technical training
- Health and nutrition—such as rehabilitating or constructing new health centers
- Government and justice—such as installing Immediate Attention Centers and houses of justice

Findings from the first experience indicated important improvements to quality of life, and pointed to the key role played by on-site upgrading and adaptation of physical infrastructure to minimize the number of project-affected households, and hence overall project costs. IUPs are a valuable example of inclusion projects that aim to improve communities' overall living conditions by not only increasing connectivity, but also enhancing access to social services and improving skills and employment opportunities.

Source: World Bank 2014b.

amenities to reach vulnerable communities. In the case of social amenities, this can be done either through the development of temporary (such as mobile health units) or permanent infrastructure, depending on population density and the frequency required for service provision. When the required school, health service, or other social infrastructure is of low/poor quality or too small, or does not exist in the community at all, it can be built, rehabilitated, improved, or extended.

Space for providing such services can also be created as part of multiple-purpose community centers, where services related to employment, health, education, child care, and other counseling and recreational activities can be jointly provided.

Alternatively, equipment can be upgraded for mobile social service units. It is essential to ensure that such investments in social infrastructure and equipment are accompanied by sufficient capacity of service providers to operate it. In case a community is spatially segregated, neighborhood connectivity improvement (mentioned above), instead of infrastructure upgrading, may be a better option.

Adequate Housing

Inadequate housing conditions can first be addressed through housing improvements. When there is shortage of housing, or existing housing structures are considered beyond repair, projects can focus on creating new housing units and/or making existing housing units available to the Roma population. Supplying an additional stock of social housing for Roma who live in marginalized communities may cost more and reach fewer people than other options, considering not only the costs of construction or rehabilitation, but also the recurrent costs associated with rental and utility subsidies.[12] An example of a low-cost housing solution is provided in box 4.6.

Box 4.6 Customized, Low-Cost Housing Solution—Quinta Monroy, Iquique, Chile

The Quinta Monroy Project provided a low-cost housing solution for families at about US$7,500 per family, and avoided burdening households with debt.

One of the project's main innovations was the way in which housing was designed, allowing households to customize and incrementally improve their houses. Elemental, a nonprofit company, proposed a variation of the traditional row house; each unit had an empty space of equal size on the side to allow the dwelling to be expanded in the future. In addition, each unit was equipped with the basic minimum infrastructure. For example, it had plumbing but no fitting for the kitchen and bathroom, and households were expected to finish and customize their spaces at their own pace, depending on their preferences and what they could afford. The project also encouraged the development of common public spaces—instead of internal roads—to foster social interaction.

For the project's implementation, households were organized in neighborhood committees. Households were consulted on how they wished to customize their future dwellings and their preferences for location (such as occupying upper or lower floors).

In order to assure construction quality, a construction advisor provided technical guidance on how households should carry out their planned internal and external renovations. As a result of the project, 100 families were resettled in situ and received basic units that they could expand according to their preferences and budget. Although the project was completed in 2004, households continue to improve their houses incrementally by adding rooms, setting up shops in lower floors, and so on. Some households are renting out the extra space and earning additional income.

Source: World Bank 2014b.

Spatial Integration

Spatial desegregation should be pursued not as an end goal per se, but as a means to removing a marginalized group's barriers to accessing services, markets, and spaces, thereby enhancing its members' ability and opportunity to participate in society. Spatial desegregation measures involve integrating deprived communities into nondeprived social groups by diversifying neighborhoods and dispersing marginalized families across integrated parts of the urban fabric. Spatial desegregation measures can take place both at the community level (addressing a whole segregated community as a group) and at the household level (supporting Roma families to live in mixed neighborhoods).

Effectively and sustainably desegregating Roma requires more than just physically moving people (Roma or non-Roma) to form integrated neighborhoods. Evidence from previous experiments with stand-alone resettlement measures suggests that to be successful, relocation interventions should consider the resettled populations' need to establish new livelihoods, build/restore social networks, and become familiar with the new modes of life (see box 4.7 for an example from Spain). Integrating disadvantaged and marginalized communities can also be achieved via improved neighborhood connectivity (see above).

Tenure Security

To ensure marginalized Roma's socioeconomic inclusion, it is critical to formalize real property rights. There are various alternatives to issuing full ownership rights. Depending on the context of the settlement, other forms of real property

---

Box 4.7 Helping People Adapt to a New Community—IRIS Subsidized Rental Housing Project, Spain

Started in 1986 in Madrid, Spain, IRIS aimed to eradicate poverty and social exclusion, particularly among the large Roma community living in the city, by providing subsidized rental housing to Roma families in need and offering beneficiaries social support in order to adjust to the new environment and livelihoods.

In addition to helping Roma families resettle, the program offered (a) educational support to children/adolescents between ages 6 and 16, in order to promote completion and prevent absenteeism; (b) pre-kindergarten schoolings for ages 0–3; (c) preventative health and campaigns for healthy living habits; (d) job training and job search assistance; (e) access to social rights; and (f) social trust-building between Roma and non-Roma in different public spaces (such as schools).

Three key program features have helped deem IRIS as a success: (a) the phased approach over a 3–5 year span, beginning when beneficiaries have not yet moved; (b) a social worker's (and implementing agency's) personalized and tailored assistance to each family, who are helped adapt to their new life; and (c) the provision of assistance with regards to children's schooling and parents' employment opportunities.

Source: World Bank 2014d.

---

rights might be more appropriate, including street addressing, possession certificates, administrative authorization, and leases. In countries such as Romania, where a large share of Roma are not considered to have access to property rights, initiatives may be organized not only at the local level, but also at the national level to facilitate the formalization of their real property rights (see box 4.8 for an example).

Box 4.8 Ensuring Legal Entitlements through Adequate Registration and Documentation—CESAR Project, Romania

The formalization of Roma's real property rights became a subject of increasing attention under the Complementing EU Support for Agricultural Restructuring (CESAR) Project in Romania. The project began in 2007 and includes a systematic registration pilot in 50 communes. As part of the systematic registration campaign, the National Agency for Cadaster and Property Registration (Agentia Nationala de Cadastru si Publicitate Imobiliara, or ANCPI) executed a local environment analysis in target communes. This analysis was also called "vulnerability mapping" because one of its main objectives was to identify vulnerable groups, assess their property rights, and ensure their rights would be taken into account during the land registration process. Specific attention was paid to Roma settlements. When vulnerable individuals or groups were identified, the ANCPI alerted the local registration offices and local authorities to ensure the vulnerable groups were fully included in the process and provided adequate assistance.

Once the vulnerability mapping was completed, a private company carried out the mapping and registration fieldwork in collaboration with the local mayor's and registration offices. Roma representatives were consulted in the process, and a local awareness campaign was carried out via posters and announcements over the radio, television, and in local newspapers. Once Roma communities were identified, special meetings were organized, followed by the land boundary demarcation and collection of legal evidence, which for Roma was often incomplete.

The registration of Roma property rights was facilitated in various ways. If Roma families had deeds, the ANCPI monitored the registration process for adequate assistance. When families had no legal basis for their rights to be formalized, the project became a starting point for negotiations with the local government. Those who resided on public land may have been offered to lease or purchase it. Also, the registration law was amended in July 2012 to allow possessions to be registered, which can be converted into ownership rights if no claim is made against the possession within five years. Those on private land were given help to reach an arrangement with the legal landowner. Communities publicly displayed the results of the systematic registration campaign and complaints were recorded. Simultaneously, a consultant undertook social monitoring to evaluate vulnerable groups' participation.

Source: World Bank 2014b.

Enabling Factors of Successful Interventions

Community-Driven Interventions

In light of the importance of locally contextualized interventions, this section emphasizes place-based interventions, which are usually prepared and implemented by local actors at the community level. Nevertheless, national and regional-level policy and program interventions also address the living conditions in disadvantaged/marginalized communities, and it is important to maximize impacts by aligning local-level interventions with national and regional ones. These may include national and regional-level regulations, policies, and sector-wide programs, among others.

The heterogeneity and needs of Roma communities call for strong community involvement to ensure intervention effectiveness. The importance of local engagement not only stems from the fact that communities have a better understanding of their situation (about what is needed, why, where the bottlenecks are, what can be done, what is affordable and can be maintained, and what opportunities exist), but also because participation increases their sense of ownership and empowerment.

The adequate participation of the Roma beneficiary group is essential to the success of integrated interventions throughout all project phases: design, preparation, implementation, and monitoring and evaluation. On the other hand, non-Roma communities' participation is also critical to avoiding their stigmatization, to foster interaction and cooperation between Roma and non-Roma on the basis of mutual interest, and to gain non-Roma's support of the project. Participation will also help empower marginalized Roma to take more assertive roles in broader social life, giving them greater opportunities to take part in decision-making processes and voice their needs and concerns.

Fostering the adequate participation of Roma beneficiaries in the design and implementation of inclusion programs has been identified as a systematic feature of successful integrated interventions across countries. Consultation with beneficiaries has played a key role in ensuring that they actually value and do not oppose the activities, and helps mitigate the risks of failure.

Focusing on Roma beneficiaries' adequate participation includes developing appropriate consultation mechanisms to capture their communities' internal social dynamics. As many Roma communities are undergoing rapid social change, tensions can emerge between those community members who want to preserve traditional values and those who want to adopt new practices (World Bank 2014b). In designing participation mechanisms, it will therefore be important to ensure that the needs and priorities of the most vulnerable members of the community—which are often women and children, but sometimes also men—are captured and reflected in the interventions' design and implementation.

In addition, engaging beneficiaries in program implementation—for instance by having them contribute (such as to building or renovating houses)—has been shown to increase their commitment, help counteract negative stereotypes and potential political pressure, and mitigate accusations that the government channels funds to these groups "undeservedly." Box 4.9 discusses an intervention that successfully engaged communities from the early stages of project development.

Political Support

A high degree of political will and public support are required if local-level interventions are to be effective. Public resistance against programs that target Roma beneficiaries is common in EU member states. Such resistance often stems from notions that Roma are newcomers to a community or accusations that they do not deserve public support. There are even fears among non-Roma that programs that successfully assist Roma may draw more of them to the settlement than the municipality can support. Given these perceptions, the presence of a strong champion institution at the national level, combined with grassroots advocacy and the involvement of local NGOs, is crucial for focusing activities and funds on Roma neighborhoods. Apart from hampering project preparation and processing, weak political will threatens programs' successful implementation and sustainability. Without a supportive political environment, local projects cannot be developed, implemented, or sustained.

Some member states have introduced incentives to build that kind of support. For example, during the 2007–13 EU programming cycle, municipalities in the Czech Republic were expected to create Integrated Urban Development Plans (IUDPs) to access funding from the Integrated Operational Programs (IOPs), while municipalities in the Slovak Republic were required to develop Local Strategies of Complex Approach to receive EU funding. These requirements

---

**Box 4.9 The Need for Local Community Leadership and Beneficiaries'
Engagement—The Social Housing and Human Resources Development
Projects in Bulgaria**

Devnya's interconnected projects are known as Social Housing and Human Resources Development (HRD). Their key objective is to improve the livelihoods of the town's marginalized groups by providing new homes and access to education, health, and social services. The projects demonstrate several good practices of an integrated approach and project design. One of the early project planning steps was to gather sufficient information about the targeted beneficiaries to know how to best serve them. Working with local NGOs, including an established Roma nonprofit organization, helped the process of identifying target populations, building rapport with them, and understanding their needs. Then, based on this information, the municipality and NGOs made a plan to conduct an ongoing information campaign among the entire population and targeted communities to inform them of the projects and the value of their participation. Cooperation between the NGOs and the municipality can ultimately ease the complex process of implementing two projects concurrently.

Source: World Bank 2014d.

---

drove municipalities to make concrete plans to address gaps faced by marginalized groups.

However, these plans and strategies often did not get fully implemented—only parts of the plan were translated into projects that mostly benefitted less marginalized and more influential groups in the municipality. Therefore, it will be necessary to more robustly promote and monitor local plans in order to hold the responsible parties accountable.

Local Capacity

Local communities are often faced with significant capacity constraints that undermine the development and implementation of comprehensive interventions. Indeed, local authorities have often been heavily burdened by complex administrative procedures, especially when they involve the implementation of European funds that have been allocated to them. Generally, local actors tend to express the need for technical assistance and training. Although in recent years many have received training and support in the areas of proposal preparation and financial management, this has often not been sufficient for them to plan and implement projects on their own. Providing assistance to local authorities and Roma beneficiaries is likely to increase the number of interventions in marginalized communities, enhance their quality, and facilitate their timely and regulation-abiding implementation. Box 4.10 outlines different options for support and summarizes international examples in this area. Networks that connect local actors can also support the dissemination of good practices.

Box 4.10 Helping Communities Develop and Implement Local Interventions

Assisting local communities in the development and implementation of inclusion interventions may require focusing on different junctures of the project cycle, and across different areas or activities, including (a) needs identification and prioritization, sensitization of communities (outreach, advocacy, and awareness raising), selection of top priority needs through participatory methods, and community mobilization; (b) planning and application, such as preparation of investment plans, feasibility studies, and technical designs, and other required technical project documents, costing, and support in applying for funding; (c) implementation, concerning training in project management (such as financial literacy, auditing, grievance mechanisms, monitoring and evaluation, and so on), ongoing technical support (such as procurement, technical aspects in supervision, and so on) and funds management; and (d) monitoring and evaluation, facilitating information flows and providing routine technical audits.

The different types of assistance required by local communities could be provided in various forms. For example, a pool of experts with commonly required skills and expertise

box continues next page

Box 4.10 Helping Communities Develop and Implement Local Interventions *(continued)*

could be organized at the national or regional level, from which experts can be deployed to communities as needed. Alternatively, existing (organizations of) experts could be mobilized to assist local communities. In addition to local authorities, support and training could be provided to other stakeholders involved in the development and implementation of projects, including civil society organizations and the target beneficiaries (such as users associations).

The **Poland Post-Accession Rural Support Project**, for example, supported the recruitment of 27 regional consultants that provided technical assistance, new project ideas, and support in monitoring the implementation of projects. The consultants were embedded in the local government offices they were assisting, but also acted as liaisons between the local authorities, regional social policy personnel, and project implementation units. The project impact evaluation found that their contribution acted as an outside spark that helped energize the existing actors.

The **Azerbaijan Rural Investment Project (AzRIP)** provided support and expertise to communities through two types of actors: project assistance teams and technical design companies. PATs assisted communities throughout the subproject cycle, providing "hand-holding" support with (a) sensitization; (b) local initiative identification; (c) community mobilization; (d) investment plan preparation with the help of these design companies; and (e) implementation stages. These companies contributed technical expertise at relevant junctures of the projects. For example, they assisted with (a) preparing preliminary project designs, including feasibility studies; (b) costing out these plans; and (c) providing routine technical audits and implementation support to communities throughout the project cycle.

Source: World Bank 2014c, 2014d.

Disadvantaged and marginalized communities can also benefit from the on-the-ground presence of community social workers who interact with community members and monitor their needs and issues on a day-to-day basis. Community social workers, especially when permanently based in a community, can serve as an open channel of communication between the community members, service providers, and local project planners. They can help enhance the provision of services and relevance of interventions by facilitating the identification of needs, while also gathering the most current information on the conditions of existing infrastructure, services, and development opportunities. Continued and direct communication with community members, including local NGOs and government representatives, is also essential to monitoring project implementation, keeping track of project priorities and results, and introducing course-correction as necessary. Community social workers who come from the communities they serve not only facilitate the reflection of the knowledge and the context of the communities, but also enhance partnerships and communication through trusted relationships with community members they have built over the years (see also the discussion in chapter 5 on the role of social workers).

Options for Sustainable and Effective Interventions

The impacts or results of a project should not dissipate with its completion or end of national or EU funding. Projects are too often designed without sufficient consideration of the operational arrangements and recurrent (operation and maintenance) costs beyond the life of the project, and thus results cannot be sustained. Projects need to be designed with a realistic exit strategy and activities that address the root causes of the issues. Without an exit strategy, local communities are likely to become dependent on the project (and financing), and risk losing the gains achieved once the project ends. Addressing root causes means not only improving the quality and coverage of infrastructure and services, but also removing demand-side (users') constraints to accessing them. Demand-side bottlenecks, such as those related to users' awareness, affordability, capacity constraints, opportunity costs, social norms, and risks (safety, dignity, reputational, and others) may be the root causes of the gaps in living conditions, and need to be assessed and addressed.

Many disadvantaged and marginalized Roma communities are highly impoverished, and merely providing new infrastructure or services will not necessarily result in their utilization. If people are not aware of a service's benefits, or if it is too costly to access, they will not be able to utilize it. In a periurban community of Kaposvár in Hungary, for example, most owners in municipal and private homes cannot afford gas for heating or cooking; most simply use wood-fueled furnaces. Moreover, even when a service itself is provided free of charge, people may decide not to access it if the transactions or opportunity costs (such as transport, lost time for income generation and family care) are considered too high. Fear of being mistreated by service providers or associated exposure to humiliation could also discourage them from accessing a service. As an example, Roma from a segregated community in Kyustendil, Bulgaria, expressed their discomfort in visiting a medical facility in nonsegregated areas of the town out of fear of being mistreated. The design of any project must be accompanied by the question, "If we build it, will they come?" Depending on the context, community-level projects would therefore need to be accompanied by activities that adequately help tackling the issues listed in the following subsections, through both hard and soft measures.

Awareness-Raising Activities

If the target populations are not aware of the availability and benefits of an intervention (or activities, services, or facilities provided by it), it risks being underutilized by the target population. Insufficient information could also generate concerns, questions, suspicions, and resistance to interventions, which would render them largely ineffective. Awareness raising and consultation are thus essential to keep stakeholders informed, provide feedback, contribute to and have ownership over the process.

Being Fair, Faring Better • http://dx.doi.org/10.1596/978-1-4648-0598-1

By informing both Roma and non-Roma neighbors about the nature, impacts, and implications of the interventions, their understanding, take-up of, and support for interventions can be increased. Stakeholders' awareness of the availability and benefits of particular interventions, services, or practices/behaviors can be raised through (a) public awareness campaigns and (b) outreach activities carried out by social workers and mediators, including consultations with stakeholders. Examples of the effective use of such activities in the context of Roma inclusion are provided in box 4.11.

Focusing on Social Integration

Social integration outcomes must be given priority if a program is to be effective; otherwise, historic grievances or mistrust between the Roma and non-Roma might prevent the community from collectively and efficiently benefiting from interventions. This may especially be the case where decades of segregation may have hindered interaction and communication between Roma and non-Roma and made mutual understanding between both groups difficult. Different customs, perceptions, and circumstances may lead each group to behave differently, which could make it difficult for the other group to understand or accept. Such differences could lead to misunderstandings, mistrust, and mutual disapproval, which could in turn fuel tensions and conflicts between different groups. These perceptions and attitudes could also result in discrimination. It is important to increase the capacity of Roma and non-Roma to understand and respect their differences through interaction, training, and awareness activities.

For example, collaborative activities that require responsibility sharing in maintaining a community facility have proved to yield that kind of result. Indeed, recent research in Slovenia and Croatia provides evidence that ground-level activities aimed at improving relations between Roma and non-Roma can be more effective in reducing discrimination than larger scale and

---

Box 4.11 The Relevance of Awareness-Raising Activities—Govanhill Service PUB Partnership Project in Glasgow, Scotland

The main objective of the Govanhill Service HUB Partnership Project in Glasgow, Scotland, is to understand and address Roma migrants' current needs and empower them to move out of poverty. To that end, the project adopted an integrated approach involving activities such as refurbishment and infrastructure upgrades, a multiservice drop-in center, general social-economic support for newly arrived Roma, and language translation and interpreting services. One of the initiative's design features was the development of a media campaign to overcome stereotypes about Roma. This involved project implementers regularly meeting with reporters on the social and economic barriers that constrain Roma from fully participating in society, along with disseminating information, good practices, and positive outcomes through media channels.

Source: World Bank 2014d.

---

broader policies (such as the EU integration process) (Bracic 2013). Additional literature also indicates that intergroup contact usually reduces prejudice (Pettigrew and Trop 2006) and intergroup anxiety (Blaire, Park, and Bachelor 2003).

In the Human Resources Development (HRD) Project in Dupnitsa, Bulgaria, the inclusion of other marginalized groups helped avoid singling out one group (like the Roma) for new housing at the perceived expense of another (the Karakachani ethnic minority). This improved social cohesion and expanded the possibility for integration among all peoples. Similarly, in the "A House, A Future" Project in Bălţeşti, Romania, volunteers from the local community and beneficiaries themselves were mobilized and engaged in home building, which fostered increased trust between Roma and non-Roma, who do not necessarily have many occasions for intergroup interaction.

Increasing the general appreciation for Roma culture can also boost self-esteem and empower Roma to take a more affirmative and active role in social and economic life. In addition, when a Roma or a non-Roma moves to a new neighborhood, they need to be familiarized with the new community's rules and accepted codes of conduct. When conflicts or tensions continue to arise from groups' differences in customs, codes of conduct, perceptions, and values, a mediation service could be provided to help resolve or ease them.

Tackling Affordability Constraints

Ensuring that services and facilities are sustainably operated and maintained generally requires collecting user fees. But when users have difficulties paying these, projects must find a way to either lower the fee or help the user pay. Even if a service is extended, people cannot use it if they are unable to pay for it. According to the RRS, 74 percent of Roma households are having difficulty paying their mortgage, rent, or utility bills. In one town in the Czech Republic, although measures were introduced to prevent the indebtedness and eviction of Roma and low-income families from municipal housing, increases in rental fees resulted in pushing low-income households out of municipal housing, making their housing situation even more vulnerable. In Výborná, the Slovak Republic, households were given access to water and sewerage, but some residents continue to use outdoor spring water for washing, as they lack the resources to pay the new bills associated with the infrastructure upgrades.

Affordability constraints can be addressed by reducing the costs of initial investments, operation, and maintenance, and by helping raise the population's opportunities to generate additional income, when possible. Some options include (a) involving local labor in project activities, such as in infrastructure upgrading, which not only reduces the initial investment costs but also creates temporary job opportunities and develops skills for future employment; (b) training the local population to be hired in the future to operate and manage projects; (c) providing microfinance interventions for affordable housing renovations; and (d) making sure that existing targeted utility subsidies (or social welfare programs) reach these communities. Examples are presented in boxes 4.12 and 4.13. Overcoming affordability constraints stresses the importance of helping marginalized Roma families to access employment and sources of sufficient and regular income.

Box 4.12 Ensuring the Affordability of Improved Housing, Infrastructure, and Services—Flood Protection Project, Argentina

The Flood Protection Project was developed to protect the livelihoods of about 5.5 million people living in flood- and disaster-prone areas. It featured the construction of flood protection structures and strengthened institutional mechanisms to manage prevention and response measures. As part of the project, 5,636 new houses were constructed for people who had to be relocated to safer areas, in addition to 99 shelters that were built for people affected by floods. The project was targeted to very poor, vulnerable populations in the flood disaster areas.

The project applied the assisted self-construction approach to building houses, which was intended to lower construction costs, increase employment skills, and promote community cohesion and cooperation without generating a sense of entitlement or charity. Under the project, participants were led to form groups of 20 families (approximately 100 people). Each group worked as a team to build 20 houses. Although most had little or no experience with construction, the project's provincial subunits—which consisted of architects and social workers—trained them on the necessary skills to build the houses. Those who could not participate in the actual construction contributed through other tasks.

The project provided construction materials for free through vouchers, which were given in tranches as the work progressed; these were up to US$6,200 in value per household. The vouchers could only be used to buy materials at each stage, and were not transferrable. They were managed under strict supervision with serial numbers and detailed records of quantities, amounts, and recipients. The houses were built on lots provided to the participants for free by the local government and prepared by the housing institute in line with the urban development plan. After the lots were proposed to the participants, they were given the choice to accept or reject the location. Only when they accepted in writing that the new location would not weaken their livelihood or social networks, they could participate in the project.

The self-construction scheme enabled houses to be provided at a lower cost, culminating in the construction of the new houses. As a result, 92 percent of participants who had no prior experience with construction acquired new skills, and income has increased for 41 percent of them who now hold construction-related jobs. About two-thirds of participants reported that the training and experience increased their chances of finding employment. More than 90 percent of participants also reported improved quality of family life with more living space and privacy, as well as a greater sense of security and opportunity. The self-construction in groups also resulted in boosting the beneficiaries' self-esteem, sense of belonging to the community, neighborhood solidarity, and spirit of cooperation.

Source: World Bank 2014b.

Box 4.13 Technical and Financial Assistance to Improve or Expand Housing—Patrimonio Hoy Project, Mexico

Patrimonio Hoy targets people with immediate needs for housing and home expansion, low-income households, single mothers, young adults, and inexperienced builders. It provides (a) collateral-free microfinancing through a membership system based on small monthly fees; (b) engineering and architectural expertise to customers undertaking construction as part of the membership benefits package; and (c) space to store construction materials, as a lack of storage had been a major obstacle for families trying to improve their houses at their own pace. In addition, it serves as an intermediary for distributors of building materials—by bundling together the requirements of several families, it ensures good quality materials at cheaper prices to its members. The table below illustrates the solutions offered by Patrimonio Hoy to the numerous problems faced by lower income groups in accessing decent housing.

Problems	Solutions
1. Lack of savings	No financial collateral required; draw on social capital created in groups
2. Limited access to financing	Ability to make payments in installments
	Microlending/microfinance by project
	Letters of recommendation for credit purposes
3. Limited knowledge of building technology and lack of planning skills related to home building	Assistance by architects as part of the membership package
	Masonry training program
4. Lack of access to quality building materials	Project executor negotiations with distributors and development of quality controls
5. Inability to store materials	Unlimited, free storage of materials
	Regular deliveries of materials

Benefits from the Patrimonio Hoy initiative include access to design services for better room/house layouts, cost savings, locked-in material prices, material storage and delivery, and financing.

Source: World Bank 2014b.

Promoting Organizational Capacity and Active Citizenship

Users often need to be organized (such as in the form of a water users' association, homeowners association, or neighborhood association) to collectively make decisions and perform necessary actions to operate or manage a new community infrastructure. If an intervention's target population cannot coordinate the use of the service or facility, it could end up benefitting certain users unequally at the expense of others. The service system or facility also risks breaking down if the community's administrative and management capacities are inadequate. Many informal settlements lack such experience and capacities.

Their capacity could be increased by (a) supporting the formation and running of service users' associations/committees (such as legal and facilitation support to form associations) and (b) providing training to users' associations or committees (such as training on accounting, basic financial literacy, and participatory approaches to budgeting and monitoring).

In addition, facilitating the local population's engagement can increase their ownership over the project and their capacity to demand service providers' accountability. Box 4.14 summarizes some international examples of interventions that adequately address citizenship concerns and incorporate these

---

Box 4.14 Fostering Active Citizenship of Beneficiaries—Post-Accession Rural Support Project, Poland

Poland's 1989 transition to a market economy resulted in several waves of strong economic growth, though these did not benefit all of society equally. Economic liberalization exposed structural poverty and long-term unemployment, which contributed to a self-perpetuating cycle of social exclusion, especially in rural and underdeveloped gminas (local districts). Active policies to encourage inclusion at the local community level were needed. The Post-Accession Rural Support Project (PARSP) initiative was designed to actively engage local government actors and civil society organizations at the municipal level in the development and implementation of social programs that directly addressed the causes of exclusion.

PARSP supported local actors in planning and implementing services for marginalized groups in the 500 poorest gminas (municipalities) selected for the project. Special attention was paid to particularly vulnerable individuals, as identified by the communities, such as youth, children, the disabled, and the elderly. Initial priority needs that were identified included better access to health care, education, and communications services.

The project recruited 27 regional consultants to provide expertise, advice, and a link between local government authorities and other project stakeholders. The dynamism and innovative ideas they provided enhanced the work and strengthened other actors' capacity, contributing to the success of the project.

One project in a rural community, for example, financed the establishment of a kindergarten for local children. With support from the mayor, local civil society organizations, and input from residents, those involved made a plan, retained an unused building for space, and purchased educational materials. This project provided a safe place for children and succeeded in socializing their mothers, who were then free to look for jobs and contribute to their community's development. PARSP's overall positive impact is reflected in the active participation of gminas, strong prospects for project sustainability, and strengthened capacity to implement initiatives and absorb funds.

Inclusion Program in Pécs, Hungary

The Inclusion Program of Pécs City is one of several "area-based" and "community-led" development pilots that were set up with the help of a pilot partnership with UNDP. As part of the

box continues next page

Box 4.14 Fostering Active Citizenship of Beneficiaries—Post-Accession Rural Support Project, Poland *(continued)*

program, community interventions were conducted to mobilize local stakeholders and all local resources, and to empower the disadvantaged local communities. Through the active involvement of two community coaches, local communities were empowered and resources were mobilized in Pécs-Kelet, mainly in the Szabolcs segregate.

With the facilitation of the community coaches, an Urgent Needs Plan was developed for solving the most critical problems in the target area. The development of this plan was critical for generating motivation, providing a framework for activities, and teaching participants how to think through solving small but urgent problems faced by the communities of the Szabolcs segregate. As a first step, members of the targeted community established a working thematic group to identify problems, needs, and ideas for solutions. As a second step, focus groups and coordination meetings were organized, with the participation of the municipality, relevant companies, institutions, and local NGOs, where democratically elected representatives of local communities presented challenges and solutions in a constructive, coherent way.

The development skills and organizational capacities of the local stakeholders in Pécs strongly improved with the help of organizational development training provided in the course of the program. Specifically, the development and communication training aimed to establish and facilitate the cooperation of local stakeholders, NGOs, and local government departments, institutes, and authorities. The trainings were essential in bringing together local stakeholders, developing a common vocabulary, and understanding the development process and vision for the inclusive city. Beyond any critical skills development, the various stakeholders' participation in some of the trainings had a special bonding effect.

Results of these initiatives, based on a robust impact evaluation, were not available at the time of this writing.

Source: World Bank 2014b.

---

kinds of activities. Parents' increased engagement in school activities (through parents' associations, for example) can not only increase the quality of education provided by schools and children's educational performance, but also empower parents to participate in community life. Social workers and mediators can also play a central role in helping the local community voice their demands. They can improve their communication skills and enhance both the quality and uptake of social services.

Facilitating Civil Documentation

While the majority of Roma possess personal identification (a birth certificate, identity card, or passport), the lack of civil registration in some cases constrains community members' eligibility to access social services like schools, health facilities, and credit. For example, many Roma in the Slovak Republic do not have valid insurance cards, and in many cases, social workers and health assistants must help them acquire new cards to access health services.

Therefore, it is important to assist and facilitate the civil registration of the target population so they are eligible to access services. If households cannot afford the cost of registration, an intervention can also be designed to subsidize the costs (see box 4.15 for an example). In Romania, one major hurdle in obtaining identity cards has been the required proof of residence, which many Roma are unable to show because of their informal housing situations. Furthermore, registration of a child older than the age of 1 could cost as much as €30 in Romania, a prohibitive price for the majority of the country's Roma households, whose median per capita monthly income is €50.[13] The challenge is aggravated by lack of literacy as well as discriminatory attitudes on the part of authorities.

Box 4.15 Civil Registration Activity—Inner Cities Basic Services Project, Jamaica

The Jamaica Inner Cities Basic Services Project was intended to holistically address the dimensions of human, social, economic, and environmental development of inner city communities. The project included a civil registration activity that aimed to enhance citizens' access to basic services in 12 prioritized communities by providing personal identification documents through community outreach fairs. In Jamaica, birth certificates are often a prerequisite to obtaining other national registration documents (such as a national ID, tax payer registration number, or national health insurance), and are also needed to access health-, education-, and employment-related social services.[a] Thus, lacking registration documents keeps people from accessing public services and reinforces existing cycles of poverty and exclusion. The civil registration component arose as a response to this reality.

The operation was particularly successful at hiring and training community liaisons who were compensated with a modest stipend. These were known and trusted community members whose function was to support the application process, community mobilization, and the distribution of newly issued birth certificates. Their participation was extremely important in overcoming trust issues, fear of sharing personal information, and demystifying barriers to service. Community demand for birth certificates was also mapped prior to the community fairs. For example, if a parent tried to register their child in an afterschool program and the child lacked a birth certificate, the program community liaisons would take down the child's information and ensure he or she was prioritized during the certification fair. This type of cooperation provided both a way to establish and meet the existing need in the community before the fair, and also prevent people from being barred the service.

Outreach fairs were widely advertised a month in advance, both through community-based organizations and door-to-door surveys. This included sensitizing people to available services, and often convincing people who were part of the "informal sector" of the importance of being officially registered and making them aware that "free public services" were available to them upon registration.

As a result of the civil registration activities, close to 4,675 people from 12 inner city communities received registration documents. Beneficiaries ranged from newborns to elderly

box continues next page

Box 4.15 **Civil Registration Activity—Inner Cities Basic Services Project, Jamaica** *(continued)*

community members. Communities reported a heightened awareness of services available to them. The fairs also helped the city capture vital statistical data to assist the national planning process.

The intervention could be used to provide registration documents to facilitate vulnerable communities' access to or use of social services and programs, while also generating a heightened sense of inclusion. Results of the initiative, based on a robust impact evaluation, are not available at the time of this writing.

Source: World Bank 2014b.
a. Until 2007 it was not required for women to register their children after giving birth, which resulted in many unregistered births. In 2008 Jamaica approved the Bedside Registration Law, which allowed for birth registrations to be carried out at hospitals.

Conclusions

The heterogeneity of living conditions in disadvantaged and marginalized Roma communities calls for a customized mix of interventions that are tailored to each community's priority needs. The large scale of European Structural and Investment Funds that will be available during the 2014–20 cycle is a great opportunity to fund these interventions. Different targeting strategies can be adopted to implement these initiatives. Among these, the principle of explicit but not exclusive targeting would allow a focus on disadvantaged and marginalized communities in general, so as to avoid further stigmatizing and segregating Roma. Neighborhood-level collection and analysis of additional data, such as those related to the formality of tenure, housing conditions, and access to basic infrastructure can enhance how these interventions are targeted and prioritized.

Annex 4A: Spotlight on Territorial Targeting

This spotlight introduces an approach to identifying the territorial distribution of poverty and marginalization in EU member CEE countries. It takes an in-depth look at the specific case of Romanian Roma, with a view toward assessing whether investments targeted through a "de-ethnicized" territorial approach are likely to reach the majority of Roma families in need.

Mapping At-Risk-of-Poverty in European Union Member Countries
Today, close to one-quarter of the European Union's population is at risk of poverty or social exclusion. Many Roma are among the most marginalized, and many Roma communities live in extreme poverty. The rates of poverty and social exclusion vary widely across EU member states, and there is also a high degree of variability in living standards *within* member states. In its 2014–20 multiannual financial framework, the EU budgeted one trillion euros to support growth and jobs and to reduce by 20 million the number of people who live at risk of

poverty or social exclusion by 2020.[14] Success depends on developing the right policies and programs and targeting them effectively.

Until recently, the European Commission (EC) relied on subnational data at a relatively high level of aggregation for program planning and EU funds allocation. The EC and the World Bank, in cooperation with individual EU member states, have developed a set of high-resolution poverty maps.[15] The greater geographic disaggregation of the new poverty maps allows users to identify which parts of these larger regions have particularly high rates of poverty and social exclusion and thus require greater attention from poverty reduction programs.

A closer look at the poverty maps for Romania and Hungary confirms existing knowledge about poverty in both countries, but also reveals several new insights. In Romania, previous surveys have shown that the northeast region has the highest rates of poverty (map 4A.1, left panel); the county-level poverty map (map 4A.1, right panel) shows that all counties of that region (with the exception of Bacău) have a high incidence of at-risk-of-poverty rates. In contrast, the South is heterogeneous, comprising counties with very high poverty rates (such as Călăraşi and Teleorman), as well as counties with relatively low ones (such as Prahova). Similarly, Cluj county has the second lowest poverty rate in Romania (after Bucharest), but its neighboring counties in the northwest region (Bistriṣa-Năsăud, Maramureş, Sălaj, and Satu Mare) experience higher poverty than the Romanian average. Knowing which counties have higher poverty rates can help efficiently target resources toward development and poverty reduction.

Map 4A.1 At-Risk-of-Poverty Rates in Romania at the Development Region and County Levels

a. Development region level (NUTS2)

b. County level (NUTS3)

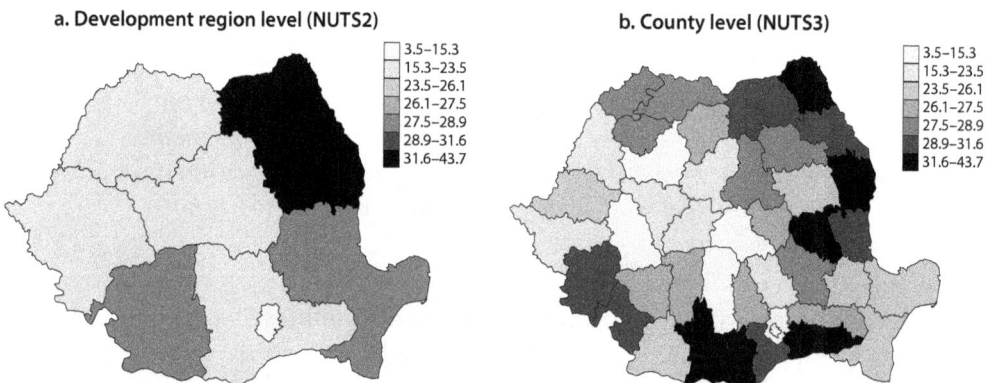

Legend (both panels):
- 3.5–15.3
- 15.3–23.5
- 23.5–26.1
- 26.1–27.5
- 27.5–28.9
- 28.9–31.6
- 31.6–43.7

Source: World Bank estimates using the 2011 Population and Housing Census and 2012 EU Statistics on Income and Living Conditions (EU-SILC) data collected by the National Institute of Statistics (Romania). EU-SILC = EU Statistics on Income and Living Conditions.
Note: "Risk of poverty" is defined using the EU standard of 60 percent of median national equivalized income after social transfers. The development region is classified at the second level, or NUTS2, and the county is set at the third level, or NUTS3, statistical region of the European Union—referred to as the Nomenclature of Territorial Units for Statistics or NUTS. For panel a, direct estimates from EU-SILC suggest limited poverty heterogeneity across development regions. For panel b, predicted NUTS3 estimates reveal considerable variation in poverty incidence, both across the country and within development regions.

In Hungary, the highest rates of poverty were measured in the northeastern region (map 4A.2, left panel) in earlier surveys. The statistical subregion level (LAU1) poverty map (map 4A.2, right panel) shows that many of the subregions in the northeastern corner have high incidence of at-risk-of-poverty rates, although Eger, Miskolc, and Nyíregyháza stand out as areas with only moderate poverty incidence. In contrast, southern Transdanubia is a heterogeneous region, comprising low poverty incidence in subregions such as Pécs, with relatively high poverty incidence in nearby Siklós, Sellye, Szigetvár, and Szentlőrinc. More generally, there is a much higher degree of heterogeneity in poverty incidence at the statistical subregions level vis-à-vis the estimates that are directly available from the EU Statistics on Income and Living Conditions (EU-SILC) survey for the seven planning and statistical regions. Knowing which subregions have higher poverty rates can help improve how resources for development and poverty reduction are targeted.

Drilling Down to the Community Level—Mapping Urban Marginalization in Romania through Census Data

While poverty maps can help CEE countries identify at-risk-of-poverty at the subregional level, these tools cannot reliably identify small pockets of marginalized communities (say, around 100 households) that exist within cities or towns. At the same time, official municipal maps used by local government decision makers often do not show all of the marginalized (Roma) settlements, as these are often of an informal nature. As a result, these communities' needs are frequently overlooked in local development plans, including those funded with EU structural funds. Some new member states have a particularly poor track record in using these funds to effectively target marginalized communities, especially to benefit ethnic minorities such as the Roma. This also contributes

Map 4A.2 At-Risk-of-Poverty Rates at Statistical Region and Statistical Subregion Levels

Poverty rates higher in northeastern Hungary, but differences across regions are not large

Poverty rates vary widely and are highest in the northeast

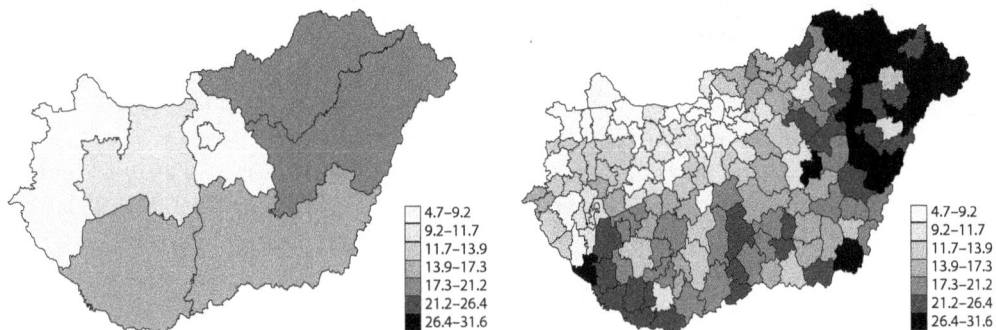

4.7–9.2
9.2–11.7
11.7–13.9
13.9–17.3
17.3–21.2
21.2–26.4
26.4–31.6

Source: World Bank staff estimates using 2005 microcensus and 2005 EU Statistics on Income and Living Conditions data collected by the Hungarian Central Statistical Office.
Note: "Risk of poverty" is defined using the EU standard of 60 percent of median national equivalized income after social transfers.

to a widening gap between planning social inclusion policies at the national level and actually implementing activities on the ground. However, a new approach for spending EU funds—community-led local development (CLLD)—allows EU-funded activities to be explicitly targeted to pockets of deprived communities. To help the Romanian authorities design their CLLD program, the World Bank developed a methodology that highlights the location of severely marginalized communities for each town and city in Romania—the Atlas of Urban Marginalized Areas in Romania, which presents maps that are based on data from the 2011 population and housing census.

This tool uses a typology and corresponding indicators that are based on qualitative research and a review of earlier analysis and indices of urban marginalization. The maps use indicators at the individual, household, and dwelling levels (such as education, employment, access to electricity, and so on) from the 2011 census. For each of these indicators, the values at the urban census sector level (areas of typically about 200 people) are determined for all urban census sectors and an urban threshold is then defined as the 80th percentile. For each urban census sector, it is subsequently determined whether its value is above the threshold for that indicator. If a census sector has a particular combination of indicators that are above their threshold, it is regarded as disadvantaged or marginalized. For a number of cities, maps at the census sector level were produced, displaying the typology of urban marginalized areas as determined by applying this methodology to the census data.

An additional series of maps were produced that reflect information collected directly from urban authorities in Romania on whether marginalized communities existed in their municipality, and if so, where. For a subset of cities, maps were available from both the census-based method and the information gathered directly from urban authorities. Using census data to identify urban marginalized communities is a promising approach. However, further work is needed to assess its validity, including beyond urban areas.

While poverty maps or maps of marginalized communities in urban areas can provide more finely tuned information about subnational or within-city variations in poverty and marginalization, and improve resource allocation, they cannot solve all development problems. To make the most of the information, it must be complemented with local, context-specific knowledge by drawing on local expertise and community demand. In other words, after identifying the areas or populations in greatest need, it is necessary to understand *why* these places are poor. The reasons are likely to vary from place to place, and may include inadequate infrastructure, lack of economic activity, insufficiently skilled work force, or other reasons. While the right combination of approaches will vary by country, the maps provide important information to help improve policies and programs to combat poverty and social exclusion.

Will Investments in Marginalized Areas Reach All Roma Families in Need?

The Atlas of Urban Marginalized Areas in Romania can be used as a robust way to identify people in need and target resources toward them, regardless of their ethnicity. However, it is yet to be determined whether this instrument captures the specificity of the problems faced by Roma who live in concentrated areas, and whether its use as the sole targeting instrument might exclude parts of the Roma population who live in difficult situations.

To answer these questions, an analysis of 2011 census data from Romania finds that:

- *The larger the share of Roma population within the community, the higher the probability that the community is marginalized.* While only 1 percent of the urban communities with no self-declared Roma is marginalized, 47 percent of the communities with large shares of Roma are disadvantaged in all three dimensions (human capital, employment, and housing) of marginalization.

- *The larger the share of Roma population within a marginalized community, the worse the values of all social exclusion indicators, for both Roma and non-Roma.* If, for example, in marginalized areas without self-declared Roma, 31 percent of youth ages 16–24 are not in school and have at most lower secondary education, in marginalized communities with more than 40 percent of the population Roma, this percentage is 65 (see figures 4A.1–4A.3).

- *At the same time, within the same types of communities, Roma are much more often excluded from education, employment, or housing.* For example, among working-age, not-in-school Roma who live in urban marginalized communities with less than 20 percent Roma, 68 percent are not working or retired; the percentage is only 39 for non-Roma who live in the same communities. The gap between Roma and non-Roma is larger in communities with lower shares of Roma (regardless of whether these communities are marginalized).

- *However, residence in a marginalized or non-marginalized urban area makes little or no difference to Roma's situation.* Regardless of whether they live in a marginalized or non-marginalized urban area, Roma score significantly lower on human capital and employment indicators compared to other ethnic groups—see figures 4A.1–4A.3—and the gap between Roma in marginalized areas and those in non-marginalized ones is much lower than the gap for non-Roma. The situation is similar when looking at housing indicators other than those used to identify the marginalized areas (overcrowding, lack of electricity, or dwelling ownership); no matter where they live, Roma face similar difficulties in terms of access to potable water or connection to sewage disposal systems.

Being Fair, Faring Better • http://dx.doi.org/10.1596/978-1-4648-0598-1

The aforementioned analysis suggests that interventions that exclusively target marginalized areas could only partially reach vulnerable Romanian Roma. Such interventions need to be complemented by further investments specifically targeted at Roma communities, particularly those with higher proportions of Roma, strongly focused on human capital (education, skills, and health care), formal employment, and access to basic utilities (water, sewage).

Figure 4A.1 Roma Youth (Ages 16–24) with at Most Lower Secondary Education and Not in School, by Roma versus Non-Roma Marginalization of Urban Area

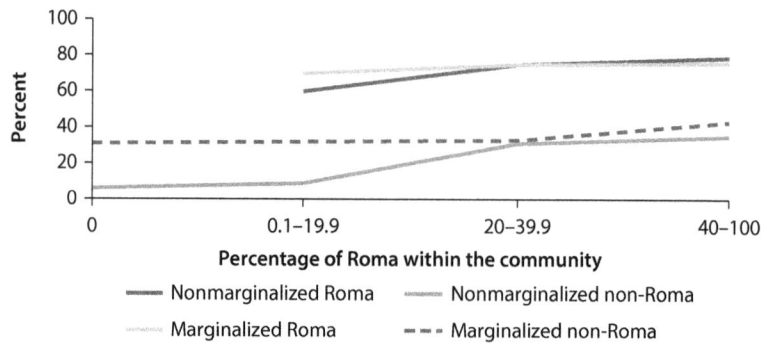

Source: Estimates on the 2011 census, carried out within the Reimbursable Advisory Services for providing input to the Romanian Strategy for Social Inclusion and Poverty Reduction.

Figure 4A.2 Roma Population (Ages 15–64) Either Not in School, Not Retired, or Not in Employee Status, by Roma versus Non-Roma Marginalization of Urban Area

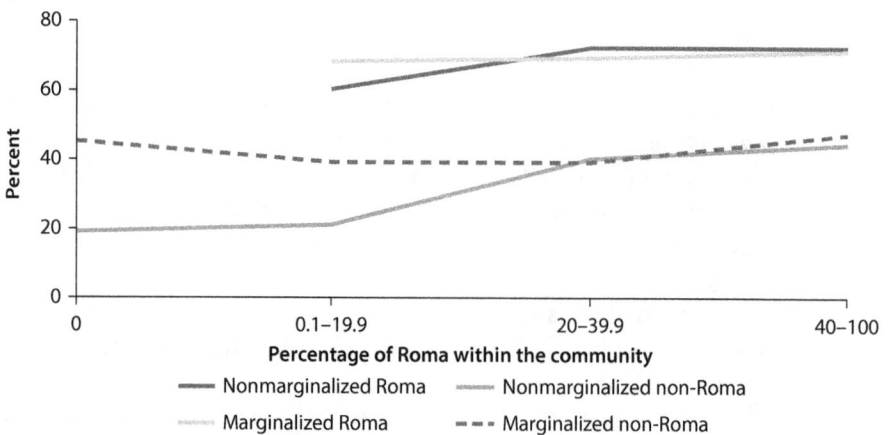

Source: Estimates under the Social Inclusion and Poverty Reduction RAS on 2011 census.

Figure 4A.3 Roma Residing in Housing without Access to Utilities, by Roma versus Non-Roma Marginalization of Urban Area

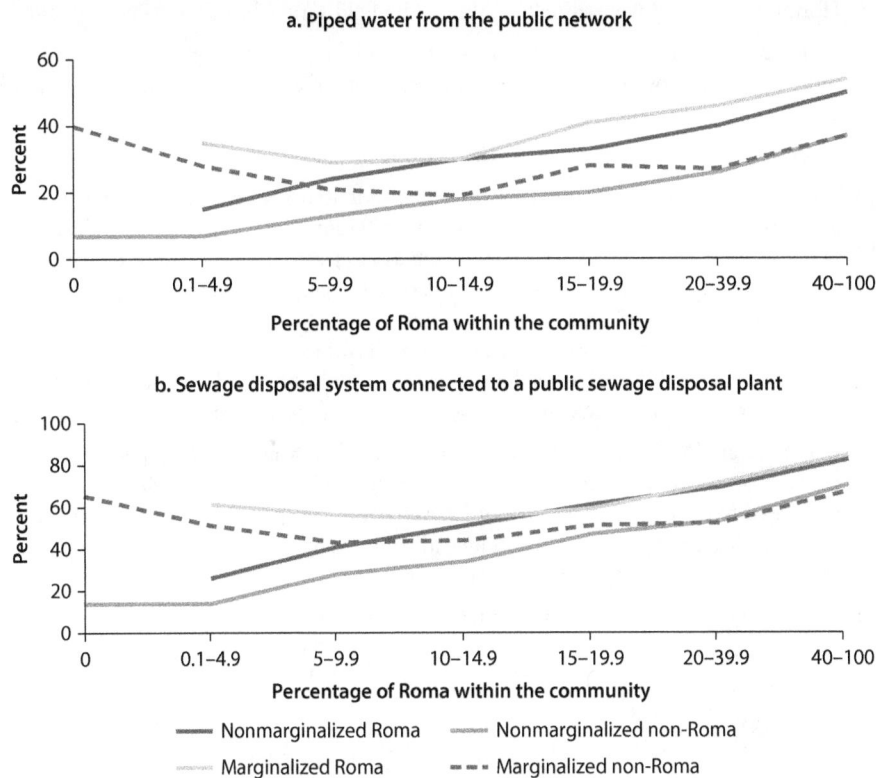

a. Piped water from the public network

b. Sewage disposal system connected to a public sewage disposal plant

Source: 2011 Population and Housing Census and National Institute of Statistics staff estimates.

Notes

1. These factors combine with limited access to health services and relatively higher incidence of risky behaviors, such as smoking and unsafe reproductive health practices to result in worse overall health outcomes and lower life expectancy for Roma, which appears to be on average much lower than a non-Roma's—by six years in the case of Romania, for instance.

2. This indicator is calculated using the question, "Which of the following is the main source of potable water your household uses: piped water inside the dwelling; piped water in the garden/yard; public tap; covered well or borehole?" The values "other," "refused," "don't know," "missing/NA," and "DK/DNUQ" were defined as missing.

3. This indicator is calculated using the question, "Does this dwelling in which you live have... toilet in the house; shower or bathroom inside." The values "other," "refused," "don't know," "missing/NA," and "DK/DNUQ" were defined as missing.

4. Neighborhoods where more than half of residents are Roma.

5. In general, more than two persons per room is considered overcrowded in the European context. This can be considered a rough proxy for EU standards. See the

following link for more information: http://ec.europa.eu/eurostat/statistics-explained/index.php/Main_Page

6. Housing conditions were visually evaluated by field surveyors of the RRS.

7. Some 54 percent of urban Roma in Romania report having difficulty paying rent, versus 39 percent of rural Roma in Romania (UNDP, World Bank, and EC 2011).

8. Most urban Roma do not live in social housing.

9. This chapter focuses on Roma's spatial or residential segregation, in which Roma and non-Roma are physically separated in different neighborhoods. It is different from segregation in service provision, such as in classrooms and health care, which is not the focus of this chapter. While spatial segregation could often be a key source of segregation in service provision, it is not always the cause of service segregation, and desegregation in service provision (for example, school desegregation) may not necessarily require residential desegregation. Avoidable service segregation should not be justified or continued on the basis of spatial segregation.

10. Duminică and A. Ivasiuc (2013), on the other hand, indicate that 12.5 percent of the Roma have no property papers. This is down from 37 percent in 1998, but still high compared to the comparator figure of 1.6 percent for the non-Roma. The report states that the desirability effect may induce distortions in how respondents choose to answer, so the percentage might be misleading.

11. See spotlight on territorial targeting for a nuanced discussion.

12. In some cases, especially when there are already social housing units available, costs could be lower than other housing interventions.

13. Until 2007 it was not required for women to register their children after giving birth, which resulted in many unregistered births. In 2008 Jamaica approved the Bedside Registration Law, which allowed for birth registrations to be carried out at hospitals.

14. "Statistics Explained: People at Risk of Poverty or Social Exclusion" (accessed February 1, 2014), http://ec.europa.eu/eurostat/statistics-explained/index.php/People_at_risk_of_poverty_or_social_exclusion.

15. These maps combine information from the 2011 population censuses and EU-SILC household surveys to estimate the rates of monetary poverty for small geographic areas such as counties, districts, or municipalities.

References

Berry, B. 2007. "Disparities in Free Time Inactivity in the United States: Trends and Explanations." *Sociological Perspectives* 50 (2): 177–208.

Blaire, I., B. Park, and J. Bachelor. 2003. "Understanding Intergroup Anxiety: Are Some People More Anxious than Others?" *Group Processes & Intergroup Relations* 6 (2): 151–69.

Boardman, B. 2004. "Starting on the Road to Sustainability." *Building Research and Information* 32 (3): 264–68.

Boyle, P., P. Norman, and P. Rees. 2004. "Changing Places: Do Changes in the Relative Deprivation of Areas Influence Long-Term Illness and Mortality Among Non-migrant

People Living in Non-deprived Households?" *Social Science and Medicine* 58 (12): 2459–71.

Bracic, A. 2013. "EU Accession, NGOs, and Human Rights: Discrimination against the Roma in Slovenia and Croatia." SSRN. http://ssrn.com/abstract=2335125.

Breysse, P., N. Farr, W. Galke, B. Lanphear, R. Morley, and L. Bergofsky. 2004. "The Relationship between Housing and Health: Children at Risk." *Environmental Health Perspectives* 112 (15): 1583–88.

Bronfenbrenner, U., and P. A. Morris. 1998. "The Ecology of Developmental Processes." In *Handbook of Child Psychology, Volume 1: Theoretical Models of Human Development*, 5th ed., edited by W. Damon and R. M. Lerner, 993–1023. New York: Wiley.

Brooks-Gunn, J., G. J. Duncan, P. Kato Klebanov, and N. Sealand. 1993. "Do Neighborhoods Influence Child and Adolescent Development?" *American Journal of Sociology* 99 (2): 353–95.

Brooks-Gunn, J., G. J. Duncan, and J. L. Aber, eds. 1997a. *Neighborhood Poverty I: Context and Consequences for Children*. New York: Russell Sage Foundation.

———. 1997b. *Neighborhood Poverty II: Policy Implications for Studying Neighborhoods*. New York: Russell Sage Foundation.

CABE Space. 2005. *Decent Parks? Decent Behaviour? The Link between the Quality of Parks and User Behaviour*. London: CABE Space.

Capon, A. 2007. "*Health Impacts of Urban Development: Key Considerations.*" *New South Wales Public Health Bulletin* 18 (10): 155–56.

Cattaneo, M. D., S. Galiani, P. J. Gertler, S. Martinez, and R. Titiunik. 2009. "Housing, Health, and Happiness." *American Economic Journal: Economic Policy* 1 (1): 75–105.

Clark, R. 1992. *Neighborhood Effects on Dropping Out of School among Teenage Boys*. Washington, DC: Urban Institute.

Connell, J. P., and B. L. Halpern-Felsher. 1997. "How Neighborhoods Affect Educational Outcomes in Middle Childhood and Adolescence: Conceptual Issues and an Empirical Example." In *Neighborhood Poverty I: Context and Consequences for Children*, edited by J. Brooks-Gunn et al. New York: Russell Sage Foundation.

Dekker, K., and G. Bolt. 2004. "Social Cohesion in Heterogeneous Neighbourhoods in the Netherlands: The Cases of Bouwlust and Hoograven." Paper presented at City Futures Conference, Chicago, July 8–10.

Duminică, G., and A. Ivasiuc. 2013. "The Roma in Romania: From Scapegoat to Development Engine." Report, "Impreună" Agency for Community Development, Cluj-Napoca. https://www.academia.edu/6037269/IN_ROMANIA_ROMA_From _Scapegoat_to_Development_Engine.

Ellaway, A., S. Macintyre, and X. Bonnefoy. 2005. "Graffiti, Greenery, and Obesity in Adults: Secondary Analysis of European Cross-Sectional Survey." *BMJ* 2005 (331): 611–12.

Ellen, I. G., T. Mijanovich, and K.-N. Dillman. 2001. "Neighborhood Effects on Health: Exploring the Links and Assessing the Evidence." *Journal of Urban Affairs* 23 (3–4): 391–408.

Ellen, I. G., and M. A. Turner. 2003. "*Do Neighborhoods Matter and Why?*" In *Choosing a Better Life? Evaluating the Moving to Opportunity Social Experiment*, edited by J. Goering and J. D. Feins. Washington, DC: Urban Institute Press.

Ensminger, M. E., R., P. Lamkin, and N. Jacobson. 1996. "School Leaving: A Longitudinal Perspective Including Neighborhood Effects." *Child Development* 67: 2400–16.

Evans, G. W., S. Saegert, and R. Harris. 2001. "Residential Density and Psychological Health among Children in Low-Income Families." *Environment and Behavior* 33 (2): 165–80.

Flournoy, R., and I. Yen. 2004. *The Influence of Community Factors on Health: An Annotated Bibliography*. Oakland, CA: PolicyLink.

Galster, G., D. E. Marcotte, M. Mandell, H. Wolman, and N. Augustine. 2007. "The Influence of Neighborhood Poverty during Childhood on Fertility, Education, and Earnings Outcomes." *Housing Studies* 22 (5): 723–51.

Gephart, M. A. 1997. "Neighborhoods and Communities as Contexts for Development." In *Neighborhood Poverty*, edited by J. Brooks-Gunn. New York: Russell Sage Foundation.

Jencks, C., and S. E. Meyer. 1990. "The Social Consequences of Growing Up in a Poor Neighborhood." In *Inner City Poverty in the United States*, edited by L. E. Lynn and M. F. H. McGeary. Washington, DC: National Academies Press.

Kawachi, I., and L. F. Berkman, eds. 2003. *Neighborhoods and Health*. New York: Oxford University Press.

Lavin, T., C. Higgins, O. Metcalfe, and A. Jordan. 2006. *Health Effects of the Built Environment: A Review*. Dublin and Belfast: Institute of Public Health in Ireland.

Leventhal, T., and J. Brooks-Gunn. 2003. "Moving to Opportunity: An Experimental Study of Neighborhood Effects on Mental Health." *American Journal of Public Health* 93 (9): 1576–82.

———. 2000. "The Neighborhoods They Live In: The Effects of Neighborhood Residence on Child and Adolescent Outcomes." *Psychological Bulletin* 126 (2): 309–37.

Lund, H. 2002. "Pedestrian Environments and Sense of Community." *Journal of Planning Education and Research* 21 (3): 301–12.

Macintyre, S., A. Ellaway, and S. Cummins. 2002. "Place Effects on Health: How Can We Conceptualise Operationalise and Measure Them?" *Social Science and Medicine* 55: 125–39.

Macintyre, S., and A. Ellaway. 2003a. "Ecological Approaches: Rediscovering the Role of the Physical and Social Environment." In *Neighborhoods and Health* edited by I. Kawachi and L. F. Berkman. New York: Oxford University Press.

———. 2003b. "Neighborhoods and Health: An Overview." In *Neighborhoods and Health*, edited by I. Kawachi and L. F. Berkman. New York: Oxford University Press.

New South Wales Department of Health. 2009. *Healthy Urban Development Checklist: A Guide for Health Services When Commenting on Development Policies, Plans and Proposals*. Sydney: New South Wales Department of Health.

Pettigrew, T. F., and L. R. Trop. 2006. "A Meta-analytic Test of Intergroup Contact Theory." *Journal of Personality and Social Psychology* 90 (5): 751–83.

Roux Diez, A. V., S. S. Merkin, D. Arnett, L. Chambless, M. Massing, F. J. Nieto, P. Sorlie, M. Szklo, H. A. Tyroler, and R. L. Watson. 2001. "Neighborhood of Residence and Incidence of Coronary Heart Disease." *New England Journal of Medicine* 345 (2): 99–106.

Semenza, J. C. 2003. "The Intersection of Urban Planning, Art, and Public Health: The Sunnyside Piazza." *American Journal of Public Health* 93 (9): 1439–41.

Solari, C. D., and R. D. Mare. 2012. "Housing Crowding Effects on Children's Well-Being." *Social Science Research* 41 (2): 464–76.

Staniewicz, T. 2009. "Thematic Study: Housing Conditions of Roma and Travellers." FRA RAXEN Report Slovakia. https://fra.europa.eu/sites/default/files/fra_uploads /596-RAXEN-Roma-Housing-UK_en.pdf.

UNDP (United Nations Development Programme), World Bank, and EC (European Commission). 2011. *Regional Roma Survey.* Report, UNDP, World Bank, and EC, New York.

Weich, S., M. Blanchard, M. Prince, E. Burton, B. Erens, and K. Sproston. 2002. "Mental Health and the Built Environment: Cross-Sectional Survey of Individual and Contextual Risk Factors for Depression." *British Journal of Psychiatry* 180 (5): 428–33.

World Bank. 2014a. *Gender Dimensions of Roma Inclusion: Perspectives from Four Roma Communities in Bulgaria.* Report, World Bank, Washington, DC.

———. 2014b. *Global Case Studies: Lessons from Interventions for Improving the Living Conditions of Marginalized Communities.* Report, World Bank, Washington, DC.

———. 2014c. *A Handbook for Improving the Living Conditions of Roma.* Report, World Bank, Washington, DC.

———. 2014d. *A Review of 36 Projects Improving Roma Living Conditions in Bulgaria, Czech Republic, France, Hungary, Italy, Romania, Slovakia, Spain, and the United Kingdom.* Report, World Bank, Washington, DC.

PART 3

Implementing Policy Responses

Life Story—Going to School: After Getting Help, She Works to Help Others

The story of a young Roma university graduate from a non-segregated rural area in the Slovak Republic

I was born in the capital of the Slovak Republic. We lived there until I was twelve or thirteen years old when we moved to another city. We stayed in that city until my grandfather, who lived in a village, got sick and we moved to his village, and we are still living there. About 1,800 people live here and most work in factories not far from the village, and they commute every day. There are about 150 Roma in my village. None of them speaks Romani, and they are assimilated or integrated. Most of the Roma in my village have very little education, and they barely survive on occasional low-skill manual work in the factories. There are about eight Roma families living in the center of the village; they are very poor and live on social assistance. I have never heard of or experienced tensions between the Roma and non-Roma in my village.

My father is Roma and my mother is not. My father has some secondary education. He works in a car factory outside the village. My mother has some vocational schooling, and she works for a local company that makes motor oil. I have four younger sisters. My second sister graduated from secondary school, and even though she had very good grades, she preferred to work. Since she finished school she's been working for the same company. My third sister only finished primary school. She couldn't stay in school because of her disability, which doesn't allow her to commute to the secondary school in the town or carry anything heavy like books. My two young-est sisters are studying to be nurses. One is in her first year at university and the other one is in her first year in nursing school.

I studied in mainstream primary and secondary schools, and I am happy about that, because if I went to a segregated school, I would probably not have studied past grade school. I commuted an hour and a half to my secondary school in town. In both primary and high school my teachers and classmates were nice. I was ambitious and I always got good grades. I was good in all my subjects except math and my mother always helped me with my math homework.

I wanted to go to university since primary school, and I knew I would go, but I didn't know what exactly I wanted to study. In high school I developed an interest in social work, and I did my BA and MA in social work. My parents were unemployed while I was getting my BA, and I got support from the state, which was enough to cover my expenses. I heard about the Roma Education Fund scholarship, and I applied, but I didn't get it and I didn't apply again. When I started doing my masters, I got a job as a social worker helping the local Roma community. So I was studying and working at the same time. Around that time my parents both also got jobs. After the Roma project ended, I started searching for another job. I registered as a job seeker at the employment agency, but I never did get offered a job.

Then I applied for a master's program at a university abroad. I was accepted with a partial scholarship, but I couldn't cover my living expenses. I applied for and got grants from REF and OSI so I could finish my degree. I wouldn't have been able to do it without the two grants. Then I did a three-month internship with an interna-tional organization, supporting their work on Roma. Soon I will start an internship at another international organization, again supporting their Roma work. In the meantime, I keep looking for a job. I'd like to keep working on Roma and Roma inclu-sion projects.

Life Story—From an Orphanage to a Graduate Degree: Teachers and a Scholarship Make the Difference

The story of a young Roma man from Romania who lives in a non-segregated urban area

I was born in a small village in Central Romania into a very poor Roma family. When I was three or four years old, my parents put me in an orphanage in the nearest town. In the orphanage we were many kids and it was impossible for the teachers to watch after each of us and protect us all the time. Sometimes the older kids bullied the younger ones, including me. My life in the orphanage was not that bad because I had food to eat, I had a bed and clothes, and it was interesting for all of us to live together. We made friends and we grew up together. Half of the orphans there were Roma, like me, but they did not like to be called Roma because no one likes the Roma, they wanted to integrate and didn't want to be seen as different from the other orphans. Growing up in the orphanage I loved theater and reading books.

I finished primary and high school while I was living at the orphanage. The teach-ers could not work individually with us because we were 25–30 children in a class, but I think that the education at the orphanage was great. We had expert teachers who did not leave the orphanage after school, like in regular schools, they were working with us after school in both the primary and the high school, and when we grew up we learned a lot. I wasn't the best student in school, but I had talent and I studied well. My two favorite teachers—my chemistry and physics teacher and my Romanian language teacher—motivated me and worked with me after school.

At school, I developed a passion for social work and I wanted to go to university to study. All my classmates and most of my teachers did not believe that I could be accepted to university, but I knew that I was a good student. And if others could do it, then I also could do it, and it was hard for me that they didn't believe in me. At the age of 18 I left the orphanage, and before applying to university, I went to the village where my parents lived to search for them. I was very happy and excited that I was about to finally meet them and see their faces and hear their voices for the first time. But when I arrived in the village, I was shocked when I was told that they had died. This was a very hard time for me.

Later, I met a social worker from an NGO which helps orphans, and she believed in me. She believed that I could be accepted into a university, and she supported me. This was very important for me. And I did it. I was accepted to study social work at university. At that time I heard about an NGO, which supports orphaned university students. I found the NGO and applied for a scholarship, and I got it. The scholarship was enough for my tuition and living expenses, so I didn't have to work in order to support myself. After I got my bachelor's degree, I went to another university to do my master's.

In the end of my third year at the university, I heard about the Roma Education Fund scholarship, and I applied for it and I got it. At university, many people asked me many questions about my family but I didn't know my family, and my answer always was: "I am sorry, the only thing I know is that I am an orphan, I grew up in an orphanage and I know nothing about my family."

I always liked helping people, and while I was at university I was volunteering in different social projects. When I finished university, I decided to use my knowledge and experience to help poor people living in the villages near my town. Although there are many NGOs in my town, none of them helps the poor Roma communities in the near villages. So, with five colleagues, I started a small NGO in 2013. I am the unpaid vice president, youth worker, and coordinator at the NGO, and we help Roma and non-Roma youth, disabled, and poor people in six villages by giving them food. We collect the food from local stores or get it from Germany and the U.K.

We also organize afterschool classes for local kids, using volunteer teachers. I live in subsidized housing, and I also get a little support from the state. I barely make it through the month. Sometimes one of the NGOs abroad with which we cooperate asks me to translate something for them, and they pay me for that. I also once applied for a vacancy in the local government. I sent my CV and cover letter, but when they saw that I have darker skin they told me that the job had just been filled. They hired a person whose education was lower than mine, but he was a non-Roma. My Roma identity makes it more difficult for me to find a job, and I hope that in the near future our NGO will raise enough money that I will start getting a salary for my work.

CHAPTER 5

Implementation Challenges and the Road Ahead

Sandor Karacsony and Roberta Gatti, with input from Kosuke Anan and Valerie Morrica

Summary

Chapters 2–4 document the existing and wide differences in life opportunities between Roma and non-Roma children. From a policy perspective, and despite the relevance of early education, it is evident that the family's employment outcomes and living conditions largely shape children's chances in life. Therefore, coupled with a focus on the next generation, an integrated approach throughout the lifecycle is needed.

What does such an integrated approach take? First, the role of the social workers must be emphasized, especially for the purpose of adequately coordinating all the intervening actors to work toward the overall goal of supporting disadvantaged households. Secondly, operationalizing the principle of equality of opportunity will require the involvement of the community, through the development of a cross cutting enabling platform. Finally, Governments will be key enablers of Roma inclusion, and thus their full and coordinated support will be a central precondition for success.

Adequate data collection and rigorous analysis will be particularly important to debunk the existing myths around Roma, to appropriately inform policy, and to help make the most of EU Funds through improved targeting. Impact evaluation, in particular, through randomized interventions, is a useful instrument to identify the most cost-effective actions, and to build public ownership of the Roma inclusion agenda, which is often fragile.

Addressing discrimination and negative stereotyping, two major mediating factors that determine the allocation of opportunities throughout the lifecycle, should be a priority moving forward, both through tackling the sources of discrimination and by punishing such behaviors when detected. Strengthening the cultural competency of public officials and increasing the number and capacity of mediators could help diminish discrimination at the service delivery level.

An Integrated Life Cycle Approach

The previous chapters documented striking inequalities between Roma and non-Roma in Central Europe and emphasized that these differences begin early. Some of these differences are due to predetermined circumstances such as poverty and parental education: A Roma child is much more likely than a non-Roma child to grow up in a household with severe material deprivation and to have parents who have little or no education. Other inequalities reflect limited access to basic goods and services that are necessary for dignified living, often leading to initial preconditions that are unfair.

The aforementioned early differences amount to an unfair start for the next generation of Roma. The context in which they are born and raised largely shapes lifelong opportunities and places them at a disadvantage early on. As such, promoting equality of opportunity should in practice translate into those interventions that can level the playing field for Roma children and provide them with equal chances, on par with everyone else in society. As discussed in previous chapters, facilitating access to early quality education is one such key policy, one that has recognized high returns, especially for disadvantaged children. Yet other complementary interventions are necessary to ensure that returns to investments in education are realized, especially those that promote access to productive employment and upgrade living conditions. Hence, while there is a priority emphasis on the next generation of Roma, promoting equality of opportunity for marginalized Roma children provides the rationale for an integrated approach, which can positively affect the entire family and which effectively articulates along key nodes of the life cycle (as summarized in figure 5.1).

For Children

Early childhood development (ECD) interventions can lay out the basis for cognitive development and long-term health and productivity. These include effective cognitive development in the first 1,000 days, also as supported by better parenting skills; healthy development as supported by regular maternal/child health checkups; good nutrition practices; smart incentives for immunization; and community outreach regarding learning stimulation and good parenting practices.

Expanding early childhood education (ECE) in the 3–6 age range will allow these gains to be consolidated and cognitive and behavioral foundations to be further developed. This can include investments in quality ECE infrastructure, adequate staffing, resources, and curricula; and removing financial, logistical, and administrative barriers to preschool and kindergarten attendance. Doing so will help children prepare for primary school and achieve proficiency in the national language.

In primary education, promoting equal opportunities will mean investing in accessibility and inclusiveness. Interventions should pay special attention to keeping Roma children in school by identifying students at risk of dropping out, improving teacher training, and offering afterschool programs. Support will be

Figure 5.1 Integrated Approach to Operationalizing Equality of Opportunity for Roma Children

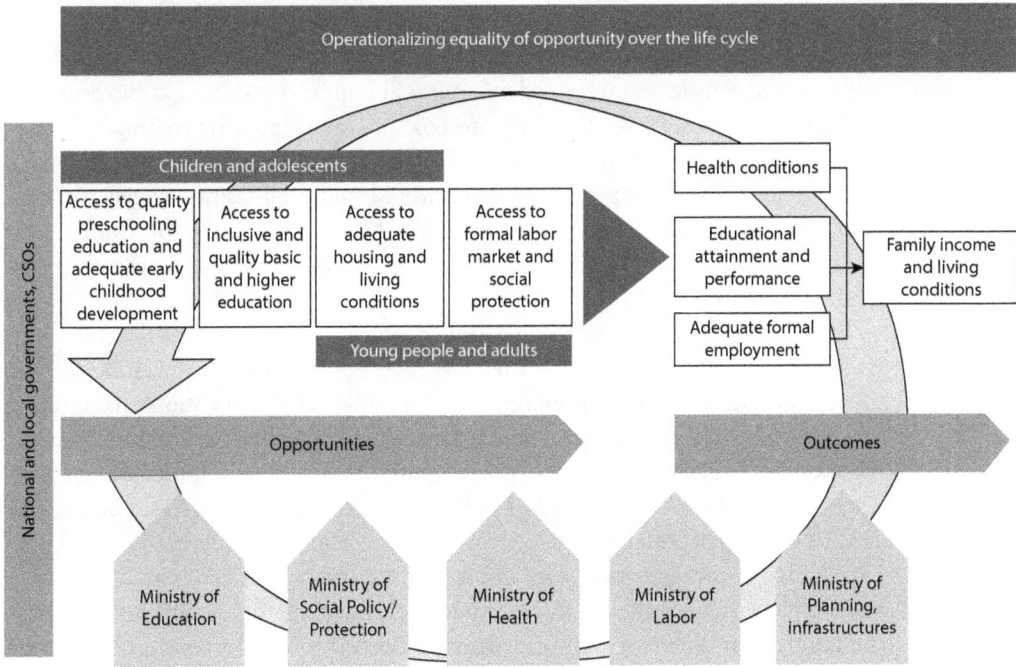

Note: CSO = civil society organizations.

particularly important during transitions between grades, when the chance of dropping out is highest for marginalized Roma children.

For Young Adults and Parents

School-to-work transition is a key moment in one's life when opportunities—which in this context means primarily access to productive employment—can shrink for those young adults from disadvantaged backgrounds, and where well-designed support can help counteract that process. Interventions that can benefit marginalized Roma include mentoring, early detection of job transition barriers, and counseling and professional orientation for youth, including in a gender-sensitive manner. Connecting with jobs and upgrading skills can support access to productive employment for working-age individuals. These interventions will range from assessing skills gaps and tailoring training and second-chance options, to technical training that caters to specific employers' needs.

For the Whole Family

These interventions aim to improve overall living conditions and combine both "hard" and "soft" measures, including (a) raising awareness among stakeholders about the availability and benefits of particular interventions, services, or prac-tices/behaviors; (b) focusing on social integration; (c) tackling affordability con-straints and connecting to benefits; and (d) promoting organizational capacity and active citizenship.

Being Fair, Faring Better • http://dx.doi.org/10.1596/978-1-4648-0598-1

What Does It Take?

The Role of Social Workers

Leveling the playing field for Roma children (and their families) and implementing interventions in an integrated manner will require a system that purposefully coordinates policies with the ultimate goal of supporting disadvantaged households. It will also need to feature capillary and field-based work that is ideally child-centered and supported by empowered and well-trained social workers, combined with community-led local action. Most importantly, the Roma communities should have a direct involvement in the design and implementation of such interventions.

In practice, such an approach would feature national and local actors who would prioritize interventions that are focused on children's well-being and development, such as conducting early childhood interventions, facilitating primary school and kindergarten attendance, and reducing early school leaving. This could be achieved if municipal professionals who are in close contact with marginalized Roma households (social workers, Roma mediators, community health nurses) organized their activities around children's needs.

The social worker—one with good training and a relatively low case load—would have the key role of coordinating teachers, mediators, health professionals, and public employment and social assistance services. The primary goal would be to promote continuity in children's school attendance and to engage the community, also through school-based activities. Box 5.1 provides an example of such an intervention from Romania.

This "reoriented" social service approach brings the role of the social workers and other community workers to the forefront, with the aim of strengthening their ability to proactively develop solutions in concert with the families that need them. Their work would focus on accurately identifying a vulnerable child's (and household's) multidimensional needs and viewing these as a unit; helping

---

Box 5.1 UNICEF Project on Invisible Children in Romania

The project Helping the Invisible Children aims to benefit children who are "disappearing from view within their families, communities and societies and ... governments, donors, civil society, the media and even other children" (UNICEF 2006).

An "invisible child" is defined as one who faces one or more types of vulnerability (poverty, neglect, abuse, violence, school dropout, abandonment, and so on); they usually lack identification and are easily trafficked and exploited. Social workers can usually only reach them through fieldwork activity—which happens in only 96 communes in Romania. Although this project helped identify more than 3,000 invisible children, many more probably exist in the country.

Source: Stanculescu and Marin 2012.

---

families be informed of and stay connected to services; and helping resolve challenges through locally generated and implemented solutions. Social workers could be trained to provide intensive psychosocial support and counseling to households. Chile Solidario (see annex 3A) is a program that successfully incorporates these elements in its working model.

Developing a Cross-Cutting Enabling Platform at the Community Level

Operationalizing equality of opportunity within an integrated life cycle approach is likely to work best if it takes into account the diversity of communities by directly involving Roma communities in the design and implementation of policies and programs. This approach could be based on incorporating priorities from the community level and further informing these interventions with projects promoted by groups within the Roma community. Such groups could collaborate with the state or municipal social service infrastructure. They would oversee the development and implementation of investments regarding the following: (a) delivering an integrated set of social services in basic health and education; (b) earning opportunities (such as employment promotion programs for parents, literacy programs, counseling, income generating activities); and (c) small community infrastructure investments that would improve basic social service accessibility and quality.

The proposed integrated model would involve mobilizing both households and communities to combine the demand (communities, households) and supply (state and local authorities) sides of social service delivery. The end result would ideally lead to relevant and complementary social service activities through both public and community-based channels through a process that would ultimately empower the communities themselves. Box 5.2 outlines the community-led local development (CLLD) approach established by a 2013 EU regulation that aims to improve coordination between European Structural and Investment Funds (ESIF).

Governments as Key Enablers of Inclusion

While an integrated approach seeks to generate immediate returns at the local level, the full and coordinated support of the government architecture—agencies in charge of Roma inclusion, ministries of education, infrastructure, labor, social policy, finance—is a key precondition to its success. Roma exclusion is a challenge that cuts across many different areas of intervention, and tackling it requires simultaneous, structural action on multiple fronts. Priority measures must reflect the legal competences of national, regional, and local institutions as established by the current law, and be aligned with both the legal framework that governs local public administration and the specific legislation that applies to local public services. At the same time, these measures must be strongly linked with the annual budget process at all tiers of governance.

Box 5.2 The EC Community-Led Local Development Approach

The EC Community-Led Local Development Approach (CLLD) approach was developed in response to adding territorial cohesion to the EU's goals by the Lisbon Treaty on the Functioning of the European Union (December 2009). Its goal was to counteract geographically concentrated problems in cities and subregions across EU member states.

The treaty acknowledged that this new goal would require better mobilizing potential at the local level, and more deeply involving local communities in designing and implementing local development plans. Legislative proposals for the EU cohesion policy for the 2014–20 period subsequently established rules for facilitating and strengthening CLLD that apply to all Cohesion and Structural Funds; these were adopted by the European Commission in 2011.

CLLD focuses on engaging local communities, including civil society, in designing and implementing locally integrated development strategies. The aim is to help disadvantaged communities develop in a manner that is smarter, more sustainable, and more inclusive, in line with the Europe 2020 Strategy.

CLLD promotes development efforts that are (a) focused on specific subregional areas; (b) community-led by local action groups; (c) carried out via integrated and multisectoral, area-based local development strategies that are designed to take local needs and potential into consideration; (d) include innovative features; and (e) emphasize networking. The five principles should be reflected in getting these action groups set up and in operating mode and in the selection of individual projects that can be funded through the Cohesion and the Structural Funds.

Source: World Bank 2014.

The Role of Data: Debunking Myths and Making the Most of European Union Funds

Data Collection and Rigorous Analytics for Evidence-Based Policy

While a focus on equality of opportunity is likely to crystallize investment efforts around Roma children, broad Roma socioeconomic inclusion has traditionally had fragile political support in many EU countries. This in large part reflects myths and incorrect beliefs associated with the Roma minority. For example, various waves of Eurobarometer surveys suggest that in countries where the lowest share of respondents report having personal contact with someone of Roma ethnicity, the highest share of respondents report that they would not feel comfortable having a Roma neighbor, or would not prefer their children to attend classes with Roma children (see figure 5.2).

Clearly, the debate around Roma exclusion is complex. This, coupled with the myths that persist about Roma, make it necessary to collect and disseminate quality data and rigorous evidence about Roma's living conditions and the barriers many of them face. The results of interventions that have benefitted them should also be closely and rigorously evaluated. Representative data on

Figure 5.2 Social Connections of Roma

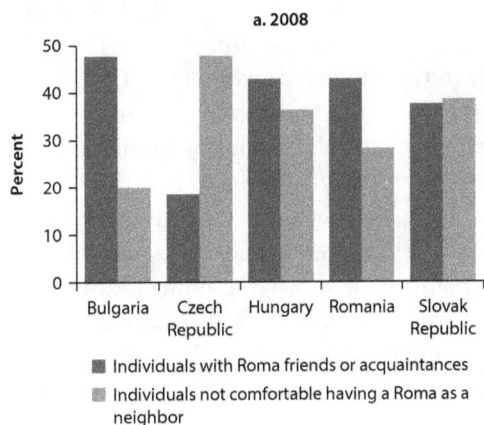

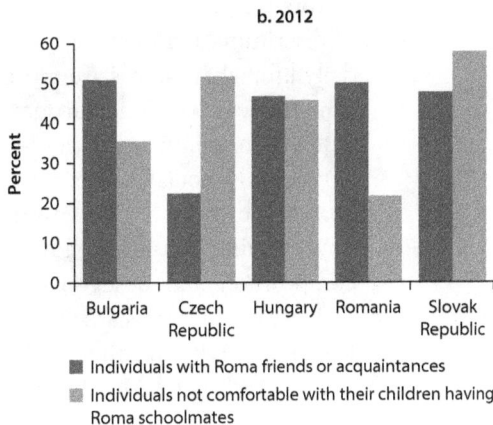

a. 2008

b. 2012

Individuals with Roma friends or acquaintances
Individuals not comfortable having a Roma as a neighbor

Individuals with Roma friends or acquaintances
Individuals not comfortable with their children having Roma schoolmates

Source: European Commission 2008.   *Source:* European Commission 2012.

Roma's socioeconomic characteristics are scarce, however. In addition, even when data on ethnicity or language are collected, Roma respondents overwhelmingly do not self-declare as Roma. At the same time, anecdotal evidence suggests that enumerators themselves might be unwilling to visit the most marginalized Roma communities. One way to address these constraints would be for Central and Eastern European (CEE) countries' household surveys to include an ethnic self-identification feature,[1] or a booster sample from the country's poorest communities to collect data from a much larger share of marginalized population groups. In line with good practices on household and multitopic survey data collection, information about spending and incomes, employment, education, housing, parental education, energy outlays, health, finance, and discrimination could be included.

Data disaggregated by ethnicity would enable stakeholders to better track Roma and non-Roma communities' progress in social outcomes and enable a much deeper analysis of determinants of poverty and social mobility. This could be done in the context of surveys such as EU-SILC, the Household Budget Survey (HBS), and the Labor Market Survey. Modules could be added to ask about particular social inclusion policy issues or important indicators related to subjective well-being, and can also include retrospective questions to fill in longitudinal information that is currently missing. Much could be learned by analyzing such data. For example, within the framework of equality of opportunity, it would be possible to understand the extent to which parental circumstances affect outcomes later in life; whether circumstances affect outcomes differently for Roma and non-Roma; and what channels mediate these mechanisms.

In part due to the scarcity of data, rigorous analytical work is also limited, despite the fact that it could go a long way in debunking myths and making the case for Roma inclusion. In particular, a number of issues are under-researched.

These include the contextual aspects and the role that cultural and social factors play at the specific country or community level; the extent and nature of discrimination in school, in the workplace, when searching for a job, and in daily life; what factors are more likely to trigger discrimination; what programs can reduce interethnic barriers and when such interventions are more effective (such as in childhood or adolescence); how new generations of Roma navigate between the social norms that are specific to their community and the rapidly changing broader societal norms; how aspirations and expectations are formed; how learning occurs and how skills are developed, especially in relation to class composition and desegregation mechanisms; and what training design and delivery mechanisms are most likely to work for marginalized groups, including Roma. Applying frontier methodologies derived from behavioral science and from social experiments could also garner important insights into these questions.

Using Data to Better Target and Use EU Funds

There is a complementary and equally important use for data. Annex 4A discusses subregional at-risk-of-poverty maps and urban maps of marginalized communities as examples of effective targeting techniques for EU funds. These maps are based on EU-SILC and census data and help identify poverty and marginalization at the subnational and neighborhood level, which in turn allows countries to take advantage of the opportunities provided by ESIF's 2014–20 programming cycle to finance interventions that promote Roma inclusion. One ex ante conditionality established by ESIF's ninth thematic objective, "Promoting social inclusion, combating poverty and any discrimination," is the need to have a national Roma inclusion strategy or policy framework in place by 2017. This ex ante conditionality comes with several requirements:

- Set achievable national goals for Roma inclusion. These targets should address the four EU Roma integration goals that relate to access to education, employment, health care, and housing.
- Use already available socioeconomic and territorial indicators (that is, very low educational levels, long-term unemployment, and so on) to identify those disadvantaged microregions or segregated neighborhoods where communities are most deprived.
- Include strong monitoring methods to evaluate the impact of Roma integration actions and develop a review mechanism for the strategy's adaptation.
- Design, implement, and monitor such efforts in close cooperation and continuous dialogue with Roma civil society, regional, and local authorities.[2]

Once poor and marginalized communities are identified, specific calls for proposals could be rolled out for integrated programs that target them. Financial allocation of the integrated program can be broken down for each locality, and local stakeholders—including municipalities, NGOs, and Roma communities—can develop a common set of project ideas that best reflect local needs. Such an integrated program offers numerous benefits. It can reflect local needs; ensure explicit but not exclusive targeting of Roma; exploit synergies between projects; strengthen partnerships between local stakeholders; and so on. This can be undertaken via the CLLD approach using European Regional Development Fund funds, combined with proposals related to human capital development using ESF funding. Managing authorities could be enabled to build capacity, help local stakeholders develop their project ideas, and facilitate strong community involvement in design and implementation. In-depth evidence from Romania also indicates that in addition to an "explicit but not exclusive" territorial targeting approach, complementary interventions that specifically target Roma communities without a geographic focus—especially communities with higher proportions of Roma—are also necessary to avoid important exclusion-related errors.

In terms of monitoring, the focal shift toward evidence-based policy making and programming also implies that EU-funded projects need to follow a clear results chain that links overall goals to clear and measurable outcomes, and to the intermediate activities and inputs that are needed to achieve them in the specific timeframe (see figure 5.3).

Figure 5.3 Example of a Results Framework of an Active Labor Market Program

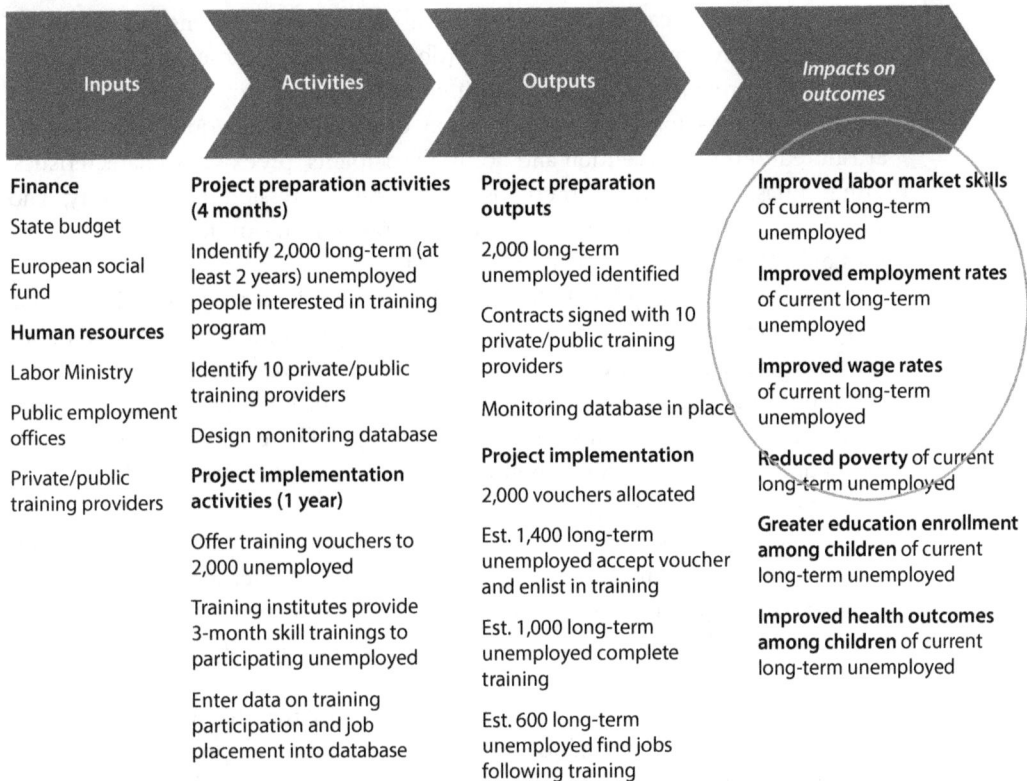

Inputs	Activities	Outputs	Impacts on outcomes
Finance	**Project preparation activities (4 months)**	**Project preparation outputs**	**Improved labor market skills** of current long-term unemployed
State budget		2,000 long-term unemployed identified	
European social fund	Indentify 2,000 long-term (at least 2 years) unemployed people interested in training program		**Improved employment rates** of current long-term unemployed
Human resources		Contracts signed with 10 private/public training providers	
Labor Ministry	Identify 10 private/public training providers		**Improved wage rates** of current long-term unemployed
Public employment offices	Design monitoring database	Monitoring database in place	
Private/public training providers	**Project implementation activities (1 year)**	**Project implementation**	**Reduced poverty** of current long-term unemployed
		2,000 vouchers allocated	
	Offer training vouchers to 2,000 unemployed	Est. 1,400 long-term unemployed accept voucher and enlist in training	**Greater education enrollment among children** of current long-term unemployed
	Training institutes provide 3-month skill trainings to participating unemployed	Est. 1,000 long-term unemployed complete training	**Improved health outcomes among children** of current long-term unemployed
	Enter data on training participation and job placement into database	Est. 600 long-term unemployed find jobs following training	

Monitoring indicators is a necessary prerequisite for tracking program impact, but an important, often essential role is often played by Roma communities themselves. Community-based monitoring is both a form of publicly supervising project implementation and an efficient way to mobilize and empower the community. Communities are in the best position to know what is happening to households in their areas, and they could be actively engaged in monitoring progresss using quantitative and qualitative data. Community members can identify areas of improvement, make suggestions for effectiveness, and provide feedback to project coordinators. This can not only help increase the efficiency and effectiveness of investments and other measures, but also help people become better informed and thus better able to exercise their rights as citizens.

Understanding Impact through Rigorous Evaluation

Evaluating the causal impact of interventions—that is, the impact that is due to the intervention and the intervention alone—is a key step in the policy-making learning process. Social policy experiments—applying rigorous research designs to determine the impact of social policy changes—can provide an important feedback mechanism for policy makers to scale up, reorient, or scale down interventions. Under the umbrella of what is known as *impact evaluation*, a variety of methodologies can be used to evaluate policy impact. Randomizing interventions into treatment and control groups offers the most robust way to draw inferences about a program's causal effect. Specifically, randomization ensures the treatment and control groups have identical (observable and unobservable) characteristics at the program's start, so that differences that arise in outcomes between the two groups—for example, education or labor market outcomes—can be attributed to the intervention and not to participants' preexisting characteristics. Other quasi-experimental methods (matching, regression discontinuity, and so on) can also vastly improve on inferences drawn from simple ex post comparisons of outcomes among program participants.

Promoted by the EU PROGRESS facility and implemented around the globe by governments, civil society, and international organizations, impact evaluations can help identify cost-effective interventions and showcase the results of Roma inclusion programs. This is particularly important for building public ownership over an agenda where such support is often fragile. There are many examples of evaluations that have allowed political choices to be reoriented and successful programs to be scaled up (see box 5.3).

The local dimension of an EU-funded project provides a dynamic ground for social experimentation, which could be leveraged for better learning and scaling up over time, especially if evaluation strategies are designed with projects themselves. This would allow building (be it in a randomized or nonrandomized manner) suitable counterfactual for evaluation.

Finally, local-level peer-to-peer learning networks, together with ways to systematically feed this information to the national level, can promote knowledge sharing and convergence toward a consensus of what works, where, and why.

Box 5.3 Designing and Implementing an Impact Evaluation

A recent and ongoing example from Bulgaria shows how impact evaluations can be embedded in project design and implementation. On June 30, 2014, 236 communities, many of which are Roma settlements, were randomly assigned to the following interventions: (a) intervention type A—A1: free preschool; A2: free preschool + 7 leva/monthly conditional on attendance; A3: free preschool + 20 leva/monthly conditional on attendance; A4: status quo; and (b) Intervention type B—B1: information and awareness-raising intervention (five community sessions) and B2: status quo. The communities were previously selected via a listing exercise in which different stakeholders and a community member were surveyed.

The project is implemented by two dozen NGOs and financed/supervised by the Trust for Social Achievement under the America for Bulgaria Foundation. A short baseline survey on nearly 6,000 households in the 236 communities took place between April and June 2014. A detailed follow-up survey measuring ECD outcomes was planned for May 2015.

Addressing Discrimination and Negative Stereotyping

Discrimination is a central mediating factor that can reallocate opportunities over the life cycle by distorting access to services and can help explain persistent inequalities in outcomes for Roma children and their families. One commonly observed mechanism of discrimination of Roma in CEE stems from broader society's belief that the Roma do not want to lift themselves out of poverty (World Bank 2014). Such ethnic stereotyping leads to disapproval and contempt and results in disrespectful and discriminatory treatment of Roma. For example, in Romania, this understanding was common among local authorities and various types of service providers, as shown in the PHARE Program and National Roma Agency study from 2008 (Fleck and Rughinis 2008).

Discrimination is also perpetuated by poverty profiling, or when service providers profile Roma via assumptions about their lack of financial resources or their high risk of default. Social status and perceptions regarding ability to pay are important factors in the accessibility of health facilities and quality of treatment.

The historical mistrust between Roma and non-Roma in some countries may also constitute a major source of discrimination. Broader society's mistrust of Roma is often the result of failing to understand elements of Roma culture. In the collective memory of broader society, Roma culture could often be associated with selective traits that reinforce negative stereotypes about Roma. The dominant group's cultures and norms could often actively disrespect groups they consider subordinate. The dominant group could prevent the nondominant one from fully participating in society by treating them disrespectfully, assaulting their dignity, stereotyping them, and holding their cultures and practices in contempt (World Bank 2013).

Being Fair, Faring Better • http://dx.doi.org/10.1596/978-1-4648-0598-1

In addition, without proper recognition of cultural identities, Roma can feel unaccepted by society, leading to self-exclusion and inactive citizenship. Adequate recognition of Roma's cultural heritage and identity is therefore critical for helping them be treated as equal citizens, empowered to fully enjoy their rights (see box 5.4).

Prejudices, poverty profiling, and historical mistrust are perpetuated by the reproduction of negative stereotypes. For example, the media's contribution—including television, movies, and advertising—to negative images and stereotypes of the Roma has been well documented in research (Bernath and Messing 2011; ERRC 1999; European Commission 2008). Researchers and civil society experts[3] also argue that international institutions—including the World Bank—contribute to the negative stereotyping of Roma by leading a policy discourse on poverty

---

Box 5.4 Participation and Empowerment

Public discourse around Roma inclusion activities often focuses on the need for participation. However, participating in and of itself is but the first step, where the ultimate aim should be empowerment. Empowerment is the process of enhancing individuals' or groups' capacity to make choices and transform these into desired actions and outcomes. Empowered people have freedom of choice and action, which in turn enables them to better influence their life course and the decisions that affect them (World Bank, n.d.). Perceptions of being empowered vary across time, culture, and the domains of a person's life. For example, in India, a low-caste woman might feel empowered if she is given a fair hearing in a public meeting that is comprised of men and women from different social and economic groups; in Brazil, citizens—both men and women—feel empowered if they are able to engage in decisions on budget allocations; in Ethiopia, citizens and civil society groups report feeling empowered by consultations undertaken during the preparation of the poverty reduction support program; in the United States, immigrant workers feel empowered through unionization, which has allowed them to negotiate working conditions with employers; and in the United Kingdom, a woman who is the victim of domestic violence feels empowered when she is freed from the situation and able to make decisions about her own life. Empowerment is self-determined change; it implies bringing together the supply and demand sides of development to change the environment within which poor people live, and helping them build and capitalize on their own attributes. When looking at empowerment in the context of Roma inclusion, Kocze (2012) highlights that, according to the RRS (UNDP, World Bank, and EC 2011), low levels of participation persist by Roma respondents in civic and political fields at local levels. This in turn suggests a lack of Roma participation in local decisions and policy making, which can contribute to social and political exclusion. The RRS also highlights that the Roma (as well as their non-Roma neighbors) trust family ties more than institutions, including local NGOs. Kocze (2012) concludes that the lack of NGO presence and the lack of trust in civil society organizations disempowers local Roma communities, which limits their opportunities to initiate changes.

and social exclusion of marginalized Roma in CEE and ignoring both success stories and the diversity of the Roma community in general.

Discrimination can be combated by adopting a two-tiered approach: (a) tackling the sources of discrimination and (b) punishing acts of discrimination. The roots of discrimination, such as negative stereotypes and mistrust, must be tackled by reducing negative portrayals of Roma in media and research, and by increasing interactions between Roma and non-Roma to foster mutual understanding. Acts of discrimination need to be strictly prohibited through effective and consistent application of the law.

At the service delivery level, discrimination should be reduced by strengthening public officials' cultural competency (including teachers, health care providers, police, mayors) and increasing the number and capacity of mediators who serve as a bridge between Roma and service providers. For example, in collaboration with the Association for Development and Social Inclusion, Romania successfully implemented an innovative and sustainable health antidiscrimination project on ethics and nondiscrimination of vulnerable groups that focused on Roma: A study revealed that medical students are aware of the fact that discrimination occurs, but they are not trained to prevent it and do not know how to address it. Based on this finding, the project initiated and conducted a comprehensive campaign to design and include such training in medical curricula. The course is delivered in an interactive way and includes presentations of real discrimination cases, role playing, and debates.

Conclusions

Investments in children's chances—especially when these children come from disadvantaged socioeconomic backgrounds—generate the highest returns. Equal opportunities for marginalized Roma minorities matter. These statements respond to a moral imperative based on a widely recognized concept of societal fairness and at the same time can promote growth and productivity. Recent evidence shows that more equality is associated with higher growth, and investing in the skills and productive inclusion of the young and growing Roma population can herald important economic benefits in those countries where aging, low fertility, and outmigration contribute to a rapid shrinking of the labor force.

The ESIF 2014–20 funding cycle provides a unique opportunity for making progress through more and smarter investments in the marginalized Roma population.

However, improving these investments' effectiveness requires continuous learning: Countries need to generate more data, evidence, and knowledge in order to (a) better understand community and household needs at the local level; (b) align with the national level to provide a more enabling environment; and (c) better use EU funds to achieve smarter and more inclusive growth.

Just as importantly, more and better social investments and knowledge will help progressively break down barriers for Roma and contribute to more integration, equality of opportunity, and social justice in Europe.

Being Fair, Faring Better • http://dx.doi.org/10.1596/978-1-4648-0598-1

Notes

1. For self-declared ethnic identity, questionnaires may follow the practice of the 2011 Hungarian census, which included two separate questions that allowed respondents to opt for dual ethnic identity. The reliability of ethnic data could be further strengthened through third-party identification or the use of Roma enumerators.

2. Considerable efforts are underway to improve results-based monitoring and evaluation (M&E) on Roma inclusion in the EU. A working group of member states, led by the EU Fundamental Rights Agency (FRA), is developing a model aimed at adopting a set of common rights-based indicators that can comprehensively assess Roma inclusion efforts at the EU level. It applies a so-called structure-process-outcome (S-P-O) indicator model that assesses (a) the legal and policy framework (structural indicators); (b) the concrete measures to implement it (process indicators); and (c) the achievements, as observed for the target group(s), for example, Roma (outcome indicators). A recent transnational workshop on M&E organized by ESF Roma Inclusion Learning Network in Madrid (November 13–14, 2014)—has also provided an opportunity for member state participants to share the past Roma inclusion investments, M&E experiences, and plans for the next programming period. The workshop has highlighted the fact that all countries are aware of the past programming period's weak M&E systems, and that some progress is being made with regards to M&E in the 2014–20 programming period, particularly in the areas of (a) better targeting of resources (such as using information on disadvantaged localities—the Czech Republic, the Slovak Republic, Hungary) and (b) monitoring whether projects are reaching Roma (in Hungary, Bulgaria) using self-identification. Participants discussed concrete ways to improve results targeting and monitoring using modern IT technology, and by making the M&E systems much more inclusive toward the implementing organizations and final beneficiaries.

3. For example, http://www.opensocietyfoundations.org/voices/who-defines-roma; and comments received from NGOs Romani CRISS, Amare Rromentza, and O Del Amenca during a learning event organized by the World Bank in December 2014.

References

Bernath, Gabor, and Vera Messing. 2011. *Pushed to the Edge*. Research Report on the Representation of Roma Communities in the Hungarian Majority Media, Central European University, Budapest.

ERRC (European Roma Rights Centre). 1999. *Roma Rights 4, 1999: Romani Media/ Mainstream Media*. http://www.errc.org/article/roma-rights-4-1999-romani -mediamainstream-media/1134.

European Commission. 2008. "Discrimination in the European Union: Perceptions, Experiences and Attitudes." Special Eurobarometer 296, Publications Office of the European Union, Luxembourg. http://ec.europa.eu/public_opinion/archives/ebs/ebs _296_en.pdf.

———. 2012. "Discrimination in the EU in 2012." Special Eurobarometer 393, Publications Office of the European Union, Luxembourg. http://ec.europa.eu/public_opinion /archives/ebs/ebs_393_en.pdf.

Fleck, Gabor, and Cosima Rughinis. 2008. *Come Closer: Inclusion and Exclusion of Roma in Present-Day Romanian Society*. Report, European Commission, Bucharest.

Kocze, Angela. 2012. "Civil Society, Civil Involvement and Social Inclusion of the Roma." Roma Inclusion Working Papers, UNDP, Bratislava. http://www.academia .edu/4134351/Kocze_UNDP_Roma_Civil_Society.

Stanculescu, Manuela, and Monica Marin. 2012. *Helping the Invisible Children*. Evaluation Report, UNICEF Romania. http://www.unicef.org/evaldatabase/files/2011_Romania _-_Evaluation_report_Helping_the_invisible_children.pdf.

UNDP (United Nations Development Programme), World Bank, and EC (European Commission). 2011. *Regional Roma Survey*. Report, UNDP, World Bank, and EC, New York.

UNICEF. 2006. *State of the World's Children 2006: Excluded and Invisible*. Report UNICEF New York. http://www.unicef.org/sowc06/fullreport/executive3.php.

World Bank. n.d. "What Is Empowerment?" http://go.worldbank.org/V45HD4P100.

World Bank. 2013. *Inclusion Matters: The Foundation for Shared Prosperity*. Washington, DC: World Bank. doi: 10.1596/978-1-4648-0010-8.

———. 2014. *Integrated Intervention Tool: Integration Strategies for Urban Poor Areas and Disadvantaged Communities*. Report, World Bank, Washington, DC. http://backend .elard.eu/uploads/wb-project-in-ro/iit_en_28april.pdf.

Environmental Benefits Statement

The World Bank Group is committed to reducing its environmental footprint. In support of this commitment, the Publishing and Knowledge Division leverages electronic publishing options and print-on-demand technology, which is located in regional hubs worldwide. Together, these initiatives enable print runs to be lowered and shipping distances decreased, resulting in reduced paper consumption, chemical use, greenhouse gas emissions, and waste.

The Publishing and Knowledge Division follows the recommended standards for paper use set by the Green Press Initiative. The majority of our books are printed on Forest Stewardship Council (FSC)–certified paper, with nearly all containing 50–100 percent recycled content. The recycled fiber in our book paper is either unbleached or bleached using totally chlorine free (TCF), processed chlorine free (PCF), or enhanced elemental chlorine free (EECF) processes.

More information about the Bank's environmental philosophy can be found at http://crinfo.worldbank.org/wbcrinfo/node/4.

green
press
INITIATIVE

www.ingramcontent.com/pod-product-compliance
Lightning Source LLC
Chambersburg PA
CBHW080419270326

41929CB00018B/3085